BEYOND THE COMMUNITY

Beyond
the Community:
Social process
in Europe

Edited by
Jeremy Boissevain
University of Amsterdam
and
John Friedl
Ohio State University

Published for the
European-Mediterranean Study Group
of the
University of Amsterdam
by the
Department of Educational Science
of the Netherlands
(Ministerie van Onderwijs en Wetenschappen)
the Hague

1975

Jacket-design by Jojada Verrips/Herman Govers

The publication of this volume has been made possible by the Department of Education and Science of the Netherlands (Ministerie van Onderwijs en Wetenschappen) and the European-Mediterranean Study Group of the University of Amsterdam.

Acknowledgments

These essays grew out of the discussions and some of the papers presented at a symposium on 'The meaning of small communities in the context of (supra-)national processes in Europe,' organized by the European–Mediterranean Study Group of the University of Amsterdam, June 25–29, 1973.

A generous grant from the Netherlands Ministery of Education and Science helped meet the costs of the symposium. Donny Meertens made essential organizational arrangements helped by Hanny Hoekstra. Jojada Verrips provided last minute editorial coordination.

Dirk Jan Beukenhorst, Robert Biagi, Anton Blok, John Cole, Carla Jonker, Peter Loizos, Roger McConochie, Jolanthe Van Opzeeland-De Tempe, Melba Ramos and Hans Vermeulen also attended the symposium and played an important part in the discussions.

Contents

I

Introduction:
Towards a Social Anthropology
of Europe

Jeremy Boissevain
University of Amsterdam

ABSTRACT

This volume examines national and supra-national processes in Europe. These include the paradoxical centralization of power at higher levels of integration, and the gradual decline of the autonomous power of the state. Anthropological studies of Europe have increased for various reasons, including the growing realization that anthropology is the study of all mankind, not just of primitives. The very complexity of Europe makes it an important research area for both theoretical and practical purposes, as social scientists increasingly turn to the study of change. This shift in theoretical orientation increasingly involves anthropologists in cognate disciplines, especially history.

THE SCOPE

Political, religious and economic relationships, say, in an Italian village, clearly do not exist in isolation at a local level. They are influenced by relationships and processes that lie beyond the community at regional, national and even supra-national levels. Terms such as group, village, community, culture, society have been used to indicate socially significant entities. Concepts like brokerage, encapsulation, penetration, folk-urban, great tradition and little tradition, absorption, and acculturation have been brought forward to deal with aspects of relations between these entities. These terms and concepts, which are used by most anthropologists as scientific instruments, were largely developed to describe and analyze relations in small-scale, fairly isolated communities. To polarize part and whole, micro and macro, community and nation in the study of complex European societies by reifying them as separate categories does violence to the nature of the dynamic relationships between them, and the meaning they have to the people involved. Yet here lies the rub. Anthropologists have done little to systematize their thinking on the nature of these relationships to avoid this static polarization and reification. This is the central problem to which this volume is addressed.

The authors attempt to move beyond the community, beyond the rather ahistorical, village-focused studies which have characterized much of European anthropology to date. They deal with the effects of such familiar processes as increasing industrialization, geographical mobility and urbanization. They also analyze less obvious processes. These include the growing centralization of power at higher integration levels; the progressive decline of small-scale, autonomous units; and the increasingly extensive cooperative arrangements. Most of the studies also indicate a trend towards a more equal distribution of socially valued objects, including a reduction in power differentials between classes, groups and persons. This is partly reflected in the steadily expanding public welfare activities of the state. Interestingly enough, several of the studies also indicate a gradual decline of the autonomous power of the state's central bureaucracy.

These processes are interrelated, and thus present serious analytical problems. For example, increasing centralization and the decline of the power of the central bureaucracy at first sight even appear contradictory. This paradox presents an absorbing puzzle. But there is considerable evidence that progressively more powerful configurations at the international, as well as at the grassroots level, are crosscutting state bureaucratic units, thus eroding the power of many nation-states. The interrelation between these processes is examined in more detail below.

Although all the essays are based on field research, they do not focus on local communities as objects of research in themselves. Most are 'village outward' studies. The authors have used the small community or regional locus as a scientific niche from which to examine problems of wider relevance. Six studies deal with Southern Europe. From his experience in Tuscany, Thomas Crump examines critically the traditional anthropological 'small community' approach. This, he argues, has forced the Italian nation through 'a sort of sieve to leave only a residue of relatively isolated, partly illiterate, technically retarded, rural communities.' From a grass-roots base, also in Tuscany, Robert Wade examines critically certain generalizations of political scientists who hold that Italy is a centrifugal democracy in which the political culture is fragmented and characterized by exclusive commitment to single parties. John Davis, who provides the only glimpse of the inner workings of a state bureaucracy, documents the extent to which civil servants in Southern Italy, to further their governmental masters' interests, manipulated local politics in a town in Basilicata during the previous century. In Northern Italy Phillip Katz explores the way the response of the German-speaking minority in South Tyrol to Italian law serves to maintain ethnic identity.

Donny Meertens is also critical of the traditional anthropological focus on local communities. In examining the factors influencing the growing labour unrest in Andalusia, she demonstrates the value of the regional focus. Soon Young Song Yoon examines the processes by which Provençal wine cooperatives, introduced by the government to counter rural unrest, perpetuate the class structure to the disadvantage of the small farmer.

Four studies deal with central Western Europe. Daniela Weinberg shows how the federalist structure of Switzerland provides small communities with the means to resist successfully the encroachment of the national government. The two studies set in the Netherlands highlight the unforeseen consequences of national and international processes. Jojada Verrips examines the interrelation between local and national processes. Measures designed to alleviate the plight of the small farmer merely weaken his position. He also deals specifically with the theoretical problem of the relationship between local communities and society at large. Lodewijk Brunt documents the impact that city dwellers, forced into rural communities by urban congestion, have upon local power relations. From Ireland, Mart Bax analyzes how the increasing activity of the welfare state makes more resources available to local power brokers.

Two studies of Norway conclude the volume. Waling Gorter shows that increasing integration into the nation-state does not necessarily disrupt small communities composed of various ethnic groups. Helle and Tom Snell, on the other hand, describe how the processes of national integration in Norwegian society, while initially reducing the conditions under which cultural differences can persist, have now provided the Samish minority with new tactical resources, which they use to protect and maintain ethnic identity.

THE SOCIAL ANTHROPOLOGY OF EUROPE

The fact that anthropologists in increasing numbers are turning to study Europe is itself a fairly recent development. This attention is partly explained by the sharp rise in the number of graduate students in anthropology on both sides of the Atlantic. Because anthropologists traditionally focused on primitive societies, Europe was virtually unexplored terrain, anthropologically speaking. The increased interest of anthropologists in Europe also reflects the loss of their protected status in the newly independent ex-colonies. They are no longer welcome in many of the areas they studied in the past (cf. Asad 1973). The trend to study Europe has perhaps also been stimulated by the recent shortage of research funds, for it generally costs less to study a neighbour than to mount an expedition to the New Guinea highlands. This shortage, in turn, has been caused by the increase in applicants, the reduction of U.S. defense spending on research, the reflexive tightening of government purse-strings to counter student unrest, and recent financial crises which have reduced the ability of private foundations to sponsor research.

But more important than all these is the growing awareness that anthropology is the study of all mankind, not just of primitive, tropical or non-Western man. This itself is a reflection of one of the most important long-term processes: the growing interdependence of nation-states, international organizations and continents.

Trained on literature dealing with comparatively slowly changing, isolated, undifferentiated non-Western societies, anthropologists are often ill-equipped for the complexity of Europe. This complexity, and, increasingly, that of the rest of the world, cannot be handled adequately with traditional anthropological concepts such as equilibrium, corporation, balanced opposition, reciprocity, and consensus, for example. Nor is the traditional anthropological research technique of participant observer alone any longer sufficient. New concepts and research methods are called for, yet these are only partly being provided. The high degree of centralization, the interrelation between various levels of integration, the impact of multiple long-term processes, the sweep of change that can be documented across centuries still overwhelm many anthropologists. Consequently many have sought refuge in villages, which they proceed to treat as isolated entities. They have tribalized Europe. The multitude of narrow studies of European villages prompted one anthropologist recently to exclaim: 'Five kilometers between two European villages have been, from the point of view of social anthropological comparison, longer than five kilometers in most other parts of the world' (Freeman 1973:745). Yet Europe's complexity is precisely what makes it such a fascinating and important area of research.

There are many other reasons for focusing on Europe. Because of historical circumstance, certain processes, such as state formation, national integration, industrialization, urbanization, bureaucratization, class conflict, and commercialization have generally had a longer development in Europe than elsewhere. As the studies in this volume demonstrate, Europe can thus provide a singularly important comparative perspective for those interested in the development of institutions.

There is a further reason for anthropologists to study Europe. Studies of European societies are relevant for the study of imperialism. In the analysis of the rich nation-poor nation configuration, attention usually focuses on the poor countries. Western Europe is taken as given, as not requiring further analysis. The interaction *between* rich and poor must also become an object of research if greater understanding of the interrelation is to be gained. This same perspective also requires that greater attention be devoted to Europe as an essential element in the rich nation-poor nation configuration. The nature of the interaction of Europe with the rest of the world is largely determined by power relations within and between European nations. Thus to understand how European political and business interests, using national bureaucratic governments as instruments, exploit poorer countries, studies of the operation of these institutions in European countries are essential. Studies of the effects of this exploitation on the developing nations is thus only half of the picture. It is essential to find out more about how these exploiting structures in Europe manage to maintain themselves.

All the studies show that the capitalist societies of Europe are far from homogeneous. The continuum between rich and poor, between exploiter and exploited, between metropole and dependent satellite is not just something that runs between Europe and the poorer nations. It is also present within Europe. It is present in the inequality between industrialists and workers in the Spanish corporate state discussed by Meertens. It is evident in the asymmetry described by Gorter between the middle class bureaucracy in Oslo and Finnish, Norwegian and Samish agriculturalists in the northern Norwegian province of Finnmark. And it is clearly shown in the accounts of Verrips and the Snells of the way the expanding activities of the state eliminate the traditional way of life of small farmers and reindeer breeders. Europe, too, has its neglected, oppressed and exploited minority groups, its 'primitives.' Studies of the way these smaller, marginal groups are caught up in wider social processes can thus provide a valuable perspective on internal developments in the societies draining the poorer countries. In this way the interest groups and processes which give rise to decisions that affect these poorer nations can be better understood.

Greater understanding of the structure of European societies and of processes taking place within and between them may thus help reduce the growing asymmetry between the rich and poor nations of the world. Such studies might help, for example, by indicating likely European coalition partners for poorer nations or oppressed segments in them. The support provided by certain political parties, trade unions, student organizations and minority groups in Europe for national liberation movements, unions, parties and minorities in Africa, Asia and Latin America provide cases in point.

There is yet another reason for studying Europe. The aim of social science is to gain insights into social relations and processes in order to explain the past, understand the present and predict the future. In this way it can contribute to an understanding that helps make possible a better, more equitable way of life for more people. Anthropologists working in Europe are dealing with societies at a different level of social development than most societies in other parts of the world. It seems likely than many of these poorer societies will follow part of the road already travelled by Europe. They, too, are heading for greater industrialization, centralization, bureaucratization, urbanization, differentiation, and so on. The analysis of processes taking place in Europe, and the problems of its small communities, can indicate the often unintended long-term consequences of decisions made today in societies at different levels of social development.

DEVELOPMENTS IN MODERN EUROPE

Most of the studies document the increasing centralization of decision-making powers at higher levels of integration. Concomitant with that, they show the gradual erosion of the autonomy of smaller units. Davis demonstrates that these processes were already evident shortly after the birth of the Italian state. They are particularly well documented by Verrips. He shows how, partly in response to local pressures and partly in the interest of the central bureaucracy, government bodies increasingly take over functions performed by local communities. To meet the complaints of marginal farmers who are facing financial difficulties, government consolidates land holdings to help increase agricultural productivity. The costs involved force small farmers to sell out to large farmers. Marginal farmers inevitably become the losers. To cope with increasing pollution generated by expanding industrialization and to further tourism, provincial authorities take over water control from local associations run by farmers. This further deprives farmers of status and influence. To control the competition between communities for scarce state resources, and to regulate more adequately the process of industrialization and urbanization, government amalgamates smaller municipalities. Verrips shows that the loss of autonomy does not take place without a struggle, though, at least in Holland, the smaller units inevitably lose.

The gradual shift of decision-making powers to higher integration levels is certainly not confined to government bureaucracies. Possibly to be able to resist and to influence the expanding bureaucratic power, political parties and other interest groups are also growing more centralized. Wade's study, for example, clearly shows the progressive influence of regional and national party officials on local political cadres and issues.

These examples can be repeated for most of the societies examined in this volume. Everywhere small units and enterprises have been slowly giving way to larger units. Whether they be municipalities, dairy or wine farmers, reindeer breeders, business houses or national defense organizations, the shift of more decision-making powers to more inclusive units appears similar.

The expansion of spheres of competence of increasingly larger units is linked to the reduction of power differences. Katz and Verrips describe how the asymmetry of power between landed and landless agriculturalists in South Tyrol and Holland is reduced as industrialization provides new opportunities for the poor, and rising expectations and costs of mechanization place the rich under mounting economic pressure. Brunt shows that industrial workers, driven from the cities by poor housing, are able to move to villages and commute to work, thanks to cars made possible by the general rise in the standard of living. In the villages they enter into coalition with local socialists, further eroding the power of the traditional elite of farmers and shopkeepers.

This reduction in power differentials, partly brought about by changing economic relations, is further stimulated by activities of national governments. With the exception of some areas in the Italian South, governments everywhere have been able successfully to monopolize the use of physical violence. This has deprived local power holders of an important resource for maintaining and expanding their domain. Reflecting the gradual extension of the franchise to all levels of society, the state has continually expanded its activities to further the common weal and to assist disadvantaged social categories. Education, cheap housing, medical and welfare payments, technical assistance and financial subsidies to agricultural and industrial enterprises have provided resources available to increasing numbers. New forms of association have been formed to exploit these new resources.

Many small communities are using these resources to fight for local rights the state is seeking to usurp. Gorter, for example, shows how a local community in Finnmark successfully defended its rights against the government, through local organizations and local branches of national associations founded by teachers sent up north to promote national (southern) Norwegian culture. Meertens describes how Andalusian building labourers seized upon a slight relaxation in the labour laws, brought about by E.E.C. pressure, to strengthen their organization and strike for more rights. And the Snells outline the process whereby education, modest economic prosperity, increasing tolerance in the wider society, and political stability – as aspects of the welfare state – enabled Spanish leaders to convert ethnicity into an organizational quality with which to fight for rights the state had usurped.

Other contributors document the same process. Yoon demonstrates how state-assisted cooperatives of small wine producers enter into coalition with large independent vineyard owners to fight government economic policies. Daniela Weinberg also provides an example of local communities cooperating successfully to counter government interference with local rights. Bax, too, sees a change in the balance of power in favour of the small community as a result of the expanding activities of the welfare state. These studies demonstrate that the growing concentration of power at higher integration levels can only be countered successfully by larger defensive coalitions.

Several of the studies demonstrate that the increasing geographical mobility generated by industrialization and improved communication has affected local power balances, creating categories of insiders and outsiders who vie for power. Just as increased centralization of power stimulates local communities to claim dormant rights and demarcate fields of competence, so also the penetration of outsiders leads to the crystallization of boundaries. Sames, Basques, Scots, Welshmen, Protestants and Catholics in Ireland, French- and Flemish-speaking Belgians are vociferously and sometimes violently guarding their boundaries. The same applies to Dutch urban slum dwellers,

Cornishmen, entire Italian regions, and diverse minority groups and small communities throughout Europe. Although it will take careful historical research to verify, it appears that these minorities are becoming increasingly restive. This activity would seem related to the expanding encroachment and growing impenetrability of the state bureaucracy; to the progressive penetration of outsiders; to the increasing availability of welfare state resources; and to improved communication which has made minorities internationally aware of their common interests. This unrest could well be the prelude to a more general legitimacy crisis for the nation-state. There is a structural and ideological similarity between workers striking against 'their' factory, and minorities who take similar action against 'their' country. Both feel that the demands of the owners or rulers have lost their legitimacy (cf. Galtung 1969:20). This is clearly illustrated by the way the militant National Union of Mine-workers in 1974 brought the British government to its knees by striking for higher wages. In the ensuing general election the Conservative government was defeated, and Scottish and Welsh nationalists gained in strength.

The studies in this volume thus appear to offer evidence that the power of European nation-states, which had been steadily expanding since the beginning of the 19th century, is gradually being checked. In the words of the Snells: 'Nation building is largely finished in Western Europe.' This development has proceeded roughly as follows. State formation transferred power from the local elite to the state's central apparatus, thus reducing local autonomy. In more or less democrati-cally ordered societies, centralization has reduced local differences in relative power. Progressive centralization brought with it the expansion of the state bureaucracy. This expansion involved, in its turn, a steady splitting up of decision-making powers among multiplying agencies. The pro-gressive diffusion of power at higher integration levels has made the decision-making process increasingly difficult to oversee. The spreading of decision-making powers over larger numbers of persons and agencies has also made it more difficult for single persons and small collectivities to influence decisions. Increasingly, individuals and groups are forming specialized coalitions to check the progressive reduction of local autonomy, to oversee the decision-making process, and to influence the outcome of decisions affecting members. These coalitions, with ever greater success, are blocking from below the usurpation of power from above. Their relative success is due in no small measure to the growing stream of tactical resources the state is making available, and to their success in recruiting support at home and abroad. Resources and support are expanding in proportion to the growing power of such coalitions.

At the same time that pressure from within is increasing, the nation-state is being obliged to sacrifice more of its autonomy to supranational organizations like the United Nations, the E.E.C., Nato, the Council of Europe, O.E.C.D., and so on. Moreover, international pressure groups – such as Amnesty International, the Nordic Samish Council, the World Council of Churches, and international professional and political associations – are growing more powerful. They cooperate with national coalitions to check the expansion of the power of national bureaucracies and of political and economic elites. The power of the nation-state is thus increasingly being eroded by national and international organizations, and by cooperation between the two.

The erosion of the concept as well as the power of European nation-states is also accelerated by the expanding power of multi-national corporations. These are able to evade national controls such as minimum wage legislation by operating abroad. There they can pay wages that are indecent, even by local standards, because the jobs they create are desperately needed. They also can subvert the authority of the nation-state by the use of their immense wealth. Recent activities in this field of United States multi-national corporations in Latin America as well as at home, and of British companies in South Africa, are so well known they require no further comment.

THEORETICAL IMPLICATIONS

The range of problems treated in this volume reflects the shift in theoretical orientation of the present generation of anthropologists. Up to the 1960's, the dominant question asked by most sociologists and social anthropologists was: What makes social order possible? What social institutions exist and how are they functionally related? The accent was on the description of institutions and customs, and the way they were interconnected to form a system. These questions produced many important insights. But anthropologists now are no longer concerned with merely describing what exists and explaining its existence by demonstrating how it forms part of a total system. They are asking new questions. As these contributions clearly show, anthropologists now seek to explain the events of change, to chart the forces influencing the people they study.

This shift in the questions asked, and thus in the explanations advanced, lies at the heart of much of the theoretical ferment taking place in the scientific community of social anthropologists. They are searching for nonteleological explanations for what they observe, as they seek to free themselves from the structural-functional concern with order. Hence they are increasingly turning to theoretical paradigms in which economic, political and historical elements are given greater prominence, such as those of Marx and Elias (cf. Asad 1972 and 1973, and Blok 1974, respectively).

Why the dominant question has changed is a problem which requires considerable further research. Any attempt to answer it will have to deal with both epistemological and sociohistorical processes (cf. Toulmin 1972:123). These have been dealt with in some detail, but not yet completely, by Boissevain (1974), Elias (1970), Gouldner (1970), and Harris (1968), among others. The question of what makes order possible and how it is maintained has been explored in great detail for half a century. Social scientists now want theories that explain the rapidly changing world around them and help them predict with greater accuracy the course it will take. Structural-functionalism, with its emphasis on social order, has been unable either to predict or to explain the rush of events. Rapid change is occurring in all areas being examined by social anthropologists. New theories are demanded by those affected by these processes.

SCIENTIFIC TRESPASSERS?

It is evident that all the contributors are deeply involved in cognate fields. All have had to become historians. A few also have examined problems usually treated by political scientists. Yet only a decade ago, Devons and Gluckman (1964a, 1964b) argued that it was not desirable for anthropologists to move into other scientific areas. They wrote: 'It is highly dangerous to trespass beyond the limits of one's competence . . . to exercise this competence one must abstain from becoming involved in the problems of others' (1964a:18). They argued for 'specialization and keeping to one's last in the social sciences in order to develop theoretical understanding' (Ibid.:19).

The contributors to this volume obviously do not share this point of view, but then it was generated by a different theoretical perspective. Gluckman, for example, has been concerned with social order and has made important contributions in that field, devoting himself to law, ritual and custom. The advice of Devons and Gluckman must be seen in this light, as they themselves were well aware. They noted that if the questions change, so must the activities of researchers:

We shall see that whenever we try to understand the form of certain phenomena in terms of 'why' they are as they are rather than 'how' they are interconnected with one another we are less able to take as given 'surrounding' phenomena and interpretations of the relations between these phenomena. Entry into the nature of surrounding phenomena is always relative to the problem we set ourselves: and we have particularly to be open-minded . . . when we engage in comparative and historical studies (1964b:181).

Thus it may not be possible to stick to your last if the questions asked change. And clearly they have changed. The consequence of this change is that anthropologists must rethink the assumptions, boundaries and techniques of their discipline.

The idea that past and present sociological problems should be, or can be, pursued in separate compartments by different scientific disciplines is misleading. There is a need for a more unified and integrated theoretical framework for the various social sciences. Their present boundaries and their status struggles have hindered and are still impeding our understanding of human society (cf. Elias 1972).

The implications are clear. Some anthropologists are already committed to problems and techniques of other disciplines. This means that attention must be paid to these in the universities where the apprentices in the scientific community are trained. Anthropologists can no longer rely exclusively on the traditional method of participant observation, carried out against the background of what other anthropologists have written.

Crump sums up the implications neatly: '... in the end there is no easy answer for the anthropologist interested in Italy. He must have not only a considerable command over the methods and techniques of his own discipline, but also be an expert in the history, literature, human geography and economy of Italy ... and this means searching through a wealth of material, largely in Italian, and often only accessible in Italy itself.'

THE FUTURE

This volume demonstrates that anthropologists can make an important contribution to the study of Europe. It also shows that communities of interdependent persons sharing a feeling of belonging together provide an excellent niche for the social anthropologist. From this vantage point he can study the social relations between individuals and groups, and between these and the societal processes of which they form part. Because national and international integration have proceeded farther in Europe than in most other parts of the world, anthropological studies of this continent can make a contribution to understanding the long term developments which are sweeping all societies.

The contributors to this volume thus also provide a first attempt at developing what could be called an anthropology of national and supra-national processes. This can complement the work of professional futurists such as Jungk, Galtung and others (1969).

These studies also reveal certain shortcomings inherent in the discipline in its present state of development. Overwhelmingly they show a rural bias and an interest in economically and politically marginal groups. Anthropologists would still appear to be searching for, and finding, 'primitives' in modern Europe. The studies also deal exclusively with the capitalist societies of Western Europe. Future studies must correct this bias. The world is becoming increasingly urbanized, centralized and socialist-oriented. Studies of urban-centered problems, of the interrelation between economically and politically dominant groups, including state bureaucracies and multi-national corporations, and of socialist societies are badly needed. Hopefully more studies will also focus on the role ideology and constitutional parameters, such as electoral laws, play in influencing social relations and processes. Such studies might show how, for example, in the Netherlands rival religious and political ideologies, electoral laws, the absence of regional representation, the surprising power of the central bureaucracy, and the multiplying number of action groups are interrelated. This introduction has been able to do no more than touch on some of the many theoretical issues these studies raise, and to indicate some of the general conclusions. It has scarcely done justice to the richness of the data and the elegance of their presentation by the authors. The reader must now examine these for himself.

NOTES

[1] In a sense this essay is a collective effort. M. Bax, L. Brunt, T. Crump, J. Davis, W. Gorter, D. Meertens, H. and T. Snell, J. Verrips, S. Wallman and E. Zammit provided detailed, at times sharp, but always highly constructive criticism on a preliminary draft, as did Beryl Muscat, who helped with the typing. I am indebted to them all for their advice, much of which I have followed. Errors of interpretation, of course, are mine alone.

REFERENCES

Asad, Talal
Market Model, Class Structure and Consent: A Reconstruction of Swat Political Organization. *Man* 7:74–94, 1972.
Antropology and the Colonial Encounter. London: Pergammon Press, 1973.

Blok, Anton
The Mafia of a Sicilian Village, 1860–1960: A Study of Violent Peasant Entrepreneurs. Oxford: Basil Blackwell, 1974.

Boissevain, Jeremy
Towards a Sociology of Social Anthropology. *Society and Theory* 1:211–230, 1974.

Devons, Ely, and Max Gluckman
'Introduction,' in *Closed Systems and Open Minds*, 13–19. Edited by Max Gluckman. Chicago: Aldine, 1964a.
'Conclusion,' in *Closed Systems and Open Minds*, 158–281. Edited by Max Gluckman. Chicago: Aldine, 1964b.

Elias, Norbert
Ueber den Prozess der Zivilisation. 2nd ed. Bern/München: Francke Verlag, 1969.
Was ist Soziologie? München: Juventa Verlag, 1970.
Processes of State Formation and Nation Building. *Transactions of the 7th World Congress of Sociology, Varna, Bulgaria, September 1970*. Geneva: International Sociological Association, 1972.

Freeman, Susan Tax, ed.
Introduction to Studies in Rural European Social Organization. *American Anthropologist* 75:743–50, 1973.

Galtung, Johan
'On the future of the International System,' in *Mankind 2000*, 21–41. Edited by Robert Jungk and Johan Galtung. London: George Allen & Unwin, 1969.

Gouldner, Alvin W.
The Coming Crisis of Western Sociology. London: Heinemann, 1970.

Harris, Marvin
The Rise of Anthropological Theory. London: Routledge and Kegan Paul, 1968.

Toulmin, Stephen
Human Understanding. Vol. I. Oxford: The Clarendon Press, 1972.

2

The Context of European Anthropology: the Lesson from Italy

Thomas Crump
University of Amsterdam

ABSTRACT

The object of this deliberately controversial article is to redirect Italian anthropology to studies relevant to studies relevant to contemporary industrial Italy, which is seen more as a European than as a Mediterranean land. In the era of the Mansholt Plan, the isolated backward rural community plays a rapidly declining role in modern Italy. A short demographic analysis based on the province of Siena suggests some reasons for this decline, and emphasizes factors largely in the field of human geography, which wil be most critical in determining the character of Italian society in the future.

The anthropologist intent on research into small communities in Italy is immediately faced with difficult questions of significance. His chosen field of research is in a sort of no-man's land between anthropology on one side, and Italian studies on the other. It is marginal in the *history* of either discipline. This point can easily be verified by seeing how many anthropological texts are to be found in any specialised Italian library (such as the part of the University of Reading library devoted to Italian studies, for which there is a special research institute within the university), or how many Italian texts are to be found in a general anthropological library. (When I first started looking for such texts, early in 1972, the library of the Royal Anthropological Institute had but five, which number may just have doubled since then. There might be fifty times as many texts on the anthropology of Nigeria, a country of roughly the same population as Italy.) All this could mean no more than that – by some sort of accident – scholars just happened to have neglected the field. If so, then there is nothing against proceeding confidently – and with all reasonable speed – to fill the gap. This is the general tenor of European anthropology, at least in its first twenty years or so, as exemplified by any number of studies of small-scale societies[1]. It is interesting to note, however, that the papers in this volume argue that the traditional community approach applied to Europe is inadequate[2].

It is, however, instructive to consider the possible reasons for the comparative neglect by academics – of whichever discipline – of the small Italian community. It will be assumed that the process or research is never entirely random, however much of it is influenced at any one time by prevailing academic fashion.

Here it is useful to ask two naive questions. The first is: why study small communities anywhere? And the second: why study Italy?

The first question goes to the heart of anthropology. It can be answered in two stages: the first is that the very smallness of a community may provide the best context for the study of economic, social or political organization, or of a whole range of cultural institutions. What may become extremely complex at the macro-level, becomes relatively simple at the micro-level. This leads to the second stage of the answer. The small local community – or more generally the smallest segment of any larger population – often not only illustrates the characteristic features of all other like segments, but also combines with them, according to a consistent underlying principle, to form isomorphic units at higher levels, to generate, finally, the total political organization of an entire population (vide Evans-Pritchard 1940). Even where this is not the case – as with certain peasant societies – the study can still illustrate a typical and representative example of the communities which comprise the majority of a wider population[3]. In such a case the study of the total population can be made complete by filling in the gaps – say by complementary research into local market towns[4]. The process may proceed further, to end up with specifically urban studies, such as mining communities[5], with feedback (generally considered in other quite independent studies)[6] to the local effect of emigration on the rural communities.

All this does no more than survey the more or less parallel development of the third world anthropology. At every stage the anthropologists have been only a little way behind in their study and analysis of local developments. The theme could be handled in greater detail, but the point to make is that at every stage in the academic development of anthropology – as outlined above – the historical component becomes more and more critical. Leach's criticism of the classic tribal studies of Malinowski, Firth and Evans-Pritchard (Leach 1954:7), that they relate to social systems detached from any sort of historical context, is hardly applicable to contemporary urban studies in Africa or Asia. Indeed it is arguable that the whole process will efface anthropology as a separate discipline[7].

It is now time to turn to the second question: why study Italy? Scientifically this question should be answered in the same spirit as the first. That is, there must be certain aspects of Italy which are significant far beyond the confines of any particular and specific study. This statement is so obviously trite that its truth need hardly be argued for. In the history of political and economic institutions, in the fine arts, in literature and political philosophy, in the institutions of religion, Italy must be one of the most intensively studied countries in the world. How odd then that the anthropologists should be so late in discovering it. In part it is a sufficient answer to this question that Europe as a whole has only recently been discovered by anthropology. The reasons for this late discovery are implicit in the preceding paragraph. But then, might it not also be true that there is something in the anthropological approach which in Italy – or in Europe generally – leads up a blind alley? If this proves to be so, then the approach, quite simply, must be radically modified. A good starting point is a paragraph from a study by Nadel (1951:10). (This is reasonable from the Italian point of view, since Nadel was quite open to the extension of anthropology to European and North American studies (1951:7).)

...in the kind of enquiry which is not historical but scientific we view events under the aspects of their repetitiveness and regularity, regardless of time and place, and use the observations of the individual and particular for the formation of universally valid laws.
... the scientist examines 'what happened' on the particular occasions so as to be able to state in general terms, why, or how things happen.

It may be assumed that the anthropologist working in a small Italian community is looking for the 'repetitiveness and regularity of events[8]. "(Otherwise he would be no more than a local historian: there is in fact a wealth of Italian local history[9], and it is a fair criticism that much that goes as anthropology – generally because the author professes that discipline – is in fact local history[10]. Now a piece of anthropological research is valuable tot the extent that observed repetitiveness and regularity is demonstrably the model of a general social or cultural phenomenon. At the same time, the subject matter of observation should fall within the conventional boundaries of the discipline[11] (though this is not to argue that they are rigidly fixed for all time: uncertainty about boundaries is a major preoccupation of contemporary anthropology, and it is significant how much interest there now is in marginal areas such as sociolinguistics[12]).

Now when it comes to Italy too many scholars appear to assume that the canons of *anthropological science* are satisfied by forcing the Italian population through a sort of sieve to leave only a residue of relatively isolated, partly illiterate, technically retarded, rural communities, sometimes with a non-Italian local dialect[13]. This may appear to be a harsh criticism, but just consider the subject matter of such studies as Boissevain 1966, Maraspini 1968, Davis 1969 and 1973, Pitkin 1960 or Wade 1971. Cole and Wolf really give the game away when they disclose (1974:11) that 'In fixing our attention on St. Felix and Tret, we did not choose communities representative of the wealth and often opulent life of the lowland valleys, but poor and isolated settlements with specialities and little chance to share in the richness of cultural forms so characteristic of the more prosperous Tyrolese peasantry. Poverty and isolation...' Is it that the Italian specialists feel that they have to follow the well-trodden third world path leading from traditional, technologically retarded rural populations through to the urban studies which are now appearing in ever greater numbers? There are in fact excellent Italian urban studies, such as Schnapper 1971, on Bologna, or Allum 1973, on Naples, which contain conclusions valid for the country as a whole, and which certainly leave a better understanding of Italy than do any of the small community studies[14]. To see why this is so, one must look further at the consequences of these latter studies. Of these the most critical is that the distribution of research is highly skewed. This would be tolerable only if two conditions were satisfied: first, that Italy had a substantially uniform geography; and second, that its institutional structure was generated essentially by the periphery rather than the centre.

It would be difficult to find another country as far away as Italy is from satisfying these conditions. True, the reasons for this are almost entirely historical, but this means no more than that for an adequate Italian anthropology of any kind, the whole research approach must become much broader.

The point can be well illustrated by considering the Tuscan province of Siena defined according to its frontiers at the beginning of the 19th century. This area now comprises the two provinces of Siena and Grosseto, but they are reasonably uniform, culturally and socially, particularly by Italian standards. The established bias of Italian anthropological research – as described above – has led, almost inevitably, to the neglect of this area, but there is one published study within the general tradition, Wade (1971), on 'Colombaio[15].' Now it is an implicit theme of this study (as indeed of any anthropological study) that Colombaio is seen as exemplifying a significant economic, cultural or political region. This would be the case with the Bohannans' research of the Tiv, in Nigeria, a population of much the same size as that of Siena-Grosseto. Common sense tells us that the Bohannans could not have researched every individual Tiv community in depth: with a population of a million odd, that would have been impossible. But the whole tenor of their research convinces one that in their case the parts did comprehend, and represent, the whole. Turning back to Colombaio, and looking at it in light of the 1971 census, we can see just what it exemplifies, even in the relatively restricted geographical context of Siena-Grosseto. It has a steadily falling population, particularly in agriculture. It has next to no industry, and the tertiary sector is equally unimportant. It does not lie on or near any main line of communication. Now these factors may equate it with a majority, in number, of the communes of Siena-Grosseto[16], but this does no more than bestow upon it a sort of nominal political importance, with little economic or demographic justification. The constitutional uniformity of the three-tier devolution of government in Italy, through the region, the province and the commune, does give even the smallest commune an air of civic importance, not to be found in, say, an English parish, and the political philosophy which this represents could yield an interesting subject for anthropological research. But if our interest in Colombaio has anything to do with human factors which are spontaneous rather than formal, we shall find ourselves preoccupied with a type of incomplete human geography which only informs us obliquely about the realities of Siena-Grosseto in 1973, or indeed 1273, for those with historical perspective. At the same time Colombaio exemplifies one factor which is typical neither of its province, nor of its region, nor of Italy as a whole. This is depopulation[17]. But even here the controlling factors are exogenous: there may well be an anthropology of the progressively depopulated rural community, for which Wade's study of Colombaio could be an exemplary starting point.

Here again there is an inherent problem. For all that the Italian commune, with its more or less universal formal structure, runs in all shapes and sizes, one does not have to research very far to discover that population size is the most important factor in determining the informal structures which are the anthropologist's main interest. The effect of scale on political, and even more economic institutions, has been relatively little researched in Italy. At a relatively elementary level I have discovered, in the course of my own researches – based largely on Guttman scale analysis – in the current year, for the province of Siena, that at a population level of about 6,500 there is a sharp dividing line between communes which enjoy a wide range of economic and social services, and those which do not. In the province of Siena 10 out of 36 communes now have a population above 6,500. In each of these, but not in any of the remaining 26, there will be a clothing store, an insurance agency, a car-repairing garage, a flower shop, a secondary school – to note particularly typical 20th century institutions. In these ten communes the population is increasing, whereas in the rest it is declining. The sharpest percentage declines are in the smallest centres of population. (The population of the commune of San Giovanni d'Asso fell from 2,352 to 1,421 between 1961 and 1971: one wonders if it will exist at all at the end of the century.) We are now beginning to get the right contextual setting for Colombaio, but we must proceed further. What is the distinguishing feature of the developing communities in Tuscany? Population is one answer, but this depends on the whole question of local incentive for residence, and here one is immediately brought face to face with the realities of 20th century economic development. Three things are particulary important for Tuscany.

The first is transport, with a very strong emphasis, in Tuscany, on the areas close to main-line electric railways, or more than ever in the last ten years, to the *autostrade*. The relative prosperity of the five Siena communes lying along the *Autostrada del Sole* is no coincidence.

The second critical point is the development of capital-intensive enterprise, in agriculture as well as in industry. Thus we see the rapid development of the plains of Maremma in Grosseto, which before reclamation, that is in recent historical times, were unsuitable for cultivation, and which are now intensively worked, without the demographic basis of the traditional Tuscan township. (For this area, therefore, Colombaio is quite unrepresentative.)

Third comes tourism, Italy's most important growth industry, particularly in the years of mass tourism after the end of World War II. This has particularly helped the coastal communes in Siena-Grosseto, but one should note the enormous growth of Chianciano Terme, a flourishing inland spa, which contains three-quarters of all the hotel accommodations in the province of Siena.

A flourishing tertiary sector of the provincial economies is supported by these three factors in particular. This is the only rationale of the city of Grosseto, which now contains nearly 30 per cent of the provincial population ,when at the beginning of the century it had less than five per cent[18]. It is not surprising that the latest Italian study of the province (Elia 1972) focuses almost entirely on the city.

All this leads away from traditional anthropology. I could well be accused of diverting attention from the community studies, as exemplified in Tuscany by Colombaio, by choosing my field of battle in demography or human geography. If this accusation is just, then the answer to it is that this choice is determined by the material under examination. (Blok, in his very thorough analysis of South Italian Agro-Towns (1969), is forced into just this sort of position. It is essentially a study in human geography, as witnessed by his quite explicit indebtedness to Demangeon 1927.) As an anthropologist I am, however, unrepentant. Italy, above all, is the country where the city comes first, where urban institutions permeate and dominate the countryside, which is seen as a sort of rural retreat from the city. Where else in the world, at whatever period in history, is there a place such as

Venice, the city *par excellence*? And leaving Venice aside, what does Italy mean in the context of civilization (itself a word which connotes the life of the city) but Florence, Pisa, Milan, Genoa, Rome, Naples, Palermo and so on? Almost every one of the Italian provinces is named after the city which is the provincial capital. The word by which 'peasant' (with its *rural* connotations) is most commonly translated into Italian, *contadino*, again connotes the connection with the *contado*, and the city. The traditional tenure of land by the Tuscan peasant is based on the *mezzadria*, a mercantile contract divised by men from the city who bought land in the market as an investment; this supplanted feudal tenure, based upon the hereditary rights of the lord and his subjects, as early as the thirteenth century[19].

It would be fair to argue that however dominant the city must be, its inhabitants still need to consume the produce which only their country cousins can provide. But then in Italy the organization of agricultural production has for centuries reflected the central – and essentially independent – position of the city. It is astonishing to see the intensity of cultivation which still takes place within the walls of the city of Siena. There is a sharply declining profile of profitable agriculture as the distance from the city increases, and still today one reaches a marginal region, not so far from the city centre, where primary woodland covers an area which it was never economical to cultivate (Annuario Statistica Toscana, 1971. Documentazione Cartografica, Tavola 9). For as long as the city kept all trading options open – and this has always been the secret of Italian prosperity – the social structures of marginal agriculture inevitably remained undeveloped and subordinate. The sophistication of urban institutions, and their extension outside the city walls, are historically the most remarkable common denominator of Italy as a whole. It is not for nothing that the Monte dei Paschi di Siena, the oldest bank in the world, has a branch in every commune in the province.

This is the critical factor which Italian anthropology has to take into account. A number of institutions co-exist uneasily in Italy, each one of them down to the smallest communes, and all playing more or less complementary roles: these are the church, the government, the political parties, the trade unions, the *ordini* which represent the interest of countless different professions – all with remarkably similar underlying structures. (It is astonishing for the anthropologist, and fascinating at the same time, to witness the propensity of Italians, of any recognised category, to gather together for a manifestation of quite Durkheimian effervescence: for instance, on Sunday, June 3, 1973, Siena welcomed ambulance drivers from all over Italy for a vast open-air mass in the Campo.) But if the focus of research remains fixed upon the small isolated community, the picture becomes too fragmentary, and all the wrong points are emphasized[20].

For the anthropologist, the conclusion is not so much that research should be confined to the great critics, although certainly more work could be done along the lines of Schnapper's study of Bologna (1971), but that research should have a strong thematic bias, and a deep sense of structure. So far the perspective of Italian anthropology has been too antiquarian, representing a tendency to idealise what still might be true today, if the last hundred years of history had not passed. Thus Silverman's (1968) sensitive reconsideration of amoral familism (which after all only appeared six years ago) places far too much emphasis on the *mezzadria* in central Italy, relying on statistics contained in a 1946–48 survey, but failing to take sufficiently into account that *mezzadria* holdings are rapidly disappearing, and that no new ones can be created. (This point may not have been quite as clear in the late 1960s as it is now – but no local inhabitant would have been in any doubt about the matter.) Consider also Pitkin's (1963) study, boldly titled 'Mediterranean Europe,' but which gives at least as much attention to Italy as to any other country (not surprising, actually, considering the location of Pitkin's own fieldwork). This sees the city, rightly, as the 'source of ultimate values,' but then characterises it as 'pre-industrial.' Where on earth do the Italians, with the world's seventh largest industrial economy, hide their industry? It may be arguable that 'modern history has done little to alter the basic pattern of this culture area as it was laid down in classical times and reiterated in the Middle Ages' (Pitkin 1963:123), but in this year, 1974, the argument would need qualification, to say the least. And then, how do all the small-community specialists react when they are told that '... in a pre-industrial society the countryside 'throws up' few values that are of major significance for society as a whole.'? Schnapper once again gets the perspective right when she observes (1971:85) that 'the Italians live in the decor of the past.' Even better is the way in which Davis (1973:1) sets the scene for his latest study: 'Although south Italian peasant societies can be described in ways which make them seem exotic, they are not essentially so. Pisticci and the towns like it are mixtures of the bizarre and the 'ordinary'. The Italian normal, the local idiosyncratic, the European commonplace are there combined. Like other towns in south Italy, Pisticci has many modern aspects: it is part of an industrial nation and of a parliamentary state.' But generally a mis-directed approach has led to too many superficial concepts. The whole debate about 'amoral fami-lism' illustrates this. (See Banfield 1958, and his critics: Marselli 1963, Wichers 1964, Silverman 1968 etc.) The concept is descriptive rather than explanatory: any case which exemplifies it tends to be an epiphenomenon.

The same is probably true of such favourite Italian themes as patronage or coalitions, so fully discussed in Boissevain 1974. Of course these institutions exist, but unless they occur as a result of a stochastic process (which seems improbable in any society, particularly in one so bound by tradition as Italy), there must be some order behind them, reducible to some theoretical principle. Struc-turalism may be overworked – and the present argument is not intended to be explicitly structu-ralist – but its critics (such as Boissevain 1974, Chapter 1) should consider what its alternatives add up to. The Marxists have provided one answer (e.g. Wertheim 1974: esp. 89–91), the phenomenol-ogists another (Spiegelberg 1967), and the common-sense empiricists, such as Nadel, a third. The mistake, and it is one which is easy to make in the context of Italian anthropology, is to confuse an instance, or even a multiplicity of instances, with the underlying principle.

The critic has his responsibilities. One is to be constructive, to suggest a way in which restoration may follow destruction. Since I have suggested that Italian anthropology lacks principle, and that too many of its favourite themes are superficial, I can fairly be asked to do something about the situation. Thus, tentatively, I will suggest a principle that will go a long way to explain amoral familism, brokerage, coalition and the other face-to-face reactions and relations so accurately noted in the ethnography. The Italian lives in two worlds, one profane, imperfect, disunited, and the other sacred, perfect, harmonious. Man is imperfect, but is perfectible. The two worlds constantly interact, both at a purely human level, and also, in terms of judgment, at a super-human level, which is what Dante's Divine Comedy was all about. The interaction is institutionalised, and it is not only the Church which controls the frontier between the two worlds. The idea, often stated explicitly, and surprisingly often realised in odd little corners of Italian life, is one of system, that order can always be brought out of chaos. This is comprehended by the Italian word *sistemazione*. Not only the Church as a theological ideal is *sistemata*, but so also is the state, as a political ideal, a theme at least as old as Macchiavelli. But no ideal system functioning in a human context can operate without human agents, and since the systems exist to perfect the imperfect, it is implicit that the system which these agents – themselves imperfect (theologically, because they are mortal) – actually maintain, is itself a corrupt transformation of the ideal. Thus to the Italian *sottogoverno* is more real than *governo*, and so a profane order, characterised by brokerage, coalitions, etc. repla-ces the ideal. Clergy are corrupt, not so much as a matter of observation (although clerical corrup-tion could be abundantly documented), but because in the Church as it actually is they could not be otherwise. In such a context, response to the ideal readily transforms into a cult of some figurehead – a role to be assumed, formally, say, by the Pope, or informally by one such as Padre Pio, a recently deceased friar reputed to have received Christ's stigmata. Significantly, such charac-ters are seen as entirely free from the dyadic contacts and networks inherent in all forms of broke-rage and coalition-forming. One never thinks of the Pope, or Padre Pio, as being engaged in ordi-nary conversation, let alone intrigue[21]. The Pope speaks *ex cathedra*, and Padre Pio hardly spoke at all.

All this is simplification, and in the end there is no easy answer for the anthropologist interested in Italy. He must have not only a considerable command over the methods and techniques of his own discipline, but also be expert in the history, literature, human geography and economy of Italy – and this means searching through a wealth of material, largely in Italian, and often only accessible in Italy itself.

With such a background the small community itself can most profitably be studied, and there is no reason why such studies, in Italy, should not only be creative within the discipline of anthropology, but also add to our knowledge and understanding of modern Italy. In a country where so many familiar institutions of the modern world, religious, economic, or political, originated, it would be surprising if the science which above all interests itself in such institutions had nothing to discover.

NOTES

[1] See the works cited in the bibliography under Boissevain, Davis, Maraspini, and Wade, to mention only a few such studies.

[2] See, for example, Meertens' study in this volume.

[3] There are numerous studies of this kind: see, for example, Leach 1961, and Geertz 1970.

[4] E. g. Geertz 1963, for the chapters on the market of Modjokuto.

[5] See Mitchell 1969, particularly for the contributions of Epstein and Harries-Jones.

[6] For African examples see Watson 1958 and Van Velsen 1964; for a Mexican example see Butterworth 1970.

[7] Evans-Pritchard 1963 is important on this point, and it is worth noting also the views expressed in Evans-Pritchard (1951:62). Evans-Pritchard 1968 (on the Sanusi of Cyrenaica) is as much an historical as an anthropological study.

[8] The importance of regularities in events is stressed also in Gluckman (1964:160).

[9] See for example Repetti 1933, Petri 1972, Imberciadori 1971, Cassola and Bianciardi 1956. Any local library or bookshop in Italy has a wealth of books of this character.

[10] Blok 1974 is an example of this from recent Italian studies.

[11] This is essentially the same point as is made in the quotation from Pitt-Rivers 1961 in Verrips' study in this volume.

[12] See, for example, Douglas 1970, chapter 2. For Italy see Denison's study in Ardener 1971.

[13] E.g. Maraspini 1968 (Greek), Cole and Wolf 1974 (German).

[14] An exception might well be made for Davis 1973, in which the introduction strikes just the right balance between European, Italian and purely local factors.

[15] (Wade 1971:331). Colombaio is a pseudonym, adopted by Dr. Wade, no doubt for the best of motives. The practice, which is regarded as quite normal in some anthropological circles, is inconvenient and unscientific. If one wants to develop Dr. Wade's research – which would be no more than a credit to its general value – one naturally wants to know where one is starting from. I did not have to research long in Tuscany before I discovered, from several sources, and without really trying at all, which commune Dr. Wade actually researched. Out of consideration for him, I shall not give away his secret. But the fact is that those who are interested will find it out, and to those who are not, the true name of the commune would mean nothing anyway. I am sympathetic to Dr. Wade (who may even have had to give assurances that he would not give the name of the commune away), but on balance his policy is probably mistaken. One can note by way of contrast how Davis (1973:vi) made it quite clear that he gives the real, and not invented, names of people and places.

[16] Dr. Wade sought for his research a rural commune in the hills, where there had already been considerable progress in land reform: this certainly narrowed down his choice (personal communication).

[17] There was in fact a marginal fall in the population of the province of Siena between the 1961 and the 1971 censuses, but it came exclusively from the already thinly populated isolated rural communes.

[18] I am grateful to Mr. Peter van der Werff, one of the participants in the 1973 summer programme of the University of Amsterdam, for complementing my own research in the province of Siena with his work in the province of Grosseto: see here, in particular, the 'Relazione sulla situazione economica della provincia di Grosseto nel 1970 e 1971.'

[19] Laven (1966:22). For a specifically local Tuscan study see Jones 1968.

[20] Wade (1972:190) acknowledges the role of the political parties in providing a channel of communication between the periphery and the centre.

[21] The renaissance popes were of course quite a different kettle of fish. Here I am definitely speaking about the twentieth century.

REFERENCES

Allum, P. H.
Politics and Society in Post-War Naples. Cambridge: Cambridge University Press 1973.
Annuario Statistico Toscana 1971. Firenze. Dipartimento statistica informazione e documentazione della regione Toscana, 1972.

Ardener, E.
Social Anthropology and Language. London: Tavistock, 1971

Banfield, E. C.
The Moral Basis of a Backward Society. Glencoe: Free Press, 1958.

Blok, A.
South Italian Agro Towns. *Comparative Studies in Society and History* 11:121-35, 1969.
The Mafia of a Sicilian Village, 1860–1960: A Study of Violent Peasant Entrepreneurs. Oxford: Basil Blackwell, 1974.

Boissevain, J. F.
Patronage in Sicily. *Man* N.S. 1:18-33, 1966.
Friends of Friends: Networks, Manipulators and Coalitions. Oxford: Blackwell, 1974.

Butterworth, D.
From Royalty to Poverty: The Decline of a Rural Mexican Community. *Human Organization* 29:5, 1970.

Cassola, C. and L. Bianciardi,
I minatori della Maremma. Bari: Laterza, 1956.

Cole, J. W. and E. R. Wolf
The Hidden Frontier. Ecology and Ethnicity in an Alpine Valley. New York and London: Academic Press, 1974.

Davis, J.
Honour and Politics in Pisticci. *Proceedings of the Royal Anthropological Institute* 69–81, 1969.
Land and Family in Pisticci. London: Athlone Press, 1973.

Demangeon, A.
La géographie de l'Habitat Rural. *Annales de Géographie* 36:1–24, 97–115, 1927.

Douglas, M.
Natural Symbols. London: Barrie & Rockliffe, 1970.

Elia, G. F.
Dinamica urbana di un area rurale. Instituto di Sociologia. Universita degli studi di Pisa, 1972.

Evans-Pritchard, E. E.
'The Nuer of the Southern Sudan,' in *African Political Systems*. Edited by M. Fortes and E. E. Evans-Pritchard. Oxford: Oxford University Press, 1940.
Social Anthropology. London: Cohen and West, 1951.
Anthropology and History. Manchester: Manchester University Press, 1963.
The Sanusi of Cyrenaica. Oxford: The Oxford University Press, 1968.

Geertz, C.
Peddlers and Princes. Chicago: University of Chicago Press, 1963.
Agricultural Involution. Berkeley: University of California Press, 1970.

Gluckman, M., ed.
Closed Systems and Open Minds. Edinburgh: Oliver & Boyd, 1964.

Imberciadori, I.
Amiata e Maremma. Parma: La nazionale tipografia, 1971.

Jones, P. J.
'From Manor to Mezzadria: a Tuscan Case Study in the Medieval Origins of Modern Agrarian Society,' in *Florentine Studies.* Edited by N. Rubinstein. London: Faber & Faber, 1968.

Laven, P.
Renaissance Italy 1464–1534. London: Methuen & Co., 1966.

Leach, E. R.
Political Systems of Highland Burma. London: London School of Economics, 1954.
Pul Eliya. Cambridge: Cambridge University Press, 1961.

Maraspini, A. L.
The Study of an Italian Village. The Hague: Mouton. 1968.

Marselli, G. A.
American Sociologists and Italian Peasant Society. *Sociologia Ruralis* 3:319-38, 1963.

Mitchell, J. C., ed.
Social Networks in Urban Situations. Manchester: Manchester University Press, 1969.

Nadel, S. F.
The Foundations of Social Anthropology. London: Cohen & West, 1951.

Petri, D. I.
Pienza. Storia breve di una simbolica citta. Genova: Edigraphica, 1972.

Pitkin, D. S.
Land Tenure and Family Organization in an Italian Village. *Human Organization* 18:169-73, 1960.
Mediterranean Europe. *Anthropological Quarterly* 36:120-29, 1963.

Pitt-Rivers, J.
The People of the Sierra. Chicago: University of Chicago Press, 1961.
Relazione sulla situazione economica della provincia de Grosseto nel 1970 e 1971.
Grosseto. Camera di comercio, industria, artigianato e agricultura, 1972.

Repetti, G.
Dizionario geografico, fisico, storico della Toscana. Firenze, 1933.

Schnapper, D.
L'Italie rouge et noire. Les modeles de la vie quotidienne a Bologna. Paris. 1971.

Silverman, S. F.
Agricultural Organization, Social Structure, and Values in Italy: Amoral Familism Reconsidered.
American Anthropologist 70:1-20, 1968.

Spiegelberg, H.
The Phenomenological Movement. The Hague: Martinus Nijhoff, 1960.

Van Velsen, J.
The Politics of Kinship. A Study in Social Manipulation among the Lakeside Tonga of Nyasaland.
Manchester: Manchester University Press, 1964.

Wade, R.
'Political Behaviour and World View in a Central Italian Village,' in *Gifts and Poison.* Edited by
F. G. Bailey. Oxford: Basil Blackwell, 1971.
Unpublished Ph. D. dissertation, University of Sussex, 1972.

Watson, W.
Tribal Cohesion in a Money Economy. Manchester: Manchester University Press, 1958.

Wertheim, W. F.
Evolution and Revolution. London: Penguin, 1974.

Wichers, A. J.
'Amoral Familism' Reconsidered. *Sociologia Ruralis* 4:167-81, 1964.

3

The Base of a 'Centrifugal Democracy': Party Allegiance in Rural Central Italy

Robert Wade
Institute of Development Studies, University of Sussex

ABSTRACT

Political scientists have tended to emphasise the fragmentation, polarization and alienation of Italian political life, as for example in the concept of a 'centrifugal democracy'. Local level studies, such as those more commonly undertaken by anthropologists, can help to correct the starkness of the centrifugal democracy image by showing how political party loyalty is weighed against other kinds of loyalties and self-seeking, in governmental and non-governmental contexts of action. On the basis of material from one small village in Central Italy, this paper suggests that cleavages which seem so pronounced at the national and provincial levels erode as one approaches the base.

The extension of democratic electoral systems of government constituted one of the most far-reaching changes to have affected communities in Western Europe since the turn of the century. When all sections of the adult population could be appealed to for support by groups seeking national or regional power, new lines of cleavage were introduced into communities, raising the possibility of conflicts of loyalty between party, territory, class, and individuals.

This paper asks about the relative weight given to political party loyalty in a village of Central Italy. Italy has frequently been cited as an example of a 'fragmented political culture', a 'polarized pluralist system', or most graphically, a 'centrifugal democracy'. Lijphart (1968) characterizes a centrifugal democracy as one in which party alignment determines a whole range of other associational relations; in other words a centrifugal democracy is one in which involvement in organizations is cumulative within political cleavages, not cross-cutting. But if this image is to be taken seriously we must ask why the polity does not fly apart. Neither Lijphart nor others who have stressed the fragmentation, polarization and alienation of Italian political life have much to say about this. Operating as they do at high levels of generalization, they had to ignore the question of how political allegiance operates in different contexts of action and how it is weighed against other kinds of obligation and loyalty.

It is helpful to distinguish two propositions implicit in the notion of a centrifugal democracy. First, that loyalty to a party is strong in electoral and governmental contexts, right down to the base. Second, that the spillover of party loyalty – of a partisan approach to political problems – into apparently non-political contexts is also strong, again right down to the base. The argument here is that for the Central Italian village of Colombaio[1] the first proposition, insofar as it concerns elections – national, regional, provincial and local – is broadly true; but the second proposition is not. Further, some of the reasons which account for the truth of the first proposition also account for the failure of the second. In other words, some of the forces which remove party choice at elections from cross-cutting pressures also help to keep the spillover of party allegiance into non-electoral and non-governmental contexts low.

The general conclusion – that the image of a centrifugal democracy is heavily overdrawn – is the same as that reached by Tarrow in a recent paper (n.d.). He too argues that more integration takes place at the local level than the centrifugal democracy image suggests, leaving, as he says,[6] the higher levels of the elite, with their impossible conflicts, hanging imposingly but impotently above the battle, like a still-life of warring armies above a stage on which low comedy is being played' (n.d.:3). However, he is concerned only with local political leaders – mayors of communes. And he relies on interviews for material about their attitudes and behaviour. The present paper not only addresses a somewhat different aspect of the centrifugal democracy problem, but also uses material collected by anthropological methods of intensive fieldwork in one place. The disadvantages of a community study as a basis for generalization are too obvious to need comment, but it does have the advantage of focusing attention on ongoing social processes and on the spillover from one context of social life to another. Ultimately, the conclusions reached by interview-based studies like Tarrow's, and still more the conclusions suggested by abstract formulations like Lijphart's, must be examined from a grassroots perspective.

SETTING

Colombaio lies in the western hills of southern Tuscany, about 150 kms. north of Rome. Today it has a population of 700, and the commune of which it is the municipal centre (*capoluogo*) has 4,000 people in an area of 160 sq. kms. About half the commune population lives on scattered farms and most of the remainder live in the four tightly nucleated villages with more than 150 inhabitants. In the Italian land reform of the 1950s half the commune area was expropriated and redistributed to smallholders. Before the reform most of the commune had been held in large estates worked predominantly by sharefarmers in the *mezzadria* contract (which formed the dominant kind of agricultural organization throughout Central Italy,;[2]; and in addition, part of each estate was worked by wage labourers. Something over half the population of Colombaio village lived by combining wage labour in the countryside with cultivation of their own and rented plots. Livestock and wheat were the principle products, to which wine grapes and olives have been added since the reform. From 1900 to 1940 the population grew from about 5,400 to 6,500, while the village population during the same time lay between 800 and 900. Today, less than a fifth of the village labour force (males between 18 and 65, 201 in total) depend on agriculture. A third are (nonagricultural) workers; a quarter are merchants and artisans; a fifth are professionals, office-workers and teachers; and a tenth are students. Just over a quarter of the workers, and a negligible fraction of the others (excluding students), work outside the commune, commuting on a daily or in some cases weekly basis.

PARTISANSHIP

As in the large majority of communes in North and Central Italy, voting results from Colombaio show a pattern of stable party choice, both over time and between electoral levels. Details are given in Tables 1 and 2. The principal change since 1946 has been the increasing share obtained by the two major parties, the Communist party (PCI) and the Christian Democrat party (DC), at the expense of the smaller parties. But except for the precipitous decline of the Republican party (PRI) between 1948 and 1953 this has been a slow process. For all four main parties the share of the vote received in 1972 differed from that received in 1953 by less than 10%[3]. The similarity between elections at the local level and at higher levels is suggested not only by direct figures, like those in Table 2, but also by the low frequency of the 'individual' vote, which gives the elector the opportunity to vote not

Table 1
Stability of the vote from Colombaio commune, national elections.

Constituent	Assembly	Deputati					
	1946	1948	1953	1958	1963	1968	1972
Votes cast	3,960	4,135	4,135	3,547	3,310	3,009	2,754[1]
per cent received by							
DC[2]	19	25	29	32	32	30	34
PRI	24	21	10	10	6	7	4
PSI	21	} 41	20	20	15	13	12
PCI	21		26	24	32	34	35
Remainder[3]	15	13	15	14	15	16	15

[1] Valid votes cast.

[2] DC = Christain Democrat party; PRI = Republican party; PSI = Socialist party; PCI = Communist party.

[3] 'Remainder' includes invalid and blank votes plus votes for other parties (mainly PSIUP, PLI, MSI).

Table 2
Similarity in the vote from Colombaio commune across electoral levels

	Per cent of votes cast received by	
	DC + PRI + PSDI[1]	PCI + PSI
1956 municipal council	50	46
1956 provincial council	41	47
1958 national (*deputati*)	43	44

[1] PSDI = Social Democrat party

for a party list in its entirety but for individuals who may appear on different lists. In the 1956 commune elections, only 5% of the voters cast an 'individual' vote; in 1965, 8%. This, too, is the common pattern throughout Central and North Italy, in contrast to the South where voting for the man rather than the party is several times more frequent[1].

A Communist-Socialist alliance controlled the municipal council from 1946 to 1956. Since then a coalition led by the Christian Democrat party has held power. The switch in 1956 occurred not because of a change in loyalties but because of a boundary change which removed a heavily Communist *frazione* (ward) from the commune. It should be noted that Colombaio's situation since 1956, as a DC-administered commune in a heavily Communist province, is not untypical: about half the twenty-eight communes in 1965–70 were in the same position.

Our interest is to describe some of the ways in which the party is maintained as the primary unit, even in local elections. The question acquires significance from the fact that, first, there is a strong sense of territorial identity, especially between Colombaio village and Montieri, the second largest; and second, the commune is small enough for the leading political figures to be widely known 'in the round'. How then is voting behaviour in commune elections kept free from influences of

Table 3
Party membership and party committees, by occupation, Colombaio village sezioni, 1972

Party	DC		PRI		PSI		PCI		Total	
Occupation	M'ships	Ctte	M'ships	Ctte	M'ship	Ctte	M'ship	Ctte	M'ship	Ctte
Farmers	13 } 17	1	n.k. } 27	1	8 } 31	2	27 } 46	1	} 121	15
Workers	4	1	n.k.		23	4	19		5		
Artisans, merchants	—	—	8	1	3	1	5	1	16	3
Professionals, office-workers	12	3	7	5	3	—	2	1	24	9
Others	1	—	—	—	2	—	—	—	3	—
Total	30	5	42	7	39	7	53	8	164	27

Table 4
Municipal council elections, 1965, by Frazione.

Frazione	Registered voters	Voters	Invalid votes	% of votes* received by			
				Left (PCI+ PSIUP)	Centre-left (DC + PRI + PSDI + PSI)	Liberal (PLI)	'Individual' Votes
1. Colombaio village	418	392	8	17	67	2	12
2. Montieri village	360	344	8	14	65	1	19
3. Colombaio village + countryside	587	568	6	42	46	1	8
4. Montieri village + countryside	317	289	13	39	44	1	9
5. Scarlino village + countryside	558	535	6	51	43	2	1
6. Hamlet + countryside	311	310	13	46	46	3	—
7. Hamlet + countryside	233	219	4	45	36	1	16
8. Countryside	469	450	12	62	32	1	3
Total	3253	3107	70				

* Votes cast.

personal evaluation and dependency, territorial sentiment, and questions of local resource allocation?

The first point to make is that a simple class theory of political allegiance will not take us far in explaining the general pattern of stable, impersonal choice. It is true that class differences are important in Italian politics generally. And while detailed evidence from Colombaio on who votes for whom is lacking, the influence of class can be seen from membership figures for the four party *sezioni* (branches) in the village: 80% of the professionals and *impiegati* (office-workers) belong to the Christian Democrat party or the Republicans; and 64% of the farmers and workers are members of the Communist party or the Socialists. (Table 3)

On the other hand, the village/country distinction, which cannot be reduced simply to one of class, is clearly important; the PCI draws most of its strength from country dwellers, the DC, PRI, and PSU (Social Democrats) draw theirs from the villages. (Table 4) In general, the overlap between parties and classes is too great for a simple connection to be made; nor is there much evidence to support a simple link elsewhere in Italy[5].

THE PROVINCIAL FEDERATIONS

One of the main reasons for stable, impersonal, nonterritorial voting is that choices which might conflict with party allegiance are never presented to the electorate; and one of the main reasons why such choices are not presented has to do with the power of the provincial federations over their commune branches. We can illustrate the role of the provincial federations in commune elections by describing several events which occurred during the negotiations between the commune Centre-left[6] parties in the run up to the elections of June 1970, held throughout Italy for municipal, provincial and regional councils.

A few points need to be made by way of background. First, a system of majority (not proportional) representation operates in Colombaio, as in all communes with under 5,000 inhabitants. In its usual form, the electoral competition is between two or more lists of candidates, and the list with the largest number of votes wins sixteen of the twenty municipal council seats, while the second list takes the remaining four. However, the provision for 'individual' voting (*vota individuale*), which allows the voter to select up to sixteen names from across lists rather than choose one or the other of the lists in its entirety, makes it possible for the sixteenth person in the majority list to receive fewer votes than the top person in the minority list, and in this case the minority takes five seats rather than four, the majority fifteen rather than sixteen. Such an eventuality is unusual, but as we shall see, it preoccupied many of the political leaders of Colombaio in 1970.

Second, the parties are organized into *sezioni* (sections) each with a committee; and the *sezioni* are represented at commune level in a commune committee. At provincial level, the commune organizations are grouped into the Provincial Federation of the ... Party of Grosseto. Although this table of organization is the same for all the parties, in practice there is substantial variation. In Colombaio commune only the PCI and the DC have more than two *sezioni* – the PCI has seven and the DC has six; and only they have a large-scale bureaucracy at the provincial level. The PSI has two *sezioni* in the commune, one at Montieri, the other in Colombaio; the Republican party has one fully organized *sezione* in Colombaio village, and another with a more nominal existence in another village; and the Social Democrat party (PSU) has only one *sezione*, in Colombaio village. The number of branches corresponds roughly with the parties' voting strength in the commune. It must be emphasized that the number of persons involved in each *sezione* is typically very small. Rarely do more than 10 to 15 people attend *sezione* meetings during election periods, whatever the party.

The Centre-left parties met to discuss the formation of an alliance in early April, and from then until the 13th of May, the deadline for the presentation of lists, a series of increasingly bitter meetings took place to negotiate the terms. The central question was how many of the sixteen seats should go to each party; and in the background for much of the negotiations was the question of whom the DC would nominate as mayor and whether the other parties had any right to influence the choice (it was accepted by all that the mayor should come from the DC). The matter of the seats, however, lay at the heart of the problem. The PSI was demanding five seats as the price for joining the Centre-left. This created two problems: First, if the PSI did get five seats, and if the PSI councillors then changed sides during the course of the administration, the PSI-PCI alliance would have nine out of twenty seats and the future of the administration would be shaky. Second, from the DC's point of view, a PSI total of five might cause it – the DC – to get only five seats, despite the fact that it is by far the largest party in the alliance; for if the PRI and the PSU received what they were demanding, three each, only five remained. Yet if the PSI did not join the alliance and went with the PCI, the Centre-left would probably lose the election – though since the PSI had not faced the electorate on its own for six years (in the intervening period it had been allied with the PSU) its voting strength was uncertain.

The provincial federations of the DC and the PSI exerted constant influence over the course of the negotiations and had a large part in ensuring that agreement was reached. Let us take some examples, first from the PSI.

In early March, before the Centre-left parties met, the PCI invited the PSI to form a joint list, and a majority in both PSI *sezioni* voted in favour of accepting. But a PCI-PSI alliance went against the plans of the PSI federation, for the following reason[7]: It had already agreed with the PCI federation that in communes where a majority rule of representation operated and where a PCI-PSI alliance would certainly win, it should be formed; where the result was less certain the PSI should go with the Centre parties so that the national PSI would have some defence against accusations that it had ignored the Forlani agreement, by which the national PSI undertook to encourage its provincial and local branches to form the same alliance as existed nationally, i.e., to form the Centre-left. Colombaio fell into the latter category, and so a pushy young organizer from the federation was sent in to rectify things, which he did. The PSI joined the Centre-left negotiations, and he did almost all the negotiating on its behalf, even to the point of telling local PSI leaders to shut up when they expressed a view contrary to his own.

The fact that he, rather than local people, conducted the PSI side was of some significance, for it greatly facilitated the renomination of the outgoing mayor: At the beginning of the negotiations the PRI, PSU, and the PSI all demanded to know who the DC intended to nominate as mayor. For reasons which we shall see later, Angelli, the outgoing mayor, was widely disliked, a fact which led the representatives of the three minor parties to insist that they should be able to discuss the suitability of the DC's nominee with their *sezioni*; if Angelli was renominated they would then be able to reconsider their options. But when, from the second Centre-left meeting onwards, the PSI federation man took charge of the local party a side of the negotiations, he dropped the demand because – this is the key point – at the provincial level the PSI did not much care who the mayor was, as long as it got enough seats to assure it a good deal of influence in the council. With no PSI opposition the DC felt it could risk playing for time by not deciding on its nominee, knowing that the PRI and the PSU would be less likely to join with the PCI or present their own list than the PSI would be. This is what it did, and the Centre-left fought the election without a nominee for the mayorship.

Within the commune DC, the deputy secretary of the provincial federation took an almost equally important part as the PSI organizer did within the PSI. From the time when it looked as though the negotiations would be difficult, he attended every meeting of the DC's commune council and of the Centre-left. Local DC officers were unwilling to start until he arrived; they did not want to be held responsible for what happened, they said. Meetings were sometimes delayed an hour or more, with all the local people present, until he came. While they waited, an argument sometimes developed between the local officers and a few others who claimed that what happened in Colombaio was for the Colombesi to decide, not the federation. Most people, however, were indifferent about the matter; and nobody argued that if the local officers did not want to take responsibility for decisions they should not be officers.

Like the PSI man, the DC deputy secretary cared little about the precise balance of power between the DC and the other Centre-left parties, and even less about the balance of power (in terms of seats) between one *sezione* of the DC and another. We can illustrate his influence by describing a meeting of the DC's commune council held at the end of April to discuss whether the DC should accept the only terms the other parties had been prepared to accept, which would give the DC substantially less – in terms of seats on the council and in the *giunta*[8] – than it wanted and expected. More precisely, the DC would get six seats, including the mayorship and two *assessori supplenti*[9], the PSI four seats, including two *assessori effetivi*, the PRI three seats, including one *assessore effetivo*, who would be deputy mayor, and the PSU three seats, including one *assessore effetivo*.

The Deputy secretary argued the case in favour of accepting this proposal: If the Centre-left wins the commune it will be seen as a DC victory, because the DC is the major party in the alliance. The DC will, in any case, lose several communes in the province and is anxious not to lose marginal ones like Colombaio where the result could go either way. Once lost to the communist machine, the commune would be hard to regain, especially because the DC's support comes from the villages, which are declining in population more rapidly than the countryside. The proposal under discussion at least guarantees that even if the PSI joins with the PCI, the other Centre parties will still hold the majority. And the two socialist parties feel such animosity towards each other that it is inconceivable, either nationally or locally, that they could agree to withdraw at once. Finally, he said, the present moment is the worst possible time to break off negotiations, for the general public does not understand the difference between an *assessore effetivo* and a *supplente*, and so would place the blame squarely on the DC. Better to wait for an issue where the blame could be made to fall on one of the others, such as the representation of each *frazione* in the *giunta*.

As he spoke a man named Volpi, a DC representative from Montieri, interrupted to state petulantly that under no circumstances were the 'communists' to have two *assessori effetivi* (an equation of socialists with communists which brought smiles all round); the negotiations should be broken off forthwith if the 'communists' would not give way. What happened elsewhere in the province, he continued, was of no interest to the people of Colombaio, who had to look after their own problems in their own way, just as they let other communes look after their problems themselves. The deputy secretary argued in reply that in the final analysis only two things really mattered: the Centre-left must win the commune, and the DC must provide the mayor. After that, anything else was not worth breaking off negotiations.

The deputy secretary then asked each branch to express its opinion on whether the terms should be accepted, beginning with the man sitting next to him. The latter, saying he wanted to hear what the other branches thought first, asked the representative next down the line, who said that whatever the others decide would be acceptable to him – adding with feeling, however, that a secret ballot was the only correct way to decide such an issue. The deputy secretary passed quickly on to the next man who stated that the negotiations should be broken off. But no one else supported him, and the deputy secretary took the silence to indicate approval for the terms. Without soliciting more views he announced that the negotiations would proceed, with DC accepting only six seats, including the mayorship and two *assessori supplenti*.

The deputy secretary thus used his authority and influence to ensure that the Centre-left was formed, against the wishes of many branch representatives who thought the terms intolerable. Of the three main local DC leaders, only one might have been prepared to openly recommend acceptance of the terms; for his position in the local party depends more on his position as director of the land reform agency and provincial councillor than on his local popularity and he is therefore less vulnerable to the accusation of being soft. The other two, Angelli and Bernini, are highly dependent on local popularity, and in the absence of the deputy secretary they may have been forced into opposing the terms, even though they realized the probable consequences for the balance in the municipal council.

The presence of the federation official provided them with a defence for the bad terms, for it was he, not them, who took responsibility. On a number of occasions Angelli played to the general dissatisfaction by claiming during the informal chat at the beginning of meetings that the terms were a disgrace, that negotiations should have been stopped, and that the fault lay with Bernini, to which Bernini replied that all the decisions had been approved by the DC's commune council, so fault lay squarely with all its members, including Angelli. But when the deputy secretary was present, both Angelli and Bernini kept quiet, allowing him to make the arguments about the necessity for compromise. In short, the presence of the provincial official allowed Angelli and Bernini to adopt a tough posture, in sympathy with the mood at branch level, while in fact making the necessary compromises.

Similarly the deputy secretary had an important part in Angelli's nomination as councillor from the Colombaio village *sezione* (without this nomination Angelli could not be included in the list and hence could not be mayor in the new administration). He emphasized to the local members the federation's view that a councillor should be renominated unless scandal surrounded him while in office. He also stressed that the mayor should come from the *capoluogo* (seat of the municipal administration) so that, since the DC would supply the mayor, the branch should choose someone capable of being mayor.

Once Angelli had been chosen as the branch's candidate, opposition from other DC branches to his renomination as mayor increased, and again the deputy secretary kept the sentiment in check. He warned that if Angelli was nominated as head of the list, and if DC members then said they would cast blank votes, as they had threatened, they may as well all leave the party. For the essence of a party is that once it makes a decision all members must work to realize that decision, whether they like it or not. And he emphasised that for the same reason voters must be encouraged to select one or the other of the lists in its entirety, not specific individuals in it.

When the Centre-left won the election the question of the mayor had still to be settled. The DC commune council met to decide the matter a full month later and at this meeting the power of the federation was still more evident. The provincial secretary himself directed it. Rather than have a secret ballot or even a show of hands, he simply interviewed each branch secretary alone and then announced that Angelli would be mayor (or more precisely, would be nominated by the DC and voted on by all the municipal councillors).

Why did the federation intervene so forcefully? One reason is that Angelli was identified as a supporter of the dominant faction (*corrente*) in the federation, to which the secretary and deputy secretary both belonged. Bernini, Angelli's only rival, belonged to a minority faction. But Bernini had little positive support locally; he was simply seen as the least bad of the two alternatives. How much the federation officials would have tried to insist on Angelli if Bernini had been more popular must remain an open question. A second, probably equally important reason is that the federation officials were impatient with the delays. They regarded many of the matters which most concerned local people, such as the number of DC seats in the *giunta* and the need to have each *frazione* represented there, as of little consequence. They were concerned with how the commune looked from the outside, which meant that they were concerned with who held the majority in the council and which party supplied the mayor. Hence, while allowing local decision-making to operate up to a point, they intervened at critical points to ensure the attainment of their own objectives.

It is important to note that with few exceptions the local party officials prefer to involve the federation in disputes and awkward decisions rather than use their own authority[10]. By taking responsibility, the federation allows them to escape some of the criticism which would otherwise be directed at them; and in small communities, where party officials must meet local members in nonpolitical contexts, this is an important consideration. The federation is also better able to ensure compliance from party members than the local officials themselves could. As one informant put it,

People here are like mules: they take a position and stick to it. But if a party official comes from Grosseto, a lawyer perhaps, and puts to them the same arguments as other people from here have already done, they will move into line.

Deference helps to produce this result. A lawyer from Grosseto is someone you don't argue with, not simply because you might need him one day but because he is a lawyer, is educated, and knows about politics. Further, party membership is still of considerable, though declining use, and it is therefore important to remain in good standing with the federation. Those whose party membership is public knowledge (in particular, political activists) may find themselves more dependent on their party's federation than are those whose allegiance is less certain; and being more dependent they are also more controllable.

The foregoing should not be taken to indicate that many people at the branch level have direct contact with the federations. In the case of the DC, no one other than Bernini, Angelli, and the director of the land reform office were identified with the federation's factions. The great majority of members, including those on branch committees, have little knowledge of, much less identification with, the various currents in their federation[11].

PARTY AND TERRITORIAL LOYALTY

We have seen how the federations of the main Centre-left parties, the DC and the PSI, act in commune elections to attain provincial objectives, thereby overriding (or attempting to override) specifically local disagreements. On the other hand, people have a strong sense of territorial identity; in some contexts, at least, the people of Colombaio village see themselves as distinct from and superior to the people of the surrounding countryside and nearby villages.

In the context of commune elections, it is generally believed that if a party is to be sure of obtaining votes from a given *frazione* it must have a councillor from that *frazione*, and that a representative from the *frazione* must be included in the *giunta*. This belief is used, not only by the leaders in deciding the allocation of council and *giunta* seats among the various *sezioni*, but also by people of the *frazione* in arguing for representation; they threaten that if their *frazione* is not adequately represented, they will cast blank votes.

In the circumstances of 1970 the fact that Bernini, the only plausible alternative mayor to Angelli, came from a *frazione* adjacent to Montieri, served to emphasise territorial loyalty by highlighting the opposition between Montieri and Colombaio. Bernini had most of his support within the DC from Montieri and his own *frazione*; or more accurately, most of Angelli's opposition within the DC came from these areas. And when it became clear that if the Centre-left was to be formed at all the DC would have to accept very poor terms, most of the pressure to break off negotiations came from the secretary of the DC branch at Montieri.

His calculation ran as follows: If the DC gives way to the PSI and in consequence accepts a small number of seats in the council and the *giunta*, and if the principle that each *frazione* of the commune must have a representative in the *giunta* is followed, then Montieri will be represented in the *giunta* not by the DC but by the PSI, as in the past two administrations. It is high time Montieri had a DC representative, especially because more DC votes come from Montieri than from any other *frazione*. At best, however, Montieri will have only one or two DC councillors, neither of them in the *giunta*. While if the Communist list wins, the Montieri DC might still get one of the four minority seats, and hence would not be much worse off than if the Centre-left wins. But if the Centre-left does win, Montieri's chances of having a DC *giunta* member will be much improved if the DC councillor from Colombaio village is *not* in the *giunta*. If, however, Angelli is renominated as mayor, this will guarantee that the DC will be presented in the *giunta* by its Colombaio councillor, i.e. by Angelli.

The people of Colombaio village were also sensitive to territorial questions. As the long drawn-out negotiations to form a Centre-left list proceeded, the leaders of the Centre-left parties in Colombaio village could be heard reminding each other in hushed street-corner conversations of the need to prevent Montieri from getting too many seats, because 'on something that concerns Montieri they all vote together, regardless of party'. Towards the end of the election campaign, when people began to be aware that however much they disliked the prospect of Angelli as mayor again they had to think of him in relation to alternatives, even those who had most vehemently opposed him at the beginning began to argue that whatever happened, the mayor must come from the *capoluogo* (i.e. from Colombaio village). As one of them put it at a meeting of the PRI *sezione* in Colombaio (of which he is a member): 'In the final analysis, to have an outsider (*forestiero*) come to Colombaio to be mayor goes against the grain (*gira il colione*).' ('Outsider' here refers to a person living within the commune but beyond the village). He switched from opposing to supporting Angelli on grounds of territorial loyalty alone.

Underlying this stress on territorial identity is the fact that the commune is large in area (160 sq. kms) and the population dispersed. Resources spent in one place will hardly benefit those living elsewhere. The people of Montieri, in particular, feel that Colombaio village gets the lion's share of resources. If pressed they admit it is fair that the middle school was situated in Colombaio rather than Montieri, because Colombaio is in the geographic centre of the commune; but they say there is no particular reason why Montieri should find it so much more difficult than Colombaio to get municipal funds for improving its sports ground, for example.

Yet though territorial threats are made and territorial dangers are seen, there is little evidence to suggest that territorial allegiance overrides party loyalty to any significant degree. It may be that the somewhat greater instability of the vote and the slightly greater incidence of blank or invalid votes from Montieri reflects village loyalty in opposition to Colombaio; but the magnitude is not large, and in any case it may also be due to the greater incidence of small-holding cultivators at Montieri who are likely to be less susceptible to party appeals. (Table 4) There is no evidence that councillors from Montieri (or from other villages) do in fact tend to vote together across party lines. It is a belief which fits the wider stereotype of the Montieri as pig-headed and backward, but my informants could not give any specific examples.

In the negotiations of 1970 there were numerous occasions when party representatives closed ranks to oppose representatives of other parties from the same *frazione*. For example, when the three minor parties demanded to know whom the DC intended to nominate as mayor, the DC representative from Montieri argued strongly that they had no right to interfere with what the DC decided to do; he took this position even though to have allowed the other parties some influence would have reduced Angelli's chances of the mayoral nomination, and in intraparty dealings, as we have seen, he was one of Angelli's strongest opponents. But in interparty affairs, he and the rest of the DC presented a unified front, putting territorial and personal claims to the side.

Territorial rivalry, then, is largely kept within parties rather than allowed to cut across party loyalty. And once contained inside parties its impact is reduced by the strength of the provincial federations. In this way territorial loyalty is kept out of the public political arena[12].

PARTY AND PERSONAL EVALUATION

In addition to loyalty and opposition between villages or *frazioni*, attachment to particular persons is another potentially cross-cutting influence on party voting. Especially because the voting *frazioni* contain fewer than 600 persons one might expect this to be an important force. Indeed, 20% of the votes in the 1970 elections were 'individual' rather than 'list' votes. But by postwar standards this is exceptional; as noted earlier, 'individual' votes had not risen above 8% prior to 1970. Here, then, we shall look at some of the ways by which the 'individual' vote is kept low (the 'party' or 'list' vote kept high), and why so many people changed their normal behaviour in 1970 and selected individuals within the lists.

The strength of the provincial federations of the main parties over local members, and their concern to keep local rivalries from disrupting the affairs of the commune, is the first reason. In the 1970 election it was especially the provincial officials who stressed that voters must be encouraged to vote for whole lists rather than for individuals within them; on this the DC and PCI found themselves in complete agreement. The second point, which perhaps is partly a consequence of the first, is that politics is seen as a sphere in which personal evaluations and grudges should not enter; people, in other words, are highly critical of someone who opposes others on other than party grounds in the context of elections and local government. In this sense politics is highly ideological; but it is also seen as a realm which should be kept separate from the ordinary business of life. The third and related reason is that factional conflict is almost nonexistent. The first mayor after the Second World War is accused of having benefited himself and a small circle of friends, but since then there is no evidence of coalitions or cliques which operated in the pursuit of power. The accusations directed against political leaders are made in terms of the benefits which they secure for themselves as individuals, not for themselves and their group.

The first point – the strength and interests of the provincial federations – has already been dealt with at length. The second and third points can be illustrated by events which occured in the 1970 elections.

Angelli had been mayor continuously since 1956, and by 1970 a large number of people were tired of him, less because of his policies or lack of achievements for the commune than for his failure to live up to the expectations of what a mayor should be. 'He knows how to play his part well, but ignores those he grew up with.' 'For the past 4 years, 11 months, and 2 weeks he has walked past with his head low, not greeting anyone; now he is suddenly sociable.' Some women could be heard to complain that if someone is sick or suffers a misfortune it should be he as mayor who goes to visit them, offers a kind word, perhaps a small gift – he has enough money; in fact he is never seen on such occasions. Those people who were more involved in municipal affairs (such as the PRI secretary and the schoolmaster) made other kinds of criticisms: he does things too much on his own without consulting others – he decided to extend the school building and even appointed an architect without letting the teachers know anything about it, nor were the teachers able to make comments on the architect's plans. It was also commonly said that he hogs all the benefits available to elected representatives for himself – he sat on all five of the statutory bodies in the commune which require an elected representative and which pay an honorarium, instead of sharing the positions more widely.

But no concerted opposition to Angelli's renomination developed. Baroni, bank manager and PRI secretary, was the most outspoken opponent, supported by two friends of his in the PRI. They went around the bars arguing in low voices that it would be disastrous if Angelli were to be mayor again. It must be emphasized that they themselves had no interest in holding office, nor did they support an alternative candidate. They did not serve as a focus for the general discontent, for two reasons: people in other parties did not want to be seen taking Baroni's leadership, for that might throw their own party identification into doubt. And it was said that Baroni's opposition rested on *personalismo:* on anger that the mayor had increased his taxes unfairly; on jealousy that the mayor had received a state honour (*cavaliere*) while he, Baroni, with much superior education and occupation, had not. The accusation of *personalismo,* of introducing personal grudges into politics, was sufficient to cut away much of the legitimacy of Baroni's opposition.

Likewise in the case of the PSU man who openly opposed Angelli's renomination, it was said that his antagonism stemmed from ten years ago, when he had been passed over for a job with the land reform cooperative in favour of the mayor's cousin. Moreover, eight months previously the PSU man was involved on one side of a conflict between men of two festival associations (*contrade*), with the mayor on the other. When the PSU man and one other from the same *contrada* were called to the police station the next day they received assurances of support from other members of the *contrada,* and the mayor came in for heavy behind-the-back criticism for having reported the matter to the police. But many *contrada* members who had then supported him began to criticise him for allowing such matters to condition his political attitudes. They recalled how he had said at the time of the dispute that he would take the opportunity to avenge himself on the mayor when the occasion arose; and they concluded that his opposition to Angelli's renomination was the result of nothing more than such *personalismo.*

Another reason why no concerted opposition to Angelli developed was the lack of a plausible alternative. Even around Montieri, and still more in Colombaio, Bernini was at best regarded as the less bad, rather than as one who could do the job well. The comment of an unskilled labourer from Colombaio is typical of those who, although disliking Angelli, could not bring themselves to support Bernini: After roundly condemning the way Angelli behaved and deploring the prospect of another five years of him, he said that Bernini would be even worse; at least Angelli, for all his faults, knows how to get things done (*strigare le cose*), knows how to act well (*fare la bella figura*), has contacts (*conoscenza*) in Grosseto. If there is a problem with the law, with the commune, he knows what to do. Bernini has no numbers in the head (i.e. is uneducated, inexperienced) and lacks culture. He will be manipulated by others, so it may as well be Angelli, who at least will do what is in his own interests.

But Bernini did not present himself as an out-and-out rival. His attitude was that having worked with Angelli for the past ten years in the *giunta,* he was not about to compete with him if he – Angelli – wanted to be mayor again. If for some reason Angelli did not wish to be nominated, he – Bernini – would gladly do the job. On many issues that came up during the negotiations he sided with Angelli to the detriment of his own candidacy. For example, instead of building up his support at Montieri by agreeing with the Montieri DC's demand for two councillors, he sided with Angelli in saying that no *frazione* had the right to more than one councillor if it meant that another went without. He joined Angelli in denouncing Baroni for *personalismo,* although Baroni's opposition to Angelli strengthened his own case. He was against allowing other parties an influence on the choice of mayor, although this also would have weakened Angelli's position and thereby strengthened his own. Finally, and perhaps most convincingly, they both travelled around to *sezione* meetings in the same car.

When the votes were counted Angelli turned out to have almost 100 more than anyone else, an astonishingly large lead considering that the gap between first and second had never in the past been more than about ten. A sense of outrage swept the village. It was assumed – and rumours circulated to substantiate the assumption – that Angelli had solicited the votes for himself, an action which amounted to a betrayal of the whole list, *personalismo* in the extreme. Why he did it was widely understood: because of the danger that he would get fewer votes than one or more candidates in the minority list, and would fail to be elected. In the event, many fewer deleted his name than expected, and he stood exposed. But an understanding of why it happened did nothing to moderate the criticism. His deeds served to strengthen the resolve of a number of councillors in the DC and the other Centre-left parties not to vote for him as mayor in the full council meeting after the elections, a matter which is normally only a formality. He succeeded in being elected only on the third ballot (when by law the two thirds majority rule which applies to the first two ballots is changed to a simple majority rule).

The events of 1970, however, were exceptional. In the past local politics had a blander and more impersonal flavour. But even the events of 1970 were a long way removed from local politics in South Italy. Lopreato describes a typical Southern election meeting in the following terms:

In the village square they [the candidates] alternate in singing each other's faults and defects – real or imagined. They might begin by reminding each other of their respective origin, passing quickly to accusations of robbery while in office or of intention to achieve public office in order to defraud the public. Then they might discuss the motives behind their marriage to their respective wives[13].

In Colombaio such behaviour is unheard of. It is not that people are unaware of or uninterested in social origins, or that they do not believe men take public office to benefit themselves; quite the contrary. But to talk publicly in this way would be considered outrageous. In the 1970 elections there was no debate between representatives of the two lists, nor had there been in 1965. The PCI-PSIUP list, indeed, did not even give an election address. Angelli spoke briefly for the Centre-left in the piazza late one night but did not so much as mention his opponents; he confined his speech to national matters, and when he descended to the level of the commune it was to blame the provincial administration (PCI-controlled) for not repairing the commune roads and for not bringing industry to the area. This has been the typical pattern since the early postwar elections.

Moreover, while the Centre-left parties were negotiating their alliance, very little information about the state of the negotiations circulated in the village beyond those directly involved. There was a general impression abroad that things were in a mess and that the choice of mayor lay between Angelli and Bernini, but knowledge, and indeed interest extended little beyond this point. The argument, then, is that in previous elections people have had no basis for voting in local elections other than party allegiance; matters of personal rivalry and territorial identity have either not arisen or have been kept within the party framework, and have not filtered through into the public arena. In 1970 this broke down to some extent because of the widespread dislike of the man who has been mayor for the past 15 years; hence 20% of the vote rather than the more normal 5–8% went to individuals rather than to one or the other of the lists as a whole.

LIMITS TO PARTISANSHIP

We have seen that the notion of a 'centrifugal democracy' is consistent with party politics in Colombaio, to the extent that the party is indeed maintained as the primary focus of electoral competition even in local elections, free from the potentially cross-cutting influences of personal evaluation, territorial identity, or opinion on local resource allocation. However, 'centrifugal democracy' also implies that loyalty to party spills over strongly into nongovernmental contexts, so that interaction is cumulative within political cleavages; this is not consistent with the evidence from Colombaio.

With the partial exception of a few PCI activists, one finds no obvious tendency for members of the same or adjacent parties to spend more time together than with members of more distant parties. None of Colombaio's seven bars is identified by the political colour of its proprietor or its clientele. The groups of men who play cards in the bars after lunch and in the evenings commonly contain men from across the political spectrum. Decisions about where to shop appear to have little to do with politics, much more to do with kinship, proximity, and price. A person's political party allegiance is not, in most contexts, an important means of identification; in a status ranking test, for example, party allegiance was hardly mentioned in the comments which the rankers made about each of the 68 persons to be ranked, and during my early days in the village the sketches of various local people which informants gave me made only infrequent reference to party allegiance, and then mainly in the case of communists or fascists.

Statistics describing the political composition of the committees of formal associations appear to indicate a different conclusion. (Table 5) Most of the associations have committees which are

Table 5
Political composition of committees of voluntary associations, Colombaio village, 1972

	DC[1]	PRI	PSI	PCI	Other[2]	Not Known[3]	Total
Pro loco[4]	6	4	1	2	1	3	17
Sports Club	3	3	1	—	1	1	9
Confraternity[5]	5	2	1	—	1	—	9
Band	3	2	1	—	1	—	7
Contrade[3]	6	5	5	5	2	8	31
Consumer Cooperative	2	1	2	3	1	—	9
Returned Servicemen	—	—	2	4	3	2	11
Hunters	—	3	2	3	—	5[6]	13
Total	25	20	15	17	10	19	106

[1] The classification refers to political sympathy, not necessarily to party membership.

[2] 'Other' includes Neofascist (HSI) party and Social Democrat party.

[3] 'Not known' means either that my informants did not know a person's political identity or that they knew he had none.

[4] The table includes only elective positions held by men.

[5] This is the 1969 committee. The 1972 committee is quite untypical: DC –; PRI 4; PSI 1; PCI 2; + 2 not known.

[6] All from outside Colombaio village.

fairly strongly skewed towards either the DC-PRI or the PSI-PCI side, and overall, two-thirds of the committee members whose political identity is known support the Centre-right parties. Does this mean that party affinity is used to select committee members? In some associations, this is so. The confraternity[11], for example, has always (until 1972) had a committee made up predominantly of DC supporters because of its close connection with the church. The consumer cooperative tends to attract communists and socialists for ideological reasons and the returned servicemen's association and the hunters are dominated by the PCI, as throughout the whole province. But in the associations where the DC-PRI predominates, selection is made according to occupation more than party. Committee work is commonly believed to be the business of *impiegati* and professionals, who have (it is assumed) the necessary skills to manage bureaucratic procedures. This belief, however, results in a skewing towards the DC-PRI side, for most (80%) of *impiegati* and professionals who are members of a party belong to the DC or the PRI. On the other hand, activism also influences election to committees, in a way which partly cuts across occupational considerations: a comparison between row 1 and row 2 in Table 6 shows that party committee members are more involved in associational activities (i.e. hold more committee positions) than are committee mem-

Table 6
The connection between involvement in associations, occupation, and
political activism, Colombaio Village, 1972

Number of committee positions per person	Occupation[1]		
	I	II	III
All committee members	2.5	1.4	1.3
Members of political party committees	3.3	2.0	1,8

[1] I = professionals, office-workers; II = artisans, merchants; III = workers and agriculturalists.

bers in general. In other words, political activists tend to be more involved in all associational activity than non-activists.

With one exception, however, it is difficult to detect any impact of political identity on the way committees operate[15]. The exception is the hunters' association. It is the only association in the village, apart from the political parties, where provincial events have had a substantial impact on power. This has happened because power holders in the provincial federation of hunters' associations owe their position to the votes of delegates from local branches, so that they cannot be indifferent to who holds local power. For twenty years up to 1972 the same man was president of the Colombaio branch. In 1972, however, a change occurred in the communist party faction which held power in the provincial federation of hunters, and the Colombaio president, who had been vaguely linked with the losing faction, lost his local office to another PCI member identified with the winning side. (As far as I could tell, this change has had no further repercussions within the local association. The ousted president accepted his defeat gracefully, saying that in any case twenty years is quite long enough).

One might expect to find some signs of political opposition within the Pro loco committee[16], because it controls relatively large quantities of resources, includes men from across the political spectrum, and in particular includes Angelli (DC) and his most outspoken critic in the municipal elections, Baroni (PRI). Yet not even during the late stages of the Centre-left negotiations did the animosity between these two men, or between the DC and the PCI, filter through into the Pro loco committee meetings, where village rather than party interests were under discussion. Relations between Baroni and Angelli remained, as always, formal and accommodating. One of the most militant communists in the village explained to me how he would happily vote for Marco, a well-known DC supporter, as captain of the *contrada*, and for the Pro loco council as well, for Marco has the capacity to perform such responsibilities well. But he would never vote for him in municipal elections, for that is all *politica*. His separation of two contexts, 'village' and 'politics', is the key to understanding why party allegiance has so little impact in associations.

The reaction to events in the confraternity demonstrates this separation clearly. A crisis occurred in the association in 1972 when a noted communist (the same man who commented on Marco, above) was elected to the committee. Most of the re-elected members resigned rather than tolerate a communist – this, at any rate, is how they justified their action, though almost certainly they were equally worried by his criticisms of their inactivity over the past several years. The new committee, formed by coopting those who received the next highest number of votes, had no Christian Democrats in it, two Communists, one Socialist, and four Republicans, none of whom attended church. Those who had lost their positions went around saying that the association had been 'smashed', taken over by atheists. The nuns who run the kindergarten and the mayor (Angelli, one of the re-elected committee members who resigned) were heard to say on numerous occasions that the confraternity should be closed down. But outside a small category of individuals – 'group' would imply too much cohesiveness – the reaction in the village was to say that politics and religion should be kept quite separate: the fact that one of the committee was a communist and that the others, though not communists, also did not attend church, should have no influence on the judgment of their capacity to run the association. Even here, in other words, in the association most clearly tied to the church, most people were prepared to say that politics is for one occasion, religion for another, and associations for still another.

Some evidence suggests that from the end of the Second World War up to the early 1960s the limits to partisanship were somewhat wider; schopping and recreation were coloured by politics in a way that they are not today. The land reform agency, with so many resources to distribute 'it was like a hen house at feeding time', acted for political objectives; both Centre and Left parties tried to establish local economic associations, such as cooperatives; farmers commonly gave a bushel of grain as their annual contribution to the coffers of their party; and two national labour organizations, one Catholic (ACLI), the other socialist (ENAL), sponsored bars in the village. Today – and since the early 1960s – this has all changed: the land reform agency has virtually closed down; the cooperatives failed; the farmers no longer give a bushel of grain, which they consider to be too much; ACLI closed down in 1963, ENAL two years later. But the change should not be exaggerated; there are too many accounts from the 1950s where men of very different political parties came together to spend their leisure time – in feasts, drinking sessions, even opera productions – for the idea of basic cleavages along political lines to be sustained. Evidence from the consumer cooperative strengthens this conclusion.

From after the Second World War until 1951 the consumer cooperative committee was composed largely of well-known socialists and communists. (Table 7) Even so, the first elected president in the post-war period was a *fattore*, managar of the largest estate near Colombaio and certainly not a socialist (neither had he been an active fascist). The fact that he received 27 out of 28 votes suggests he had general support. He resigned immediately, however, and the resulting committee was more

Table 7
Political composition of the consumer cooperative committee, Colombaio village

	DC	PRI	PSI	PCI	MSI	Not known	Total
1947	—	—	5	2	1	—	8
1951	2	—	4	1	1	—	8
1963	2	2	3	1[1]	—	1	9[1]
1972	2	1	2	2	1	—	9

[1] Includes one coopted member

homogeneous occupationally and politically, though it still contained a man who remained a Fascist supporter. In the 1951 elections, two Christian Democrats were elected and the Fascist supporter was reelected; from the voting figures it appears that the same voter commonly selected persons from across the major political cleavages. The balance was maintained subsequently, as Table 7 shows.

The point is underlined by the reaction to attempts by a politically-linked national organization of cooperatives to persuade the Colombaio association to join it. In 1949 the *Lega delle Cooperative*, linked to the Communist party, wrote to the Colombaio cooperative proposing membership. Dedalo Grazine, a committee member, former head of the Liberation Committee and life-long socialist, spoke strongly against the proposal:

'*Until now the cooperative of Colombaio has had complete autonomy, with satisfactory results. Given that the cooperative must pay a not indifferent subscription to the Lega I am contrary to such a link*'.

He added, however, that the choice had to rest with the Assembly of all members. In the meantime he proposed, and the council unanimously approved,

'*that the cooperative of Colombaio remains independent of all political infiltration and maintains, as it has done up to now, a direction completely above politics in the exclusive interests of the members and of the cooperative.*'

At the next Assembly meeting, it was the priest who brought this motion forward:

'*The administrative council must keep itself clean from all political and personal infiltration or ties, avoiding in this way any links with confederations of cooperatives and remaining completely autonomous.*'

No doubt the emphasis on this point reflects a tendency for political loyalties to influence the running of the cooperative. But the firm reaction from a staunch anticlerical socialist as well as from the priest suggests the strength of the desire to keep the cooperative as 'our own' and the corresponding tendency to keep party allegiance separate from village loyalty.

CONCLUSION

Despite the fact that the commune is small enough for local political leaders to be known 'in the round', and despite the strength of territorial rivalry between its villages, people vote in local elections as they vote in national elections. Local politics, in other words, does not constitute an additional source of divisiveness. This, of course, is consistent with the image of a centrifugal democracy. But centrifugal democracy also implies that people's opinions and loyalties on national issues and ideologies strongly influence their behavior in many local contexts of action. The evidence from Colombaio suggests that, even before the early 1960s when voters were in general less indifferent to local politics than they are today, the spillover was relatively low.

One reason is simply that politics is widely seen as divisive and dirty, as something which *should* be confined to a separate realm from ordinary day-to-day relationships. On the other hand, local administration is seen as a specialized business, into which disputes and grudges which arise in the day-to-day sphere should not be carried. These are no more than normative prescriptions, but the accusations against Baroni and the PSU man for *personalismo* indicate how strongly they are felt. However, the causes probably have less to do with normative prescriptions than with certain objective features of Colombaio's situation. First, its population is small. In villages which are substantially larger (how much larger is an open question) it may be more feasible for general social interaction to remain confined within political cleavages; and the sense of community and outsiderness may be weaker, with a correspondingly weaker contrast between 'village' and 'politics'. Second, the number of office-workers and professionals is small. Where they are more numerous, the number of people seeking political careers may be larger and personal rivalries correspondingly more intense. Third, arising out of the first two points, the provincial federations of the major parties exert strong control over their branches. In larger villages or towns, with a larger number of professionals and office-workers, it is possible that the power of the provincial federations may be weaker and the impact of personal and territorial rivalry stronger. Fourth, Colombaio is the largest village in the commune and is centrally situated within it. Where the *capoluogo* is smaller than other villages in the commune and/or is geographically more isolated, territorial opposition may have more impact on local politics than it does in Colombaio, for residents in the larger, more centrally situated village(s) will have grounds for objecting to the concentration of resources (the middle school, for example) in the *capoluogo*. Finally, and by no means last in order of importance, the Communist party is weak in Colombaio village (it gets only about 18% of the vote). Where the PCI is stronger, competition between it and the Centre parties may well be more intense and permeate more noticeably into voluntary associations and other leisure-time activities. These hypotheses, however, refer only to the specifics of Colombaio. But one would certainly expect – though evidence is lacking – that a village in South Italy, even if matched with Colombaio in alle the above respects, would still show a markedly different pattern of local politics, as the quotation from Lopreato above suggests. In other words, a good deal of what one observes in Colombaio is the result, not of its size, strength of Communist party, etc., but of the fact that it is situated in Central Italy, which has experienced a rather different pattern of historical development to the South since, at least, the twelfth and thirteenth centuries[17].

But the question of how typical or atypical are the patterns described for Colombaio must be left for other students of local-level politics in Italy to decide. To the extent that Colombaio is not exceptional, it would seem that the 'centrifugal democracy' image is substantially overdrawn; cleavages which seem so pronounced at the summit seem to erode as one approaches the base.

NOTES

[1] Colombaio is a pseudonym. Fieldwork was done between December 1968 and July 1970 as part of a research project on low-income communities in Europe directed by F. G. Bailey at the University of Sussex. I am grateful to the Social Sciences Research Council and the New Zealand Universities Grants Committee for finance.

This paper forms part of a wider study of Colombaio, to be published as *Economic Development and Social Change in Rural Central Italy* (provisional title). I would like to thank Sidney Tarrow, Peter Loizos and Caroline White for comments on an earlier version of the paper.

[2] See Silverman 1968:7.

[3] Galli and Prandi (1970) classify communes in Italy on the basis of the fluctuation in each main party's share of the vote in 1946 and 1963, using intervals of ten percentage points. Where the share changed by less than the interval the result is described as 'absolutely stable'; where it changed by less than two intervals in either direction the result is 'relatively stable'. They found that 87% of the communes in Central Italy had an absolutely or relatively stable DC vote between these dates, 90% and 72% had an absolutely or relatively stable PCI and PSI vote, respectively. (Corresponding figures for the South: 55%, 67%, and 84%) (Table 2–4, p. 54). Colombaio's results for the same period are 'relatively stable'. For a comparison between voting stability in Colombaio and in several towns of South Italy, see Wade 1971b:279.

[4] See LaPalombara 1965:304.

[5] See Galli and Prandi 1970:Ch. 2.

[6] Centre-left refers to the coalition of Christian Democrat, Republican, Social Democrat, and Socialist parties.

[7] As told to me by two officials from the PCI federation, and, independently, by a local socialist.

[8] The *giunta* is the municipal council's executive committee.

[9] The *giunta* has seven members: the mayor, four *assessori effetivi*, and two *assessori supplenti*. By law the *assessori supplenti* may be excluded from the *giunta* if all four *assessori effetivi* are present; but in Colombaio, at least, the *supplenti* are in practice full working members of the *giunta*.

[10] The position of party officials from provincial federations resembles that of Frankenberg's 'strangers' (1966), in the sense that local officials prefer to get them to take responsibility for decisions rather than use their own authority. However, unlike Frankenberg's 'strangers', the outsider officials receive a good deal of deference and do in fact make the decisions.

[11] These findings square with Barnes' for the PSI in Arezzo, where factional identification decreases as one moves down the ladder towards ordinary party members (1967:105–110). My information about the PCI is fragmentary, but impressionistically, more PCI members at the local level know about factions within the federation than is the case with other parties.

[12] For an interesting analysis of a case where territorial loyalty is in some circumstances stronger than party allegiance, see Cohen n.d.

[13] Lopreato, quoted in Tarrow 1967:78.

[14] The confraternity is a burial society.

[15] cf. Tarrow: 'Political parties have long had an extraordinarily important role in local community life in Italy, not only in local government, but also in the interstices of local associational life.' (n.d.: 6)

[16] The Pro loco is a civic amenities association.

[17] For a development of this idea, see Wade 1974.

REFERENCES

Barnes, S. H.
Party Democracy: Politics in an Italian Socialist Federation. New Haven: Yale University Press, 1967.

Cohen, E. N.
'Political Conflict and Social Change in an Italian Commune.' Revised version of paper presented at the 70th Annual Meeting of the American Anthropological Association, New York, 1971.

Frankenberg, R.
'British Community Studies: Problems of Synthesis,' in *The Social Anthropology of Complex Societies.* Edited by Michael Banton, A. S. A. Monographs 4, London: Tavistock Publications, 1966

Galli, G. and A. Prandi
Patterns of Political Participation in Italy. New Haven: Yale University Press, 1970.

LaPalombara, J.
'Italy: Fragmentation, Isolation, and Alienation,' in *Political Culture and Political Development*. Edited by L. W. Pye and S. Verba. Princeton: Princeton University Press, 1965.

Lijphart, A.
Typologies of Democratic Systems. *Comparative Political Studies* 1:3-44, 1968.

Silverman, S.
Agricultural Organization, Social Structures and Values in Italy: Amoral Familism Reconsidered. *American Anthropologist* 70:1–20, 1968.

Tarrow, S.
Peasant Communities in Southern Italy. New Haven: Yale University Press, 1967.
n.d. Partisanship and Local Political Exchange in Italy and France: A Contribution to the Typology of Party Systems. *Sage Professional Papers in Comparative Political Sociology*, Vol. 1 (forthcoming).

Wade, R. H.
'Colombaio: Collective Action and Social Change.' Unpublished D. Phil dissertation, Sussex University, 1971a.
'Political Behaviour and World View in a Central Italian Village,' in *Gifts and Poison: The Politics of Reputation*. Edited by F. G. Bailey. Oxford: Basil Blackwell, 1971b.
'Colombaio,' in *Debate and Compromise: The Politics of Innovation*. Edited by F. G. Bailey. Oxford: Basil Blackwell, 1973.
Rural Social Organization and Centre-Periphery Relations. *Institute of Development Studies Bulletin* 5:4:67-77, 1974.
n.d. (forthcoming) Economic Development and Social Change in Rural Central Italy (provisional title).

4

Beyond the Hyphen: Some Notes and Documents on Community-State Relations in South Italy

John Davis
University of Kent

ABSTRACT

The author argues that anthropologists should try to write the ethnography of the state administration: neither the social construction of reality nor the discovery of national processes gives an adequate picture of the social forces at work. He presents some documents and anecdotes to make the point that government officials act, and fail to act, in terms of their own categories, and in response to pressures which may have nothing to do with local communities. Even if such information is hard to find, every effort should be made.

A conference of anthropologists on the topic of national process flirts with danger. There is a heady intoxicating elixir held out to us by the macro-men, sociologists and political scientists, who have not merely convinced us that national process exists, but also seek to tell us what it is: modernisation, integration, mobilisation, all the nations bred by nations are on offer, with the promise of eternal youth for our discipline which indeed does have to come to terms with the simple incontrovertible fact that the communities we study are parts of nations. In this paper I propose that we should attempt an ethnography of the nation – or at least, that we should recognise that the state apparatus, the higer levels of segmentation, consist not simply of depersonalised macro-processes, but of people interacting, playing roles, occupying offices, operating within a structure of rules, categories, norms. There is little doubt in my mind that to replace our current treatment of the state, which I hold no brief for, with macro-process of one kind or another, would be substitute one mystification for another. And I hope to show this by discussion of the ethnography of the state.

The evidence we collect about politics in South Italian towns is mostly about what goes on within the town. We make gestures towards the state; we explain that some people are more powerful than others because they mediate with the outside world, and that people struggle to become mediators. But our picture of the state, the state beyond the hyphen, is obscure: we cannot do fieldwork at the committees and councils which embody the more-inclusive levels of segmentation; because we are forced to rely on uncheckable gossip, rumour, we are forced to conclusions of the kind which hold truth irrelevant. 'Whether these rumours were justified or not, the X certainly believed them, with important consequences for their political behaviour.' Stirling's point (1968) is well-taken: we cannot be certain, we cannot print, and we therefore lapse into the social construction of reality.

This has serious consequences for our analyses of politics, which are already fairly nebulous because of the intrusive ambiguities of exchange theory and networkism: the safety-clause of social construction of reality adds a new dimension of mist. We are entitled, as a profession, to reject the risks involved in pursuing rumours of angels to another world; but we should not accept quite so readily that the state is in that class. 'What men define as real is real in its consequences' – absolutely; certainly; – no-one would question that. But suppose it is real not simply because men define it so, but because people have done things, written things, said things which could have been observed. Do we not fail when we put them together with angels? When we allocate the state's interventions to the dream-world of social construction our communities become isolated: the hyphen becomes a vaporiser, a mystifier, a cloud of obfuscating symbols. Even those who put most emphasis on community-state links describe their community in moderately concrete terms and then add an insulated supra-world inhabited almost indifferently by Prefect, Ministers and Blessed Virgins who distribute largesse and grant favours at the intercession of mediators, brokers, gatekeepers and the like. So long as there is a mediator the networks, factions and quasi-groups will get their secret life-giving ingredient, and the local systems we so carefully delineate will start up, work, function. This paper is an attempt to identify some real features of the hyphen. What I have done is reproduce some documents from the political files of the Prefect at Potenza from the period 1861 – ca. 1900. These relate to episodes when the government intervened, apparently without supplication from below. The documents are mostly dispatches from the Prefect's subordinate in Matera. Built on a limestone bluff, Matera was a city of ecclesiastics, merchants and land-owners – the peasants and labourers living in caves cut into the sides of the hill. Without a railway, it was linked to the outside world only by the via Appia – the Rome – Brindisi road built about 2,000 years before: it was real backwoods.

In the early years of unification, when the government was still located at Florence, and before the Papal States were incorporated into the new nation, the Ministry of the Interior was perturbed by the flourishing political life of the big cities – Genoa, Bologna, Milan – which had subversive elements. Accordingly, the Minister sent out circular enquiries to all field-officers – including the increasingly chagrined sub-Prefect at Matera. What was the Action Party doing in each district? How were Republicans behaving? And the Mazzinians? How many people, on the occasion of the lying-in of the ex-Queen of Naples, had been to Rome to congratulate the Bourbon? From Matera a brusque negative in each case, until finally a demand for information about the activities of Freemasons provoked the following reply:

Sub-Prefect, Matera, to Prefect, Potenza, 16.10.1869
There is scarcely any politics at all in this District. Indeed, very few people receive or read newspapers, as is clear from the restricted number distributed by the Post Office. By that, I do not mean to say that every-one likes the present complexion of government: the choice of Deputy De Boni, one of its most violent opponents in the Chamber, is enough to prove that. Nevertheless, with their apathetic and diffident mentality, no-one thinks of a popular uprising. And even of anyone did think of such things there would be nothing to fear since we have no person with the capacity or influence or popularity to win proselites – let alone excite the tranquil masses who, by ancient lassitude, wait for their benefits to come from government.
That said, although it has been impossible for me to discover what the plans of the society of Masons might be, or even, whether there are any Masons in this District – for there is a dull tonelessness which reigns over every aspect of politics here – nevertheless I feel obliged to rejoice that, from the facts I have described, I can be sure that the Society, had it indeed incorrect or subversive plans, would find here only sterile fields to propagate itself or to broadcast its opinions. (Arch. State Pot. Gabinetto 1870 facs. 171)

Although we may feel some sympathy for the Savoyard exiled in the South, provoked by constant reminders of the political excitements to be had by colleagues in Districts where Post Office spies had some information to provide, perhaps we must make an immediate adjustment to our picture of reality across the hyphen: Government is a political organisation, supervising, controlling, manipulating local politics – that is true enough. But there is a precondition of government concern, which is that is has to recognise local activities to be political activities before there can be any response to them. The sub-prefect was not an anthropologist of the new sort, and we may therefore forgive him for saying that there was nothing deserving the name politics, even though we know *a priori* that each and every of the 50-odd towns under his control was a pulsating throbbing mass of networks, transactions and quasi-groups, We may be less inclined to overlook his forgetfulness of the Bourbon partisans, financed from Rome, and on the rampage in his District at that time (e.g. Nitti 1953) – though before he is condemned on that count, remember that he called them not partisans but bandits, and reported their activities not under 'Politics' but under 'Public Order.' So, when we discuss the Community-State assemblage we should remember that some things are, others are not, politics; some things are below the threshold of perception. When they are noticed, and are regarded as political, the government may begin to supervise and try to control. In the early 1870s the Prefect and his deputy began to collect the books of statutes of the Mutual Aid societies which sprang up in a number of towns. Potentially socialist, and elsewhere than in this province actually socialist, they were a threat to good order. The notes about them in the files are replete with good sense: for example, in August 1874 the prefect received a letter from Stigliano:

'The commune of Stigliano, model of peace and concord, sustained by the most worthy Mayor Signor Correale (who unfortunately for the town has lived in Naples for the last year, constrained by absolute family needs) has lost that harmony for which it was so noted... By a terrible calamity the principles of socialism, of internationalism (in the form of a Society of Workers or Mutual Aid) have intruded themselves...'

The society was trying to organise votes, was trying to exclude 'intelligent landowners' from government and administration. The Prefect should take note that public order was threatened. In fact the Prefect sent the letter to Matera with a note that the letter seemed based on electoral pique, but that nevertheless the deputy should look into it. A fortnight later, the deputy replied: the letter was signed with a false name; the town was quiet; the Society was 'rather cultivated and composed'; 'it is true that thirty or so members meddled in the administrative elections but apparently not with political motives.' The officers were either good honest men or without influence. 'It is a pity that the Society should meddle with elections', he concludes, 'but it's hard to catch them when they do not pass resolutions about it. I have reason to believe that there's a rule in their Statutes which forbids the President to hold political meetings but I've not been able to lay my hands on a copy. We could then see if it would be suitable to do as we did with the Matera Mutual Aid, that is, to give discreet advice that they should reform their rules.' And so on: the eventual conclusion was that no further steps should be taken, since there was no threat to public order, just as the Society itself was not political, although some members might dabble in elections.
The same care was taken with other societies of the kind: in Pisticci the society was potentially socialist but responsible people had rallied round and, by taking positons of leadership, had effectively disarmed the danger. This might be called preventive politics: it is designed to check the growth of subversion. The collection of general political intelligence comes into this category:

Sub-Prefect, Matera, to Prefect, Potenza, 5.3.1873.
The only party which exists here is the Clerical-Bourbon one, of which the most influential member, sustaining the others with hope, is the Archbishop. Otherwise there are no parties: no International, no Republicans – there are only a few persons without influence who make a point of their republican opinions.
(Arch. Stat. Pot. Gabinetto 1872–88, fasc. 15)

On 16.11.1873 the sub-Perfect wrote again listing the names of the four influential people in the District (with, 1 repeat, some 50 towns) who were hostile to the government: two Republicans, a Radical and another Republican 'member of the Emancipation Society of Genova, perhaps an Internationalist but without any inclination to action.' In April of the following year he replied to a circular which noted that the International was trying to infiltrate the conscript army (*Gab. 971, 20.2.1874*).

Sub-Prefect, Matera, to Prefect, Potenza, 19.3.1874
From Pisticci... I am informed of one Giuseppe Delfino, son of Giuseppe deceased, and of Grazia Plati,
born in 1852, who, by his character, his lazy vagabond way of life and his upbringing, might be capable of
sowing the seeds of subversion in the lowest proletariat. However this could be no more than a suspicion
founded on the frightful political behaviour of his uncle Berardino Plati.[1]

He noted that some people said Delfino had reformed, and that the Carabinieri would keep an
eye on his comings and goings. The preventive side of political administration, the protection of
the army, of local councils against subversive elements, is matched by an interventionist activity in
which the administration is used to secure support for the government. It is most apparent at
election times, and I present extracts from the files on the bye-election held in 1883 for the Matera
college, and on the 1900 general election for the whole province.
Following the election of 1882 the Deputy for Matera, the Hon. Correale, was made junior Minister
at Public Works. By the rules of the day he had to stand again for election. He had had a large
majority in 1882, and with the resources of his Ministry available it was not difficult to secure his
re-election. But the pride of the prefecturate, government and candidate was that the majority
should be overwhelming – a resounding acclamation: he should be elected by a plebiscite – a word
which, in Italian political rhetoric, has lost the sense of referendum, and assumed that of 'unanimous'
(hence, *plebescitariamente* = 'unanimously'). The electorate in Basilicata in the 1880s seems to have
been about 5% of the population).
On 6.8.1883[2] the sub-Prefect informed his superior that Correale was assured in Matera itself: the
burning issue was the route of the new railway and 'who does not think that his aspirations might
be fulfilled now that Commendatore Correale is at the Ministry of Public Works?' At Stigliano
and Tricarico (which would not benefit from the railway if Matera did) there was some possibility
of opposition, but this would be minimal since Cavaliere Michele Gattini in Stigliano had been
induced to withdraw his support from the oppostion candidate. Writing again on August 12 the
sub-Prefect noted that at Matera Correale was assured of a 'plebiscite': the Minister had signed a
decree, given wide local publicity, authorising government railway engineers to survey private
land indiscriminately round the city. At Garaguso 'everyone is proud to have a fellow-townsman
in this most honorable office of Secretary General.' In Montepelosa there was some discontent, but
it would be easy to appease it. In Pisticci 'every counsel of prudence' would persuade the opposition
to abstain from voting. At Tricarico the Democrats will abstain unless Correale makes a public
'declaration that he is not numbered among those Deputies called followers of *trasformismo*[3].'
On August 16th the sub-Prefect wrote again. Correale was assured of re-election; there were many
friends working for him – but the poll might be low since polling-day coincided with the anual
livestock fair at Potenza. That would be unseemly, and the sub-Prefect recommended that various
influential electors should be given leave from government service to return to the district to
register their votes. The Prefect accordingly sent off a number of telegrammes, marked for ciphe-
ring, requesting the return of a soldier from Bari, and official of the Ministry of Agriculture from
Gallipoli, and so on.
The sub-Prefect's last letter, dated August 19th, reports that opposition has been eliminated at
Pisticci, Tricarico, Stigliano, S. Mauro Forte and Pomarico. In Matera there was a possibility that
the immigrants from Montemurro would vote for another candidate, also from Montemurro –
but the most influential member of his group had recently married into a Correale-supporting
family. In Grassano some members of the Materi family were urging abstention; however, the
branch of that family established in Matera had been mobilised by their affine, Cavaliere Michele
Gattini of Stigliano, to dissuade their Grassano kinsmen from such a negative procedure. In Bernalda it had become clear that the anti-Correale vote registered in the election of 1882 was the
result of local disputes: 'Every indication now is that Bernalda desires to have its (earlier) really
scarcely satisfactory performance forgotten.''

On August 26th Correale was re-elected by a 50 per cent poll, almost *plebiscitariamente*.
In the general election of 1900 the same mobilisation of administration to secure the withdrawal of possible opposition candidates occurred. The main threat was that a socialist, Ettore Cicotti, would stand. Cicotti was to speak at Pisticci. Certain dissidents there invited their friends from neighbouring Montalbano to attend, but the Mayor of Montalbano intercepted the postcards and destroyed them – a loyal act which he quickly told the sub-Prefect about. The same mayor requested a letter from the sub-Prefect in which he would mention favourably the name of a particular candidate. The mayor could then show it to doubtful electors drawing government salaries, to convince them where official support lay: 'the government employee . . . does not have the right to *vote against he who employs him*.' (original emphasis) The sub-Prefect also sent the following letter to the mayors of Bernalda, Pisticci, Pomarico, Irsina and Montescaglioso:

'*Quite apart from our official relations we are also true friends, and I therefore allow myself to ask you to busy yourself on behalf of the Hon. Torracca, to get a good strong vote. If you could act for him in other Communes, or for the Hon. Materi in the Tricarico College, you would do me a great favour . . .*
Post Scriptum: *I ask you to return this letter to me when you have read it.*'

These and other measures assured that although Cicotti did stand, he collected only 67 of the 1500–odd votes cast. Torracca and Materi were elected.
Government intervention is a response to the needs of government: action through the hyphen is not in these cases stimulated by town patrons, mediators and that sort. Observe how it is done. First, in the 1883 election there were promises of major expenditure on public works, but these were subtly unspecific: because the government decree authorised surveyors to survey *any* land in the Matera area, every man might hope for the compensation and improved access which he would get if the railway passed across his land: no-one was disappointed before polling-day. Then, the way in which government pressure is brought to bear: influential people are helped to vote; other influential people are induced to withdraw support and to abstain; the affinal alliances of oppositon groups are noted, and pressure is brought to bear on them through their in-laws. The pressure, incidentally, is not to get men to switch their support to another candidate, – that would be too much to ask? – but simply to abstain. Friendship, the duties owed by government employees are used to drum up support. While government intervenes for its own purposes, it intervenes in ways which fit the local idiom.
Of course, I am not pretending that the government and its representatives are only either preventative or interventionist in the way I have sketched: undoubtedly, government is compelled to respond to pressure from below sometimes. But we might hesitate before we attribute all government largesse to the pressures brought to bear by parish worthies. It is also possible that parliamentary concerns may inspire a government to disburse resources. I was once present when an official was asked by his Minister to make sure that a vote in committee went the right way: the official telephoned the deputies offering them minor development projects in their constituencies. The vote was won, some of the projects were realised – but it was almost at random, not concerned with local pressures, the demands of patrons at all: parliamentary necessities determined the distribution. That vivid memory of an occasion when I saw one of the realities which could underlie the appearance of careful planning, on the best expert advice, prompts questions about continuities. Are the manoeuvres of 1883, 1900, also the manoeuvres of 1963, 1973? The archives are not open, and so the answer must be speculative, based on circumstantial evidence if on any. In Pisticci in 1965 a new petrochemical factory was due to open: tens of thousands of people from Pisticci and the neighbouring towns applied for jobs; the announcement of who had got jobs was not made until after the local elections (see Davis 1973 for further details). The technique of timing distribution of largesse seems to have changed not at all since 1883. I suspect that other manoeuvres have changed

or been discontinued: the electorate is now so large that the most energetic Prefect could not hope to keep track of their affinal alliances, although it is quite clear that individual Deputies in Parliament are very sensitive to the nuances of local politics (Colclough 1969; Sacco 1965). The impulse to secure plebiscites, the abstention of opposition voters, seems also to have disappeared.

The purpose of this paper has been to make an obvious but I hope not trivial point: that the world beyond the hypen is a real one, and that, consequently, those who people live in it act in accordance with their own categories, constrained by their own cultures. If we wish to talk about Ministers and Prefects as if they are not Virgins but real people we must pay attention to their interests and impulses as well as to those of the local patrons whose influence we may tend to exaggerate. Our sources are not perfect: historical records raise difficult questions about continuities; participant observation of government action occurs by chance;[1] the writings of political scientists on the states do not usually contain the kind of information we require, and when they do they permit us to argue only by analogy. Nevertheless some attempt on these lines has to be made if we are to avoid the vaguenesses of the social construction of reality.

It is clear that our present analysis of the state as it impinges on local communities is inadequate, and that if we continue to be blind, helpless, impotent when confronted with nations, our discipline is unnecessarily restricted. But national processes of modernisation, integration and the like are not a remedy. Macro-sociological constructs are not an elixir, just monkey-glands. A few years ago most of the incidents recounted in this paper would have been acceptably analysed in terms of the pressures within local communities, the struggle to obtain access to resources. If we take the monkey-glands we shall, in a few years, convince ourselves with analyses in terms of such struggles occasioned by national processes: as railways are built, as state intervention increases, so the prizes become bigger and the struggles more intense – and so on. A good example of this kind of nebulosity is present, in embryo, in *Land and Family in Pisticci* (Davis 1973) at pages 155–6. But what is needed is a greater awareness of the social structure, relationships, networks even, of the administrators and politicians: we should always assume that these men too have – for example – categories which allow them to see some things as political, others as merely troublesome. And that they are not merely responsive to local pressure, but have needs within their own communities and cliques – needs for parliamentary votes, for making a good show of unanimity – which can push them into taking an active, manipulative role in local communities. By all means let us put this into the over-arching framework of processes which are peculiar to large aggregates of people: but without the ethnography or, failing the accidents which allow us to gather it, without the assumption that there is an ethnography there to be gathered, the framework is no more than just another trendy panacea, lacking even the advantages of the old ones, which at least are local constructs, made by indigenous craftsmen.

NOTES

[1] Berardino Plati was a Notary born in 1817 and elected to the Pisticci Council in 1862 with 49 votes. He was re-elected in 1864 when his property qualification was noted as L. 40,000; again in 1866 (L.50,000), 1872, 1876 (L.100,000), 1882, and 1887 (L.120,000). He was a member of the Giunta (executive sub-committee) from 1862–4 and 1878–83. When he died in 1888 his place was filled by the man who had polled the next highest number of votes: it was none other than his lazy vagabond nephew, Giuseppe Delfino, who was elected in his own right in 1889 and again in 1895, after the electoral reforms, when he had a declared wealth of L.150,000. He was a member of the Giunta 1890–3, and resigned, together with a majority of councillors, in 1896. He never held office again.

[2] The documents for this election are in *Arch. Stat. Pot. Gabinetto 1872–88 Fascicule* 41.

[3] Indeed, the hey-day of *trasformismo* was approaching: Giolitti's mode of securing a parliamentary majority was by Namier out of Barth. (See, e.g., Salvemini 1962).

[4] Bailey (1973) observes that students do not have easy access to authority in western European countries.

REFERENCES

Bailey, F. G.
Social Change in Selected European Communities. Report submitted to the Social Science Research Committee of Great Britain. Lodged in National Lending Library,1973.

Colclough, N. T.
'Land Politics and Power in a South Italian Village.' Unpublished Ph. D. dissertation, University of London, 1969.

Davis, J.
Land and Family in Pisticci. L. S. E. Monographs in Social Anthropology, 48. London: Athlone, 1973.

Nitti, F.
Lettere inedite sul brigantaggio Materano. *Arch. Stor. Calab. Lucan.* I–II:55–77, 1953.

Sacco, L.
Sindaci e ministri. Milan: Communita, 1965.

Salvemini, G.
Il ministro della malavita e altri scritti sull' Italia giolittiana. *Opere* IV:1. Milan: Feltrinelli, 1962.

Stirling, P.
'Impartiality and Personal Morality,' in *Contributions to Mediterranean Sociology,* 49 64. Edited by J. G. Peristiany. The Hague: Mouton, 1968.

5

Village Responses to National Law: A Case from the South Tyrol

Phillip S. Katz
University of Massachusetts, Amherst

ABSTRACT

This paper examines the response of highland Tyrolese villagers to several areas of national law. Contacts between village and state are viewed in terms of their effect upon the maintenance of Tyrolese cultural forms and identity.

In recent years social scientists have shown an increasing awareness that village communities in Western Europe, as in many other world areas, are bound by many important links to the larger nation-states of which they are a part. A number of these enduring links include involvement, either direct or indirect, with regional and national markets, as well as various forms of contact with state political and legal institutions. Following the theme that village communities cannot be studied as entities isolated from national and supra-national forces, this paper considers some aspects of the impact of national law upon processes of dispute management and access to social and economic resources in a highland Tyrolese village. As will be shown, villagers eschew regional and national courts in favor of local forms of dispute settlement which operate in accordance with principles far different from those employed by the courts. Also, state financial assistance programs and the rise of a locally resident group of wage laborers have had the net effect of reorganizing village social and political ties while strengthening local traditional life. I will stress that although state-village contacts may be important sources for change, they may also provide the stimuli for the *maintenance* of ethnic and cultural identity amongst rural Tyrolese.

A number of recent examinations of community responses to national law have focused upon the 'new', developing states of Asia and Africa (e.g. Singer n.d.; Jaspan 1965; Rheinstein 1963). These studies have focused upon the problems related to the adoption of uniform law codes within plural societies, particularly when these new codes are imported from western nations. In such cases the state population must deal with legal institutions which may be based upon alien value systems, and which may be contrary to customary law at the village level. The development of uniform law codes in the new states often functions as an important symbol of newly-won independence and nationhood (cf. Geertz 1963), but there may be many unforeseen legal and social consequences for the diverse groups within these nations. For, as Nader and Yngvesson have noted:

Those who often suffer (under nation-building through legal change) are the preliterate, the illiterate, the common people closest to urban centers–people whose indigenous systems of law are sabotaged under modernization pressures and for whom the imposition of centralized, professionalized law has decreased traditional access to law, at least until they learn by various means how to manipulate or use the newly introduced systems (Nader and Yngvesson n.d.:2).

Problems relating to the presence of uniform national law within plural societies are not found simply within the developing nations of Asia and Africa. Anthropological studies of social and cultural pluralism have been predominantly concerned with formerly colonial areas (e.g. Smith 1960; Kuper and Smith 1971) and have paid relatively less attention to those areas in which pluralism has developed in a noncolonial context. There are, for instance, few nations in Europe which do not have significant ethnic and cultural groups within them. It is an interesting fact that as the European nation-states have become more integrated among themselves there has been a corresponding rise in the visibility and influence of the ethnic minorities which they contain (cf. Pi-Sunyer 1971).

An examination of the ways in which these ethnic minorities have responded to national law, as well as to broader processes of social and economic change, can give us valuable insights into the ways in which their identity has been maintained and, in some cases, strengthened in recent years.

THE SETTING

Dornstein, the community under study, is located in a high valley in the Italian South Tyrol, which together with the Trentino constitutes a semi-autonomous region within the Republic of Italy. This area was once part of the Austrian Crownland of Tirol but was ceded to Italy in 1918 at the time of the breakup of the Austro-Hungarian Empire. Italy thus gained a cultural minority of some 220,000 German-speaking Tyrolese within its borders.

Relations between the Tyrolese and the Italian administration reached a low point during the Fascist era, when there was a concerted effort on the part of the state to forcibly Italianize the population of the South Tyrol. A number of measures taken by the state included the Italianization of local place names and many family names; the state-subsidized immigration of Italians from the south to the area; the appointment of Italians as clerks throughout the administrative bureaucracy; and the enforcement of Italian as the official language. By royal decree, all civil and criminal cases were to be carried out in Italian only, and those who could not understand Italian were not to be put on jury lists (cf. Alcock 1970: 33–45). Since World War II the Tyrolese have won the right once again to have German taught in their local schools, and the administrative apparatus of the state is supposed to be operative in both the Italian and German languages. Nonetheless, one finds that in practice much of the state administrative and legal machinery is conducted primarily in Italian, which has caused difficulties for the majority of rural highland Tyrolese who are not bilingual.

Within the South Tyrol as a whole one finds a clear dichotomy between a rural Tyrolese population based in the mountainous countryside and an urban-centred Italian population.[1] This dichotomy is more than simply a demographic fact – the distinctions drawn between life in the cities and that of Tyrolese *Bergbauern*, or mountain peasants, form an important boundary which affects the ways Tyrolese utilize national institutions and perceive the world about them. Villagers in Dornstein often noted that 'city life' represented a system of values completely alien to their own way of life. Whether or not this statement is entirely true, the lines drawn between urban and rural life provided categories through which the different values and cultural expectations of Tyrolese and Italians were viewed.

Dornstein is one of five villages making up a *Gemeinde*, or civil parish, which is the smallest politically and judicially independent unit recognized by the Italian state. Within the total parish population of some 1400 persons there are fewer than ten Italians present, all of whom are employees of the parish center or work as the local *carabinieri*.

Dornstein's population of about 400 persons is presently made up of both subsistence-oriented farmers and workers who derive their principal income from wage labor outside of the community. Prior to the construction of a road from the parish center to Dornstein in 1968, the village could only be reached after an hour's walk from the valley bottom. The outstanding feature of the community's ecologic setting is altitude: with households spread out between 1200 and 1800 meters elevation the village lies well above the zone in which the principal commercial crops of the surrounding valleys can be grown. This, combined with remote location, has kept the village marginal to, although certainly not isolated from the economic and cultural forces emanating from the lowlands.

Interpersonal ties in Dornstein have traditionally existed within a hierarchical structure in which landholding farmers dominated a dependent, landless *Knecht* ('farmhand') population. Access to land resources has been *the* most important criterion in determining an individual's ability to attain economic independence and political power locally. Within the past two decades a number of forces, including a general surge in postwar European economies, rural industrialization and tourism, have greatly increased the number of viable economic alternatives open to the village *Knecht* group. They are now forming a locally resident group of workers who are economically independent of their farmer siblings. The growth of a resident worker population in Dornstein has also been fostered by state subsidies and loans offered to cash laborers wishing to construct homes locally, as well as child-support payments offered to both farmer and worker families.

Recent economic changes and the subsequent rise of a local group of workers have broken down the hierarchical and farmer-dominated structure of village political and social relations. Workers and their farmer siblings now exchange goods and services on a more egalitarian basis. While farming is still seen as the life which is most fitting and satisfying for a Tyroler, farmers are willing to take on some cash labor when it is available. Indeed, farmers recognize that the viability of their estates, and in some respects the ongoing viability of local traditional life, is related to the local market for farm produce which workers provide and the availability of occasional wage labor (Cole and Katz 1973).

RESPONSES TO NATIONAL LAW: DISPUTE MANAGEMENT IN DORNSTEIN

In a general discussion of the utility of studying law in Western societies, Vilhelm Aubert has rightly noted that the principles and values according to which disputes are settled are often 'suggestive of pervasive structural features' in a society (1969a:277). In examining the response of Tyrolese villagers to national law it has been useful to observe whether the principles and values surrounding conflict resolution at the village level are consistent and compatible with those employed by state agencies. Research in Dornstein indicates that while national agencies for dispute settlement are available to villagers, they are not frequently used, in large measure because of the principles of settlement which they employ.

Both Aubert (1969b) and Gulliver (1969a, 1969b) have directed their attention toward an analysis of the various modes of dispute settlement available to disputing individuals, as well as the social implications of their use. Gulliver has distinguished negotiation and adjudication as the two dominant modes of dispute settlement. Negotiation generally involves compromise agreements, while adjudication is based upon binding decisions given by a third party. Such decisions are

in some way coercive in that the adjudicator (judge or the like) has not only both the right and obligation to reach and enunciate a decision but also the power to enforce it (Gulliver 1969a:17).

Aubert is also concerned with negotiation and adjudication as dominant modes of settlement; adjudication is considered in his analysis of the 'legal model' of conflict resolution. Settlements which follow a legal model involve third parties and are strongly oriented toward the establishment of guilt and matters of fact. Negotiated settlements, on the other hand, do not require the presence of third parties, nor must there be total agreement on the actual facts of the case (Aubert 1969b:286–289).

Nader and Yngvesson (n.d.) suggest that there is a correlation between the nature of the relationships binding people and the mode of settlement they will choose in resolving a dispute. They propose that where disputing individuals are bound by multiple, cross-cutting ties they will attempt to resolve their disputes through negotiation and compromise, so that the disputants will be reconciled and their relationships remain viable. Where parties to a dispute are bound by simplex ties, they will be more likely to opt for settlements based upon adjudication and will attempt to 'win' as much from an opponent as possible. One of the goals of my research in the South Tyrol was to test the views of Nader and Yngvesson, particularly in light of recent social and economic change.

Disputants in Dornstein have a range of potential agencies for dispute settlement available to them, including local mediators and public arenas for negotiation as well as formal, state-affiliated courts. The local parish government is headed by a Burgermeister and a council of fifteen men drawn from the parish. The council may resolve land and border disputes, although it may not handle cases in which restitution is sought by a party. The parish court, or *Friedensgericht*, is the lowest link in the formal court system; this court does not meet regularly and is only brought into session upon the request of a disputant. The mode of settlement in the parish court is adjudication. The judge of the parish court is a local schoolteacher with close ties to members of the parish. Acting as a private person, the schoolteacher often attempted to effect negotiated, compromise agreements between disputants, warning them that if negotiation failed and if they appeared before him in his capacity as judge, he would have to render a win/lose decision in which one party might lose all.

At the next level in the national court system are the courts of Meran (Merano) and Bozen (Bolzano). Within these settings settlements follow the legal model described by Aubert: judges are impartial observers of each case; only the facts directly relevant to a case are considered before the court; the decision handed down by the court is not so much concerned with the continuing relations of disputants as with determining right or wrong according to well-defined legal rules. The appearance of a dispute before a national court generally implies that attempts to resolve the conflict informally at the village level have failed.

Since 1900 there have only been seven instances in which Dornsteiners have been involved as litigants in the urban courts. In each of these cases litigants sought control over farm resources, and in three of these cases outsiders with few close ties to villagers were involved. There are at present no documented cases of villagers from Dornstein appearing before the parish court[2].

The reluctance of Dornsteiners to use the courts to resolve disputes is related to a number of factors. These include: the cost of court and lawyers' fees, which often outweigh the potential gains of a court suit; economic dislocation caused by court appearances and other time spent with lawyers and state officials; the villagers' perception of the courts as tools of the Italian state which are not attuned to the needs of rural Tyrolese; and, quite significantly, the recognition by Dornsteiners that the courts employ principles of settlement which may be damaging to the continuing relationship of disputants.

In contrast with the courts, village-level agencies for dispute settlement seek the re-establishment of harmony between the parties to a dispute and are less concerned with assigning guilt or innocence. Also, while the courts only consider those facts directly relevant to a case, negotiated and mediated settlements in Dornstein are concerned with all aspects of the disputants' ties.

The management of conflict in Dornstein is usually accomplished within a number of public arenas, such as the *Gasthaus*, or inn. While Dornsteiners stress affability and mutual accommodation in their day-to-day social relations, informal activity in the *Gasthaus* and some celebrations, such as those before a wedding, are marked by much consumption of wine, and by aggression and arguing. An important aspect of the drunken aggressiveness one witnesses in the *Gasthaus* is an open atmosphere coupled with the belief that disputants should ultimately be friends again, no matter how heated an argument might become. This attitude that disputants ought to be reconciled prevailed in almost all cases witnessed between two villagers. When outsiders with few close ties to Dornsteiners enter into disputes, however, the 'ground rules' change somewhat and people seemed less concerned as to whether or not disputants' relationships were damaged.

Dornsteiners operated under the fiction that arguments in the *Gasthaus* are 'only brought on by the wine,' although there are usually very real issues underlying disagreements. This belief that 'only the wine is talking' allowed individuals to make direct accusations and air all aspects of a dispute. In normal social intercourse outside of the *Gasthaus* aggressiveness and an argumentative nature are severely condemned.

Serious disputes which cannot be resolved within the village are often brought to the Burgermeister who, acting in an informal capacity, studies all aspects of the case and renders a compromise agreement. The aim of the dispute settlement process employed by the Burgermeister, as within the *Gasthaus*, is the mending of a broken relationship. In a large majority of cases the Burgermeister's unofficial settlements are abided by and the disputes do not go on to the courts.

Economic and social changes of the last two decades, particularly the growth of a group of wage laborers able to set up households locally, have broadened the political base of the village and have to some extent altered the hierarchical structure of domestic units. Farmers now maintain a broader range of functionally significant ties with their siblings than in the past, including bonds of fictive kinship and labor and gift exchanges. The appearance of a local group of workers, and the broadening of economic alternatives which they represent, has paralleled a decline in recent years of disputes over land, particularly the inheritance disputes which were relatively frequent in the past. It is not surprising that all of those cases which escalated to the courts involved access to land and forest resources as the central issue of conflict, since until recently it was only access to farm resources which assured an individual economic independence and high social prestige.

Multiplex ties throughout Dornstein remain strong. The importance of these ties is reflected in villagers' attempts to resolve conflict at the village level through negotiation whenever possible. Despite the very real differences in economic and political power which still separate Dornsteiners, especially farmowners and the few dependent *Knechte* remaining, all men have equal access to the *Gasthaus* as a setting for the airing and settlement of disputes. Women do not have access directly to the *Gasthaus* as an arena for settling disputes, although their husbands may air a dispute for them. While the disputes between women often fester for some time, they rarely escalate beyond the village level.

The data from Dornstein presented here bear out the general validity of Nader and Yngvesson's model of dispute settlement. The presence of strong multiple, cross-cutting ties does appear to influence villagers toward compromise settlements which stress renewed harmony between disputants. In examining patterns of dispute behavior it is important that we look at the central issue of conflict as well as the nature of disputants' ties. In light of the data from Dornstein I would add, as a corollary to Nader and Yngvesson's model, that when strategic or limited resources which allow for power differentials are at issue, disputants will be likely to disregard their multiplex ties and seek an adjudicated settlement.

In assessing the use of the national courts by villagers in Dornstein, it becomes apparent that villagers do not perceive the process of dispute settlement employed by the courts as suiting their needs. Villagers recognized that adjudicated settlements, particularly in a court setting in which the problems of rural Tyrolese might not be understood, could be damaging to the continuation of disputants' relationships. Villagers only seemed willing to go to court when the stakes were high enough, that is, when access to farm resources was at issue. While the courts are avoided by villagers in most dispute cases, it would be wrong to assume that the impact of their presence as part of the national legal system is minimal – in many ways it is the presence of the courts, and local opposition to their use, which compels Dornsteiners to work through negotiation and compromise at the village level[3].

NATIONAL LAW, SOCIOECONOMIC CHANGE, AND ACCESS TO VILLAGE RESOURCES

While the influence of national courts upon the process of dispute settlement in Dornstein has largely been indirect, the impact of other areas of national law, particularly tax and commercial codes as well as government-sponsored aid programs, has been direct and considerable. Within the past twenty years there has been a notable increase in the number of codes affecting villagers' control over local resources. The effect of these codes has been to remove control of local land and forest resources from the hands of the community to those of the state. Whenever an animal is butchered or a stem of wood cut in one's forest, a tax is levied. Moreover, the amount of wood which may be cut each year as well as access to grazing areas is now closely regulated by state agencies. Until recent years access to local forest grazing areas was regulated by cooperative associations of farmers who were bound by kinship and economic ties and whose forest borders were often contiguous. These local associations are no longer operative, as it is now the local forest warden appointed by the state who controls access to forests and grazing areas. Nonetheless, several villagers consistently take a 'mini-max' game approach in dealing with codes regulating use of local resources: they knowingly permit their animals to graze illegally and cut more wood than is allowed, hoping that any fine or penalty incurred is outweighed by the potential profit of the animals or wood for local use or sale. The forest warden, a Tyroler from an urban center, is responsible for levying fines, and since fines are negotiable to an extent villagers often attempt to cultivate and maintain positive relations with him.

Dornsteiners do not condemn a man who allows illegal grazing or cuts too much wood on *his own* land, for any potential conflict from such actions is seen as involving the state and not other villagers. Indeed, a number of local people expressed pride in their 'battle' against state control over their land. One of the most direct consequences of recent controls over local resources has been to proling the period over which farmers have given the obligatory inheritance payments due to siblings leaving the estate. In the past, farmers were able to cut large portions of their forests for sale in order to pay off their siblings in a relatively short period of time, but this is no longer possibe. The encroachment of the state over use of local resources is part of the larger process by which village communities are becoming integrated into national-level institutions throughout Europe. The problems associated with this more general movement have been exacerbated in Dornstein by presence in a plural society. Villagers feel most threatened by state controls over their economic lives, and their thoughts are often articulated in terms of their fears over the state's desire to 'Italianize' them. Extremely costly state registration fees for local dances as well as controls over the evening celebrations which follow certain religious observances are viewed as attempts by the state to restrict and weaken local tradition.

National laws are sometimes manipulated by villagers to fit local custom and needs, as in the case of inheritance laws. Italian law states that all of the children of an estate heir must receive a portion of the estate property, although this is an area of impartible inheritance in which the eldest son ideally inherits the farm land intact. High priority is given to keeping the estate landholding together, for continued division over time might threaten the balance of land types needed to run a farm properly. The state does not define different types of property, however, and so while the land is given intact to the one chosen heir, the other siblings are given payments which in the eyes of the state may have a value equal to that of the land. Those *Knechte* who remained on their natal farm received only their room and board and sometimes a token sum as their inheritance payment. Although national laws have assured that all heirs received a share of the estate property, the land, which until recently was the principal source of economic independence and political power locally, remained undivided and in the hands of one heir.

One of the most influential areas of national law at the village level has been the state assistance of the growing worker population in Dornstein. Since about 1960 worker families have received payments of from $30–50 per month per child under fourteen years of age, and this has provided a major source of income. Farmers, on the other hand, have received child-support payments from the government only since 1968. Also crucial to the permanent settlement of worker households have been loans and state subsidies available to workers wishing to construct their own homes. (cf. Cole and Katz 1973:58).

In spite of generous support for workers and the subsequent rise of a worker group locally, life as a farmer working on the land remains the ideal for a 'proper' life in Dornstein. Thus, while one finds farmers taking on some wage labor when it is available, most workers are eager to purchase land and keep a number of animals for family use. In fact, most of the worker families keep a number of chickens and goats and many keep a cow to provide milk for their families. Workers receive grazing and stalluse rights, as well as hay from their farmer siblings in return for their occasional contributions of labor to the farm, strengthening still further the ties between farmers and their siblings.

Within the process of social and economic change which has affected life in Dornstein in many ways, there remains an essential continuity with the past. Villagers cling to Tyrolese traditions, particularly the subsistence-oriented economic strategies of farming and keeping livestock. Moreover, they are aware that it is the availability of wage labor and the presence of a locally resident worker group, as well as state aid, which underwrites the ongoing viability of the local economy and traditional life.

The areas of national law considered in this paper have affected village life in both direct and indirect ways. In the area of conflict resolution, villagers retain a form of dispute settlement which is compatible with the continuation of ties locally. The courts are viewed as impersonal state agencies which are not attuned to the needs of rural Tyrolese. Local opposition to use of the courts serves to compel villagers to resolve disputes at the village and parish level through negotiation and compromise whenever possible. Of more direct impact has been the redefinition of local resources so that they are no longer communally held and regulated, but are now controlled by state agencies. This has been accomplished through tax laws and codes governing villagers' access to forests and grazing areas. State assistance programs, in the form of child-support payments and subsidies and loans for the construction of homes, along with possibilities for wage labor outside of the village, have been crucial in fostering the growth of a locally resident group of workers. The appearance of this worker group has served to realign political, social, and economic ties within the village, but has not altered significantly the ideology and practice of Tyrolese tradition which gives meaning to the lives of Dornsteiners.

One major aim of this paper has been to stress that village communities be studied as entities which interact with the nation states of which they are part. Indeed, the continuing viability of traditional Tyrolese culture in Dornstein is to a large extent a function of the ties which villagers maintain with the larger national economic, political, and legal institutions about them[4].

NOTES

[1] While the number of Tyrolese in the major cities of the South Tyrol has actually dropped in the past forty years, there has been a tremendous rise in the migration of Italians to urban areas. Thus, while Italians comprised only five percent of the total population of Bozen (Bolzano) in 1910, they now represent over seventy-five percent of the city's population (Cole and Katz 1973).

[2] Although disputes between villagers are generally not settled in the courts, in several cases court action was initiated as part of a strategy to pressure an opponent. The eventual resolution of these disputes was achieved locally through negotiation, however.

[3] The relationship of village and state with regard to conflict resolution in Dornstein is in some ways a passive one: a form of resolution is offered by the state but is not used often by villagers. Also, the form of conflict resolution employed at the village level is viewed as acceptable by the state.

Under different circumstances in which the state views the local forms of law and conflict resolution as unacceptable, the reaction to local law is less benign. For instance, the use of the vendetta as a part of the local law system of Sardinia is viewed as being in conflict with the laws of the Italian state and is proscribed (Pigliaru 1959).

[4] Fieldwork for this study was carried out in the South Tyrol between January 1972 and January 1973, and was assisted by a Research Fellowship from the European Studies Program at the University of Massachusetts, Amherst, Massachusetts.

REFERENCES

Alcock, Antony E.
The History of the South Tyrol Question. London: Michael Joseph, Ltd., 1970.

Aubert, Vilhelm
'Introduction: Case Studies of Law in Western Societies,' in *Law in Culture and Society*, 273–281. Edited by L. Nader. Chicago: Aldine, 1969a.
'Law as a Way of Resolving Conflicts: The Case of a Small Industrialized Society,' in *Law in Culture and Society*, 282–303. Edited by L. Nader. Chicago: Aldine, 1969b.

Cole, John W., and Phillip S. Katz
Knecht to Arbeiter: The Proletarization Process in South Tyrol. *Studies in European Society* 1:39–66, 1973.

Geertz, Clifford
'The Integrative Revolution–Primordial Sentiments and Civil Politics in the New States,' in *Old Societies and New States*, 105–157. Edited by C. Geertz. New York: The Free Press, 1963.

Gulliver, P. H.
'Introduction, Case Studies of Law in Non-Western Societies,' in *Law in Culture and Society*, 11–23. Edited by L. Nader. Chicago: Aldine, 1969a.
'Dispute Settlement Without Courts: The Ndendeuli of Southern Tanzania,' in *Law in Culture and Society*, 24–68. Edited by L. Nader. Chicago: Aldine, 1969b.

Jaspan, M. A.
In Quest of New Law: The Perplexity of Legal Syncretism in Indonesia. *Comparative Studies in Society and History* 7:252–266, 1965.

Kuper, L., and M. G. Smith
Pluralism in Africa. Berkeley: University of California Press, 1971.

Nader, Laura, and Barbara Yngvesson
'On Studying the Ethnography of Law and Its Consequences,' in *Handbook of Social and Cultural Anthropology*. Edited by John J. Honigmann, 1974.

Pigliaru, Antonio
La vendetta Barbaracina come ordinamento giurdico. Publicazioni Dell'Instituto Di Filosofia Del Dritto Dell'Universita Di Roma, Milano, Dott. A. Giuffré, Editore v. XIII, 1959.

Pi-Sunyer, Oriol
The Limits of Integration: Ethnicity and Nationalism in Modern Europe. Department of Anthropology, University of Massachusetts, Research Reports Number 9, 1971.

Rheinstein, Max
'Problems of Law in the New Nations of Africa,' in *Old Societies and New States*, 220–246. Edited by C. Geertz. New York: The Free Press, 1963.

Singer, Norman
n.d. 'Legal Process as a Key to Legal Development.' Ms.

Smith, M. G.
'Social and Cultural Pluralism,' in *Social and Cultural Pluralism in the Caribbean*. Edited by V. Rubin. *Annals of the New York Academy of Sciences* 83:761–916, 1960.

6

South from Madrid:
Regional Elites and Resistance [1]

Donny Meertens
University of Amsterdam

ABSTRACT

The central question of this paper is the meaning of community in southern Spain, past and present. First the historical origins of 'two Spains' are outlined, with the corresponding differences in the meaning of community. We can contrast the corporate village of the north with the socially divided village and ambivalent community feelings in the south. Even in the nineteenth century the southern village was no microcosm in which all social processes could be studied. A area wider than the community, the town with its rural surroundings, provided a base for class conflicts between common people and elites. At present the location of conflicts reflecting the agrarian question has shifted even more definitely to the towns, requiring a broader scope in our investigations.

1. INTRODUCTION

To most anthropologists the small community is still an important frame of reference. Anthropological fieldwork in Spain has also followed this tradition. The result is a series of community studies, some of which belong to the classics of European anthropology, e.g., Pitt-Rivers (1961) (Andalusia), Lison-Tolosana (1966), Freeman (1970), Aceves (1971), Adams (1971), Codd (1971), and Christian (1972) (central and northern Spain). The focus of all these studies is exclusively on the small community. There are two main arguments for a focus of this kind. First, the local community is the best context for the study of 'typical' anthropological topics, such as patterns of kinship, courtship and marriage, honour, shame, and stratification and social control within a system of face-to-face relationships. Second, the community has a special meaning for the people studied. In this sense 'community' can be defined as a system of relationships with a clear boundary, characterized by identification, control of resources, exchange of labour and common social institutions. Although most studies recognize the interdependence of local and national processes, the influence of these wider processes is still studied at the local level. Such an approach may be legitimate as far as the community remains a relatively independent unit of social organization and identification. This is not equally true for all regions in Spain. We might even discern 'two Spains' in this respect. (Of course this is an oversimplification, but useful in contrasting the elements.) The historical processes of regional differentiation between northern-central and southern Spain (Andalusia) are specially important for the meaning of the small community. In contrast to the northern and central regions, the community in southern Spain never took a corporate form. In the south a real community study always remained an incomplete story [2]. The presence of a strong rural elite created divisions within the community, and the resistance of peasants against this elite stimulated bonds of solidarity transcending local boundaries. The conflicts between elites and peasants extended to a regional scale, mostly in rural areas surrounding the Andalusian towns. This area, which I here loosely call the region, is seldom studied by anthropologists[3].

This paper emphasizes the importance of the region for the study of rural conflict and resistance. It starts with an overview of the historical origins and the continued differentiation of the 'two Spains', indicating in the following sections how in Andalusia the world of community disappears more and more; how contacts between peasants and workers and 'class-conflicts' occur within a regional context, and how the town has become the centre of gravity of these conflicts.

2. REGIONAL CONFIGURATIONS AFTER THE RECONQUISTA

The influential regional elite in the south, and the relatively independent communities of central Spain, can be traced back to the Middle Ages, when systems of land tenure were established during the reconquest of the peninsula from the Moors[4]. In the first two stages of the reconquest, which took place in the ninth and tenth centuries, the King of Castile and Leon extended the kingdom across the central plateau *(Meseta)* to the borders of the Tagus. This country was sparsely populated and the King had insufficient resources for its resettlement. In the absence of a strong aristocracy the crown granted rights *(presura)* to individual settlers, mostly liberated serfs, and delegated power to democratically elected municipal councils. This gave rise to a class of small permanent leaseholders, in effective possession of the land, with no mediators between themselves and the King.

These new regions really did consist of small communities which controlled the land, exchanged labour within their boundaries, interacted as a corporate group with the crown, and were only through a rudimentary market structure connected with other villages. They held all land in common, shared out every ten years in equal portions and by lot among all the inhabitants. The commune provided the base for social organization: the council composed of all male family heads decided on crop rotation and irrigation; meadows and other lands after harvest were collectively exploited for grazing and all families participated in a rotating system of responsibilities such as mutual aid, burial societies and, occasionally, the redistribution of meat. Their democratic institutions did not begin to decay before the middle of the eighteenth century, when state influence was increasingly felt at the local level, through tax collectors, state police and state bureaucracy. In some places these local communities managed to retain their political rights, including their legal status, into the twentieth century. Some of them even practiced (but now under the banner of anarchism) their local form of autonomy and egalitarianism during the Civil War (Brenan 1962:336-340; Freeman 1970:27-47).

In contrast, vast areas of southern Spain (Andalusia) fell in one blow to the Castilians in the thirteenth century, with the kingdom of Granada following in the fifteenth century. The conquest was largely the work of military orders, or individual nobles, the latter obtaining inalieneble rights to vast territories in reward for their services. Other factors also encouraged the emergence of a latifundia structure: other regions no longer provided a surplus population to resettle the area with small-scale colonists; a relatively large population of Moors remained on the land in a subordinate position; extensive agriculture and sheep farming responded best to market demands. Common lands were turned over to pasture and became in time the monopoly of the rich, who alone had herds[5].

No trace af agricultural communes existed south of the Tagus (Brenan 1962:339). The village never functioned as a corporate group in economic and political relations. The peasants individually depended on the local elites, which consisted first of feudal lords, and later of big landowners and politicals bosses *(caciques)*. The local unit had no significant control over resources or labour. Although the biggest landowners were mostly absentees, within the village inequality still persisted through the presence of minor landlords, administrators and large-scale tenants existing alongside small peasant proprietors and landless labourers. This inequality made the identification of the village with 'community' ambivalent. This is shown in the meaning of the word *pueblo*: it is used either for the village as a local unit with the elite sometimes included, or for the community of 'common people' with the elite definitely excluded[6].

The community in the sense of a sentiment or organization embracing the whole local unit represented no present reality, but more a future utopia, which found its expression in the ideology of anarchism that became dominant in Spain's rural areas after 1888. The peasants of southern Spain in particular became the partisans of this movement. Many anarchist ideas conformed very well to the utopian sentiments of the peasantry, such as were represented by the autonomous and egalitarian community, agrarian collectivism, and the moral quality of each human being. Anarchism was, however, something more than the expression of a naive millenarian fantasy. It also contained the realistic element of class struggle, under the stimulus of an ever-growing inequality in the course of the commercialization processes that took place in the nineteenth century. Everyone was aware of the harsh class struggle that had to be fought against the elites of their own community before their ideal of local communism could be realized.

In contrast to the peasants in Andalusia, those in central Spain were far less affected by commercialization, because they operated mainly on a subsistence level, and no inequality existed such that one rich peasant could buy the common lands of the village for private use, as happened in the south (Malefakis 1972:198-199). The communal forms of organization of these villages classify a paradoxical situation: their old traditions resembled the anarchist utopia of agrarian communism, but the other element in anarchism, the struggle against existing inequality within the community, was absent. Anarchism did not take root as firmly in the central regions as in the south. The peasants of some parts of central and northern Spain even participated in the extremely conservative Carlist movements of the nineteenth century. The rather weak correlation between anarchist ideals and the existing forms of communal village organization is further illustrated by the lines of division during the Civil War. Areas in the north which formed anarchist strongholds bordered upon areas where the peasants sided with the fascists, without any underlying distinction between agrarian structures that could explain this adherence to opposite ideologies. The strong influence of urban centres can serve as a partial explanation for the spread of anarchism in some rural areas (for example Zaragoza in Aragon). The strong class antagonism, prevalent in the south, was absent in most of these communities.

This historical differentiation accounts for a whole set of interrelated characteristics of each of the two Spains. Out of the specific pattern of dominance in each region a distinct landowning system emerged together with typical forms of village organization. The sharing of communal institutions, the sense of local belonging characteristic of the villages in central Spain where the only enemy came from beyond the village borders, did not exist in the other Spain. In the south it was not a struggle of the local community against some outside power, but rather that of the *pueblo* as a class (consisting of small peasants and landless labourers) against the local landlords who constituted the main axis of opposition.

These differences between the two Spains did not disappear in the course of the centuries in which the Spanish nation-state definitely was formed. Up to the eighteenth century, the southern elites led the struggle against the tendency of the central regime to monopolize power. When under the Bourbon dynasty in the eighteenth century administrative centralization and political uniformity were finally achieved, the traditional landowning elites of Andalusia, through the personnel of the administrative bureaucracy, and through their widespread contacts in state organisms, had already obtained power in the central government itself. They continued, therefore, to play a rather autonomous role in the economic and political control of their region, using influence at the national level to protect their interests in their own power domains.

In the nineteenth century the struggle for state power continued. The processes of nation-building and state-formation in other European countries are described by Elias (1970:9-12) as 'three-cornered struggles between landowning aristocratic and court elite, rising industrial middle classes and, behind them, the rising industrial working classes.' In Spain, however, there existed a more complicated balance of power. A new industrial bourgeoisie and working classes were mainly concentrated in Catalonia. In the rest of the country, but especially in the south, the peasantry played an active role in the struggle. Ultimately the peasantry became the greatest force for polarization in the country when, during the second republic (1931–36), the weak bourgeois-democratic government was unable to enforce its promises of land reform. The government, fearing the intransigence of still powerful old elites, and hampered by a bureaucratic apparatus staffed by civil servants connected with the lower aristocracy, engaged in fruitless parliamentary discussions. This polarization culminated in the Spanish Civil War (1936–1939), which Franco won with his own particular alliance of military men and traditional Catholic elites fighting under the banner of a fascist ideology.

A most critical distinction falls between the general European pattern which Elias describes, and these developments in Spain: it was *not* the new bourgeoisie that was victorious and so dominated the processes of integration. In the Civil War the proletarian and bourgeois parties that had emerged in the nineteenth century lost their struggle for increased power.

In Spain nation-building after the Civil War changed course in such a way that economic development and industrialization were no longer to be associated with bourgeois dominance and increasing mass participation. Regional differences continue to exist as a consequence of the two-headed character of the regime. The new industrial elites lost the battle by the narrowest margin, but they already carried too much weight to be neglected in the development policies of the new 'strong' state. As a consequence, the regime shows a marked ambivalence: it fosters a strong desire for development, for an economic take-off of the nation, but *not* at the cost of the traditional elites. The result is a policy of authoritarian modernization for the southern regions, which, although encouraging economic improvements, fails to prevent southern surpluses from being syphoned off into investment in northern industries.

With this excursion into history I wanted to make clear the origin of differences between northern and southern communities. The former fit the ideal type of microcosmos in which the anthropologist can study all social processes including the influence of the state, but this is not the case in the southern Andalusian villages. For peasant movements and political control by elite and state, the community is not the most relevant unit. In the next sections I shall concentrate on one of the Andalusian regions where the scene is laid for conflicts between peasants and elite: the town Granada and its rural surroundings.

3. GRANADA: ITS PEASANT MOVEMENT AND MECHANISMS OF CONTROL

The conflicts in Andalusia before the Civil War were essentially a struggle for land that was fought in the countryside. An entrepreneurial bourgeoisie, industrial development and concentrations of urban proletariat did not exist. The Andalusian towns served the landed gentry as a principal dwelling place. The few urban workers continued to foster relationships and emotional bonds with the countryside. In the epoch of anarchism, the town served as a centre for conspiracies that set fire to the surrounding rural areas. This can be illustrated with two examples: the so-called cantonalist movement and the rise of anarchosyndicalism in Granada.

The cantonalist insurrection took place in 1874, the year of exclamation of the First Republic under Pi Y Margall, a federalist. He wanted to reform Spain into a federal republic with extreme decentralization. Many 'cantons' (towns and districts) did not wait until the governmental plans were enacted, and declared themselves spontaneously autonomous. The movement, inspired by the Paris Commune, was a mixture of liberal middle class protest against the strongly centralizing policies of the former regimes, and of peasant ideas of equality and communism. The insurrection broke out simultaneously in Granada and other towns of Andalusia and Levante. The surrounding villages started to divide up the large estates. It lasted two months. The elite needed the help of the national army to restore order, and this order brought the end of the First Republic.

There are also some data on the peasant movements in Granada during the first decades of the twentieth century (Calero 1972), a period of strong political revival, mainly anarchist, throughout the south of Spain. In spite of weak union structure at the national and regional level (which naturally accorded with anarchist principles), the movements served as a focus of class identification across community boundaries.

The contacts between Granada-town and the surrounding rural areas were important for disseminating the ideology and extending the informal organization. In the town, the construction workers (who constituted the proletariat of Granada) deliberately chose to withdraw their support for socialist parliamentarian politics and to affiliate with the CNT, the anarcho-syndicalist mass-organization. They exported their ideology to the surrounding villages, where small peasant proprietors, tenants, craftsmen and landless labourers all joined the movement.

'The idea', as it was called ,was carried from village to village by Anarchist 'apostles'. In the farm labourers' barracks, in isolated cottages by the light of oil candles, the apostles spoke on liberty and equality and justice to rapt listeners. Small circles were formed in towns and villages which started night schools where many learned to read... (Brenan 1962:157).

The participation of small peasants was important, since with some resources of their own they could afford long strikes. They joined the struggle against the landlords, who exploited them by means of burdensome rents, or bought their labour at harvest time. It was therefore in those villages where large estates existed side by side with very small ones that the strikes were carried out most energetically.

Thus, political consciousness and revolutionary tactics, stimulated by townsmen with a new ideology, made explicit the lines of division between elite and common people within the local communities. They both acted upon these divisions and combined forces with their own people: the small proprietors, rural labourers and urban workers in opposition to the landed gentry and the Civil Guard. At the local level where conflicts found their first overt expression, the old mechanisms of social and political control, such as patronage and *caciquismo*, began to fail. Waves of anarchist fervour and strikes rolled from town to villages and back, although mostly not very well coordinated. The gentry sometimes fled their landed estates, and needed the help of a supra-local power, the Civil Guard, to suppress the movement.

4. GRANADA: A MARGINAL REGION UNDER THE FRANCO REGIME

Several changes characterize the post-Civil War period. Peasant resistance was ruthlessly suppressed. The old elite returned to their villages and estates; no change ever took place in the agrarian structure until now. But in the course of the following thirty years of the Franco regime the relation between these old elites and the state apparatus has changed. Their interests (land) were never directly attacked, but they lost some political and economic prerogatives since the end of *caciquismo* and the modernization politics of the government. Their position in the regional economy also became more marginal in proportion to new entrepreneurs and bureaucratic development institutions.

The development policies of the government are directed to the creation of urban development centres for industrialization and to land reform (without changing the structure of ownership) in each district (*comarca*, a unit based on similarity in agrarian problems). In spite of this the policy is more *laissez faire* than the government pretends, for it does not try to deal with the structural problems of the south (Comin 1963:206-208). Regional disequilibrium has to be resolved through labour migration, which slowly would reduce income differentials. But the impressive national growth which started in the 1960s brought no corresponding rise in the standard of living of working class and peasantry in Andalusia.

Granada is one such centre without real development. Too many landless or minifundist peasants live side by side with a 'rent-capitalistic' elite. The reform of the *comarcas* by the ministry of agriculture intends to bring the superfluous landless labourers and too small proprietors to the town. However, the industrialization programme (the creation of more employment) did not take off in Granada. The capital invested in the few big industries of the region comes mostly from foreign companies, and the profit they make flows out of the region.

The local industry consists of small and middle-sized enterprises, with the employment of mostly unskilled labour, varying according to the season. The seasonal unemployment in both agriculture and industry gives rise to a high level of temporary migration between town and country, thus providing a link between them. Commuting, more than permanent migration, reinforces these contacts. The shared economic situation, the mixing of roles, and the extended networks which are the result of this process can be seen as creating new forms of solidarity between peasants and workers in this region.

These contacts differ from those found before the Civil War. Now nothing happens in the countryside – no conflicts, no changes in the social structures. But in the town something did change, as the commuting peasants met with a new pattern of labour relations, as explained by the general situation of labour relations and syndicates in Spain.

In the ideology of the corporate state there is no conflict of interest between labour and capital. Spain has a vertical syndicalist organization which incorporates both employers and employed. No independent formation of trade unions is allowed and strikes are illegal. Since, however, the new economic development policies of the 1950s required some liberalization in labour relations, a law was passed providing for collective labour contracts. But the possibility to enter into collective contracts did not improve the bargaining power of the workers very much. In the absence of any right to strike, and in a situation where the official syndicates are not neutral arbiters who could impose impartial compromises, the workers have no sanctions against the other party when negotiations break off. The new law had one consequence definitely not intended by those who enacted it: an enormous proliferation of labour conflicts. The contradictions in the system became all too apparent, for collective negotiation presupposes two parties with antagonistic interests, and this is exactly the opposite of the official ideology of corporate syndicalism. The enactment of the law in 1958 therefore changed conditions of class organization. Economic setbacks and the violent suppression of labour conflicts led to increased class consciousness. At the same time these conflicts tended to escalate politically.

To a certain extent collective bargaining once more stimulated regional alliances within the working class. In those industrial sectors, which are weak and fragmented, collective contracts are negotiated not at the factory but at the provincial level. This makes for a region-wide group of workers involved in the formulation of demands doomed to failure at the negotiating table in the provincial capital. This happened, as we shall see, in Granada.

In the agrarian, as opposed to the industrial, sector, the social control of the elite is still too strong to allow for anything like a collective contract. The power of latifundists in the syndicates, together with the important posts which they occupy at the provincial or district level, is sufficient to enable them to reject any petition for collective negotiation which peasants and rural workers may put forward (Martinez Alier 1968:359-387). In the agrarian syndicates, the practice of harmony between patrons and labourers is still officially maintained. Befor the Civil War the ideology of harmonious labour relations was expressed in the patronage bonds and the face-to-face relations which united both categories within the local community. Patronage as a mechanism of social control at local level has now disappeared. Instead, the agrarian elite relies on the official ideology of corporatism, using the influence which it has in the regional branches of state institutions for its rejection of the demands of the workers.

Changes for collective action and negotiations are only found in the town. Once, in the nineteenth century, revolutionary ideas were brought from town to surrounding country, where the struggle was fought. Now the town is the centre of conflict. The peasants take the misery of the countryside with them to their new, although temporary, employment. And it is also the agrarian question that is expressed in labour conflicts in the town.

5. THE STRIKE OF CONSTRUCTION WORKERS IN 1970

This mass without cohesion or stability,
in constant pilgrimage for work,
without any education, . . . this mass
lives in difficult circumstances to
reach the minimum of solidarity that
the reality of class struggle demands.
(Comin 1963:258)

This same mass showed in Granada a remarkable amount of class consciousness in the sudden outburst of a labour conflict in the construction industry in 1970, in which both urban labourers and temporary migrant workers participated.

On July 21, 1970, thousands of construction workers went on strike, gathered in front of the syndicate building and asked for the negotiations that had been broken off the day before to be reopened. The objective was a collective contract at the procincial level. The demonstration culminated in a violent clash with the police, in which three workers were shot dead, while many others fled into the cathedral. This was a deliberate political act: the clergy openly supported the fugitives and refused to allow the police to enter the church. The strikers then seized the opportunity to form a democratic council, to exert pressure on the government for the liberation of the prisoners and the reopening of bargaining. Ultimately the government won, for although the negotiations were reopened and the workers' action suspended, no positive results for the workers followed. This conflict exemplifies much of what has been said in the preceding sections. The direct cause was the breaking off of negotiations for a collective contract at provincial level.

Could it be said of this incident that it laid the foundations of a class consciousness incorporating both peasants and urban workers? Can we speak of a 'take off' in horizontal organization such as the law of collective contracts stimulated in industrial areas? These questions can only be answered by studying the course of this conflict as regional problem.

6. CONCLUSION

In the foregoing I have outlined the historical origins of the 'two Spains' and the corresponding differences in the meaning of community which we can contrast as 'corporate' in the north and 'ambivalent' (as expressed in the word *pueblo*) in Andalusia, the southern part of Spain. This ambivalence found its expression in the nineteenth century and up to the Civil War in the twentieth century in the form of solidarity of the 'common people' in opposition to the elite, for which an area wider than the community provided a base. I have characterized this area as a town with its rural surroundings. Therefore, even in the nineteenth century the Andalusian village was no 'microcosmos' in which all social processes could be studied.

This can be said with even more emphasis of the Andalusian villages in the twentieth century after the Civil War. Before this war the anarchist movement encountered severe and often crucial repression as every new conflict arose. It was able, nevertheless, to organize the working class and the peasants with a certain amount of freedom both in actuality and according to the law. In contrast, after the war, repression became everywhere more effective, particularly in the agrarian sector. At the present time, therefore, class conflicts – although covertly present in the villages and probably emanating from there – are explicit only in industrial negotiations in the Andalusian towns.

The processes of rural-urban commuting, labour conflicts and political control have to be seen first of all in the context of an economy and – more important – an employment structure of which both the town and the surrounding rural areas form part.

Under the present regime the regional elite is not completely deprived of its power and continues to dominate the agrarian sector. Its position, however, has become increasingly marginal to the most important economic and political processes of the region.

An answer to the questions put at the end of the last section depends on the pattern of development which Granada and its surroundings will follow, and especially on the role taken by the traditional elite in its modernization. Therefore we have to study local and regional elites, their power structure and relation to other economic interest groups, and their response to national policies such as those concerning development, labour relations, and agrarian reform. The location of conflicts reflecting the agrarian question has completely shifted from local communities to an area including the towns. We must broaden the scope of our study accordingly.

NOTES

[1] I am most grateful to Thomas Crump and Sandra Wallman, who kindly helped me with the English text of this paper.

[2] It is no coincidence that most community studies were carried out in central Spain, while the only study of an Andalusian village by Pitt-Rivers shows us the ambivalence of the concept *pueblo*!

[3] The only regional studies I have found are the famous work of Diaz del Moral (1969) on peasant movements in the province of Cordoba; Martinez Alier (1968), who made a study of the labour relations on latifundia in 'la Campina', a part of the province of Cordoba; and Schneider, Schneider and Hansen (1972), who concentrate on the role of elites in regional development or dependency in Catalonia and Sicily.

[4] For an elaborate account of the reconquest, see Malefakis (1970:50ff) and Vicens Vives (1972: passim). See also Brenan (1962:338-339).

[5] In this classification I omitted intentionally a third important region, Catalonia, with a history totally different from the *reconquista* and its effects. In the Middle Ages Catalonia was virtually a nation in its own right, and the Catalan elite continued to seek economic adventures outside Spain, through primitive accumulation in the time of early colonization of South America, and later as maritime merchants and as a new industrial bourgeoisie. They continued to emphasize the theme of separatism and consolidated their own resources, often in conflict with Madrid.

⁶ Pitt-Rivers introduced this ambivalence in the meaning of *pueblo* for the Andalusian village he studied. In his interpretation the cognitions of *pueblo* as community and as 'plebs' in opposition to the rich are quite compatible, 'for the rich do not really belong to the pueblo' (1961:18). He sees the village as culturally homogeneous and without clear class divisions. When the 'senoritos' (the elite) are excluded from the pueblo, this distinction is made without resentment against these people as a *class* (1961:68-77, 204). He strongly underemphasizes, however, the underlying structural inequalities. He does not interpret these cognitive distinctions as elements of class struggle. In this his argument runs counter to mine (see next paragraph in text), and is also rather incompatible with the outbursts of hatred which divided most villages during the Civil War. (And this happened most ardently in the anarchist strongholds, like the village of Alcala de la Sierra which Pitt-Rivers studied.)

REFERENCES

Aceves, J. B.
Social Change in a Spanish Village. Cambridge, Mass.: Schenkman Publishing Co, 1971.

Adams, Paul
'Public and Private Interests in Hogar,' in *Gifts and Poison,* 167–182. Edited by F. G. Bailey. Oxford: Basil Blackwell, 1971.

Brenan, Gerald
The Spanish Labyrinth: An Account of the Social and Political Background of the Spanish Civil War. Second Edition. London and New York: Cambridge University Press, 1962.

Calero, Antonio M.
Historia del movimiento obrero de Granada 1909–1923.
Granada. Unpublished dissertation. Madrid: ed. Technos 1973, 1972.

Christian, Wollram A.
Person and God in a Spanish Village. New York: Seminar Press, 1972.

Codd, Nanneke
'Reputation and Social Structure in a Spanish Pyrenean Village, 'in *Gifts and Poison,* 182–211. Edited by F. G. Bailey. Oxford: Basil Blackwell, 1971.

Comin, Alfonso C.
Espana del Sur. Madrid: E. Technos, 2nd edition 1973, 1963.

Diaz del Moral, Juan
Historia de las agitaciones campesinas andaluzas: Cordobesas. Madrid: Alianza Editorial. First published 1929, 1969.

Elias, Norbert
Processes of State Formation and Nation Building. *Transactions of the 7th World Congress of Sociology.* Geneva: International sociological association, 1970.

Freeman, Susan Tax
Neighbors. Chicago: Aldine, 1970.

Lison-Tolosana, Carmelo
Belmonte de los caballeros. Oxford: Clarendon Press, 1966

Malefakis, Edward C.
Agrarian Reform and Peasant Revolution in Spain. Origins of the Civil War. New Haven and London: Yale University Press, 1970.

'Peasants, Politics and Civil War in Spain. 1931–1939,' in *Modern European Social History*, 192–227. Edited by R. Bezucha, Lexington, Mass.: B. C. Heath, 1972.

Martinez Alier, Juan
La estabilidad del latifundismo: analisis de la interpendencia entre relaciones de produccion y consciencia social en la agricultura latifundista de la campina de Cordoba. Paris: Ruedo Iberia, 1968.

Pitt-Rivers, Julian
The People of the Sierra. Chicago: University of Chicago Press, 1961.

Schneider, Peter, Jane Schneider and Edward Hansen
The Role of Regional Elites and Non-Corporate Groups in the European Mediterranean. *Comparative Studies in Society and History* 14:3:328-350, 1972.

Vincens Vives, Jaime (with collaboration of J. Nodal Oller)
Approaches to the History of Spain. Berkeley: University of California Press, 1972.

7

Provençal Wine Cooperatives

Soon Young Song Yoon
University of Michigan

ABSTRACT

In the transition from pre-capitalist to capitalist agriculture, French (Provençal) wine cooperatives transformed the economic and political ties between small communities and (supra) national processes. A traditional social and political 'replicate structure' persisted, not despite changes in modes of production, but because of them. Through cooperatives, the peasant communities survived. A successful transition to industrial capitalist agriculture had a 'conservative' as well as 'modernizing' effect. However, the traditional structure may end because of the limitations of small-scale farming in a capitalist market. This study of three southeastern French wine-growing communities examines factors which influenced the success and possible failure of peasants to adapt to industrial capitalism. It concludes that the infrastructure of the peasant economy and contradictions of wine cooperatives were as significant as the market, state policy, class structure, and peasant coalitions in explaining the political economy of the region.

Cooperation is ideally a concession to the General Will. The social contract is a gesture of peace in times of threatening disorder. Agricultural cooperatives in France were designed to solve the problems of agrarian unrest. They were to bring civil order into chaos. This new order was both an economic and political solution. Cooperatives transformed not only the economic but also political relationships between small communities and (supra) national processes. The history of Provençal wine cooperatives in three southeastern French villages is the particular case presented here. The history of cooperatives is a specific subject dealing with a general problem: the relationship between changes in modes of production and the socio-political structure. Orthodox materialist explanations (Harris 1968:240) state that the techno-economic structure determines the socio-polotical organization. However, the persistence of traditional structures such as the class opposition of peasants and gentlemen into modern industrial agriculture challenges simplistic explanations. In her study of Brittany, Berger noted that peasants kept a strong peasant identity into the era of industrial farming (Berger 1972:4). In Provençal wine-growing communities the traditional opposition of peasants and gentlemen persisted from pre-capitalist to industrial capitalist agriculture. This class structure presented itself in the land tenure as insistently. In one commune, the larger landowners of the upper classes still owned almost 50 percent of the land, similar to the land distribution pattern since about the seventeenth century.

R. Anderson and B. Anderson suggest an alternative theory, a structural-functionalist one, in which history 'as a repetitive process' can at least receive its due. They used the term 'replicate structure' to designate formally organized voluntary associations which proliferated in Wissous. The function of these associations was to 'adapt indigenous groupings to the increasingly exact requirements of participation in a modern state' (Anderson and Anderson 1965:227). Although the authors deal with a topic similar to the one at hand – voluntary associations and nation-building –

the problem remains unsolved. We understand little about the relationship between the process of creating a 'replicate structure' and the 'silent revolution', i.e. the transition to industrial capitalism. This study suggests that the traditional structures are related to changes in relationship to modes of production. If the result is a replicate structure (classes, or voluntary associations) then there must be a basis in the political economy of the region. If, on the other hand, the structure changes, collapses or disappears, reference to the economic and political history (in this case, cooperative history) will also be useful. In Provence, changes in modes of production accounted for both the survival of the traditional class structure and the impending end of peasants.

One must examine in detail a complex set of factors such as the peasant and elite production patterns, class structure, peasant coalition, markets and state policy as well as cooperatives. The cooperative is the focus of a study which considers all these factors as they affect the history of the communities. Studies of other European cooperatives may thus be compared (see Berger 1972, Hansen 1969, Mendras 1971, Dion-Salitot and Dion 1972), although this remains beyond the scope of this work.

SOME DEFINITIONS

Before fully investigating the details of the evolution of Provençal wine cooperatives one must examine their specific form. The definition of some terms will help characterize Provençal wine cooperatives in general terms, and will facilitate further discussion. The cooperatives in the three communes (Rognes, St. Cannat and Lambesc) were 'vertical,' 'central,' capitalist enterprises[1]. This requires some elaboration.

While 'horizontal organizations (such as agricultural collectives in North VietNam) pool all land, labor, machinery and capital, 'vertical' organizations compromise collective and private ownership. Producers give a portion but not all of their resources. At the base of 'vertical' organizations are many individual farms – much like the famous potatoes in a sack – based upon private ownership of land, private capital and, in the case of Provençal wine communities, Spanish migrant wage-labor. Cooperatives keep a distance from actual production, pooling a social capital only to allow collective processing and marketing. The organization is strictly speaking a 'single-purpose' one, although in its evolution many functions could be added. Provençal wine cooperatives, for example, often were supply stores, social centers and technical counseling bureaus. Their relationship to the market was consistent with the basis of production. Cooperative sales committees sold the wine in bulk to middlemen *(courtiers)*, who then resold the goods to commercial establishments *(négociants)*. The market organization was typical of what Wolf called 'sectional' markets, with the higgling and haggling of competitive bargaining between sellers and middlemen (Wolf 1966:40)[3]. One word of caution. Whether a cooperative is 'horizontal' or 'vertical' does not preclude a specific organization of redistribution. It does seem, however, that the market has a pursuasive effect on production. As Wolf stated it: ' . . . when the peasant arrangements for the exchange of commodities become part of a market *system*, the market affects not merely the peasant's produce, and the goods and services he can command with it, but his very factors of production as well. It may attach prices not merely to pots and plowshares and potatoes but also to land and labor . . .' (Wolf 1966:48). In capitalist economies, labor and its transformation into commodities are bought and sold on an open market. This alters production to comply with the organization of markets. Capitalism at large corrects 'vertical' organizations from any socialist inclinations.

'Vertical' cooperatives accentuate class distinctions mainly in the context of a capitalist market. To add one final condition, cooperatives can be 'central' to the local economy or 'complementary.' In some French rural communities of the Alpes Maritimes farms depend on a multicrop economy. Lavender, wheat, or nature (sold to tourists in units known in French as *1e week-end*) are as important as the wine which is processed in cooperatives. The wine cooperative is a regional organization servicing several communes and is not the core of the local economy. In contrast to this 'complementary' type of cooperative, Provençal wine cooperatives in this region studied were 'central.' So cast, these wine cooperatives represented a particular type of economic voluntary association. They originated as political-social movements which successfully brought together and sustained a diverse set of class and political interests through a transition from pre-capitalist to industrial capitalist agriculture. The contract signed and sealed under state approval, the agreement to cooperate was indeed a grave commitment. Cooperative members became obliged not only to one another but, as necessity willed it, to the second major partner, the state.

CLASSES AND THE COOPERATIVE MOVEMENT

Winegrowers were predominantly males of two classes: the peasantry (*paysan*) and the gentlemen (*gentilhomme*)[4]. Although in the remainder of this study we will stress means by which the two classes got together, it is useful to have a perspective on how restricted this interaction was. In Provence of 1970 the baron was still *le baron* and aristocratic title was no light matter. Class endogamy kept the upper classes an exclusive group. The kinship network extended into the wealthier capitalist industrial classes, elite professionals (such as military and lawyers), and the traditional landed elite. The peasantry was not a homogeneous group. Some peasants had much land (up to fifty hectares), while a small minority had none. To marry a poorer peasant was not recommended but neither was it scandalous. Peasant kin networks extended to the shopkeepers, urban working class, and even government bureaucrats, while maintaining local networks between rich and poor peasants. Such economic ties as there were between the two classes weakened when peasants became wealthier through viniculture in the early twentieth century. By the 1970s, the peasants all had tractors. Their labor was absorbed in their own ambitious entrepreneurial activities. The upper class estates, particularly after World War II, relied increasingly on foreign laborers such as Italians, Spaniards, or Algerians. Economic success had resulted in further separation between peasants and gentlemen. The two classes also identified with different territories within the commune. The village (*bourg*) was the bastion of peasant democracy, egalitarianism, and self-determination. The contryside (*campagne*), on the other hand, was dotted with satellite estates of the upper classes – satellites, that is, from major cities such as Marseille. Most, but not all, members of the cooperatives lived in the village. Some owners of country estates remained staunch agrarian individualists. If the estates were commercial enterprises the owners grew, vinified and marketed the wine themselves. The economic interests and organizations of the countryside thus predisposed it to more conservative politics than the village.
But village and countryside were of the same political community. When it came to politics the classes mingled. Political and economic innovators were generally from the upper classes. They extended their influence but not full control over voluntary associations as well as municipal politics. If one were to characterize the interaction of classes in local organizations, one would find that the organizations were mixed but that the local elite provided the leadership.
As early as the sixteenth century we find a local bourgeoisie as advocates of peasant rights against a feudal lord. At this time the upper classes were not members of the village municipality. Instead, they had a syndicate (*syndicat des forains*) whose representatives interacted with the village councils. After the 1789 Revolution it was characteristic of small rural communities to have a 'mixed list' of councilmen representing different community interests: the local commercial class, artisans, peasants and upper class. At election time politically diverse municipalities could result in two ways. If three different lists were presented the voters in smaller communes could select councilmen from any of the lists. The other possibility was the election of a single list which itself was 'mixed'. It was generally presented as a package deal to satisfy the largest number of voters.

This mixing of classes and political affiliations was not exclusive to municipal politics. As Agulhon demonstrates, it was typical of Provençal sociability to bring together diverse groups (Agulhon 1968:103). From the seventeenth century on, the voluntary associations maintained this principle of heterogeneity while undergoing some changes as to purpose and title. The pattern which emerges is one of a secularization of *confréries* or religious groups and the depoliticization of secret societies such as the *francs-maçons*. By the mid-nineteenth century the *confréries* were often dropping their religious titles, assuming new forms referred to as societies (*sociétés*) or mutualities (*mutualités*). (Less is known of the *francs-maçons*, except that one gentleman suspected the Rotary Club members of being new *francs-maçons*.) Originally intended to be charity organizations for the urban aged and poor, these mutual aid associations had spread between 1849 and 1921 from Marseille to Aix-en-Provence. By 1901 Lambesc had its own mutuality and just one year before Rognes also claimed a society of equal importance. The new forms of voluntary associations had moved from city to countryside. The leaders in both cases were upper class liberals.

Prior to the cooperatives there was a pattern in which mutual aid, alliances, and formal organizations regrouped both classes. The importance of this voluntary association pattern and its relationship to municipal politics rests on the following interpretation of voluntary associations. Besides being adaptive mechanisms for national integration, they were also part of the strategy of ambitious local politicians. This strategy operated on the use of voluntary associations as political arenas. By 'collecting' offices and prestigeous titles (the best of which, of course, was founder and president) in associations, a person gained access to an organized constituency and acquired political experience, prestige and influence. For example, in tracing the political biographies of the three mayors of the communes studied we found that one mayor had held over eight administrative posts. Another was eventually (not simultaneously) president of five out of the seven societies in the commune. A third person held over six different posts while he was mayor. Hence, no doubt, the origins of a French saying: 'If you call a man 'monsieur le president' you can't go wrong.'

It should come as no surprise, then, that the beginnings of wine cooperatives in this region of Provence appeared in the guise of municipal plans to save local economies. The mayors and councils who led the movements had political as well as economic motives. And the extension of municipal organization to the cooperatives affected the latter's ideology, stability, organizational principles and economic goals. Continuing the pattern of mixing classes in voluntary associations and in municipalities, the new collectivity ignored social and economic divisions within the communities. Poor and rich peasants, and gentlemen were bound together for love or for hate, under legal, long-term social contracts. Furthermore the contracts were binding. In cooperatives, as in muncipalities, major conflicts between parties were settled mainly by the courts or by lawyers. In other words, strong patron-client relationships, shifting personal allegiances and vengeance did not characterize municipal politics. Indeed, successful bureaucratization of muncipalities was the rule. In the 1970s mayors in all three communes stated that they were mainly 'administrators' when it came to local affairs. No doubt the penetration of state authority and law to local village political organizations was significant in stabilizing cooperatives as well. The historical account was as follows.

On March 5, 1922, the wine cooperative of Lambesc, Rognes, and St. Cannat was formed. The first president and founder of this regional wine cooperative was an owner of a canning factory, a merchant, and large landowner. He was also former mayor of Lambesc in 1912 and municipal councilman in 1919. His vice president was a landowner whose main income came likewise from a can-manufacturing company.

This regional cooperative lasted two years. The resurgence of territorial community lines and process of fission was encouraged as each commune made heavier commitments to viniculture and could envision financing its wine cooperative[5]. A 'complementary' wine cooperative had become 'central,' and in the process each commune built its own cooperative. In 1924, winegrowers from

Rognes gathered to form their own wine cooperative. The first president and founder was then mayor of Rognes, a lawyer from Marseilles and landowner in Rognes. His vice president was a grain merchant and landowner. Another vice president was of the upper class from Marseilles. A wealthy peasant was elected secretary. Just three years later the same pattern was repeated in St. Cannat.

The founders of the cooperatives, being heads of municipalities, were in excellent positions to act as agents of the state in the local communes. Their municipal activities had already given them the organizational knowledge and a legitimacy in the commune. The fact that they were heavily involved in the commercial capitalist enterprises in a rural setting was also significant. They represented the leadership which was to orient the peasant communities away from traditional economies to a capitalist-credit economy. To this brief summary of the origins of the wine cooperatives a few points can be added.

The wine cooperative in Rognes illustrates the political diversity of the organization. In 1970 the president was known to be a right-wing socialist. On his cooperative administrative council were two well-known communists, one royalist and other socialists. These political differences, like the economic distances, were subordinated to an identity with the cooperatives themselves. Time and again, cooperative administrators stressed the apolitical nature of cooperatives. However, political and class differences surfaced despite the attempts to declare cooperatives apolitical and egalitarian organizations.

Although cooperatives were able to regroup a heterogeneous community of winegrowers to solve many of the economic problems, the basic contradiction was contained as an inherent characteristic, if not the organizing principle, of the cooperatives. This contradiction took the form of conflicts and administrative upsets. These were manifestations of the contradiction of a cooperative collectivity whose purpose was the protection of capitalist interests. In all three cooperatives of Rognes, St. Cannat and Lambesc, the cooperative histories were full of accounts revealing internal difficulties. Looking at the records from the 1920s to 1970, we find there were six categories of issues around which individuals and groups confronted each other: 1) marketing of wine; 2) spending of funds; 3) legitimacy of officers; 4) local cooperatives versus the government; 5) discipline of cooperative members; and 6) 'other issues.' Not all cases of conflict involved single self-interest groups in opposition to others. Sometimes the opposed parties were the individual producers against the administration or even the administrative council against the president. To interpret all problems in cooperatives as class conflicts or expressions of political factions would be an oversimplification. However, in general, individuals regrouped mainly according to economic and social groups.

In 1970 the political aspects of cooperatives were clear. Municipality remained linked to wine cooperatives by interlocking office holding. All mayors or vice mayors in the three communes were also presidents or vice presidents of the local wine cooperatives. Finally, and most significantly, cooperatives helped to establish an organizational grid for coalitions. But the content of the ideology carried to the peasantry, mobilizing peasant unrest, was, by virtue of the conservatism of the upper class liberals, a diversion toward wine politics rather than radical political change. The cooperative leaders were unlikely to demand radical changes. They would make some surprising moves in the era of the common market, but not before making important concessions to state control.

PENETRATION OF THE STATE

In this region of Provence, even the Romans had attempted to control wine production. Perhaps that was the peculiarity of French viniculture. Wine had always attracted the attention of the state. However, modern state control over production had applied mainly to high quality wines under

Appellation d'Origine Controlée (AOC)or *Vin de Qualité Supérieur* (VDQS). Through wine cooperatives the state had reached the producers of ordinary table wine, *Vin de Consommation Courant*
(VCC).

Government regulations increased after Tardive's plan to impose steep progressive taxes on winegrowers in 1931. Tardive also advocated limiting the surface area under production and instigating
price control by withholding wine from the market. In order to carry out these plans the government often used the agricultural organizations as intermediaries. State messages filtered through
national level to regional, then local organizations. Some of the most important regulations over
viniculture in 1970 were control over the addition of sugar in vinification, limitation on the total
surface area planted in vineyards, and price controls.

Working through the agricultural hierarchy was an alternative to a direct intervention by state
bureaucrats in local affairs. Nevertheless, state administrators participated in yearly cooperative
meetings. At times they actually intervened to settle conflicts in the cooperatives. The most
dramatic case of government intervention was from the early history of St. Cannat's wine cooperative. Of all the cooperatives, that of St. Cannat had the most turbulent beginnings. At least, the
records of the annual meetings from which the following account was taken leads one to such a
conclusion.

December 7, 1931, 9 a.m. in the town hall, 148 members were present or represented. They awaited
the arrival of the general inspector of the Inspection Viticole (a government agency) who entered
with the director of the Crédit Agricole Bank. M. G– , a former president, protested discussion
of the accounts, saying that the first order of the day was to determine the powers of the president.
This was followed by a protest. In a single group, sixty-six members left together, and a total of
eighty-seven walked out. After the general inspector took the floor, some of the cooperative
members re-entered the room. In utter exasperation he announced: 'This is the last time the state
wants to be bothered with the Wine Cooperative of St. Cannat!' The members were advised to
adopt the measures proposed before by the president of the Crédit Agricole Bank.

M. F—, the president, took the floor and refused to take any responsibility for irregularities in the
financial accounts. Those who had left all re-entered the room. The general inspector and the
director of the Crédit Agricole Bank left. 'Naturally the session ended before any new resolutions
could be adopted.'

However, this was *not* the last time the state was to concern itself with the cooperative of St.
Cannat. At the very next meeting, still another state bureaucrat proposed a compromise administration with 133 of the former administrators, ⅓ of the present and ⅓ newly elected ones. The
adoption of this plan eventually resolved the conflict between factions in the cooperative.

The leverage in the hands of government bureaucrats was a familiar one – money. From their
origin, cooperatives relied on subsidies from the state. These subsidies had two forms: loans for
fifteen or thirty years through the Crédit Agricole Bank, or grants. In Rognes, in 1924, the cooperative received a 572,000 franc loan (figures in new francs) in order to build its cooperative. In
Lambesc, in 1923, the entire cost of the wine cellar was 780,000 francs: 65,000 francs were part of a
subsidy, 480,000 francs were in credit, and only 240,000 francs in collective capital. At other critical
times of capital shortage the government also provided subsidies. The main periods of need were
during the expansion of the winemaking and storage space. There were two building projects in
St. Cannat, three in Lambesc, and two in Rognes from 1923–1970.

While it is evident that state control over cooperatives had numerous dimensions – subsidies, laws,
local state representatives – in each instance the cooperatives likewise gained. Without subsidies
local cooperatives would have folded financially. Without firm state law, cooperatives could not
have taken conflict cases to court. Without coordination with state representatives, the first benefit,
subsidies, would never have been so freely available. But in evaluating the relationship between
cooperative and the state, one must avoid overestimating the power of the state. True to their

respective aims of development and political stability, the partners were mutually dependent on each other's support. At the same time economic crises brought on moments of confrontation and confusion. The state that had underwritten, financed and supported cooperatives was opposed in the era of the common market by a force of its own creation.

CRISIS

A series of economic crises began in the 1950s and 1960s culminating in the implementation of the common market in the 1970s. At each crisis some winegrowers left viniculture. In the communes of Rognes, St. Cannat and Lambesc wine cooperatives survived, but in surrounding communes many closed down. However, even in these three communes producers said that the common market was the last cue for the exit of peasantry. In Rognes, two or three sons over the age of twenty-five intended to become peasants. In Lambesc there were only five or six; in St. Cannat, only a handful. The reasons for the crisis could be seen from two points of view. Leaders of the wine coalition in the 1970s regarded the state as the instigator of an anti-wine campaign. National policies discriminated against all producers of ordinary table wines. According to M. de B—, president of the regional committee of the wine coalition, the winegrower was victim of three sources of competition: 1) internal competition from clandestine sales at low prices of industrial-type wines, 2) competition from the Third World countries and 3) competition created by fiscal, social and legal disparities within the common market.

The French market alone could absorb 70 million hectoliters per year, but the average of the production in France from 1960–70 had been only sixty-four million hectoliters. Yet within this period of time, importations from Algeria, and in the 1970s from Italy, had allied the Third World and Italy with commercial enterprises in France.

These imports from the Third World were not to enter below a price fixed by an agreement in Luxembourg. Algeria would abide by the principle of quantitative complementarity. That is, imports would be limited to the amount necessary to compensate for wine shortages in the common market countries. The Third World was also to be subject to the special price of nine francs per hectoliter rather than the domestic price of 7.10 francs.

M. de B— recognized that Algerian wines were imported because they had a particular function in making French industrial type wines. For example, in the Camargue wine merchants and winegrowers faced the problems of a wine which was often low in alcohol content (around eight per cent) When mixed with the high alcohol wine of Algeria (or some Italian wines) the product was a legitimate wine cocktail. Thus, no matter how much wine was withheld by government order, prices could not be maintained at satisfactory levels.

The irregularities and disparities in national policies were putting France into an inequitable race. Italy had just barely finished a wine cadastral census in 1970, something which in France began in the 1940s. For the last ten years, prices of the same quality wines in Italy had been considerably less than French wines. Taxes on French wines were also higher[6]. In Italy producers did not have to pay a planting tax (*droit de plantation*), nor was there a limitation on the cultivated area in vineyards. The Italians could add sugar in bad years. Their cooperatives received larger subsidies. The Mediterranean regions of both France and Italy were ecologically similar, but the regions were divided into two economic systems, each with different relationships to state control.

Another explanation is broader in scope but requires a closer examination of local production. Cooperatives and family monopolies withstood pressures of the market differently. And blaming the market or wine policies of the state left the question unanswered: Why, in similar economic environments, did some winegrowers prosper while others envisioned quitting viniculture? For writers such as Mendras (1967), Perceval (1969) and Mandel (1962) cooperatives for small producers would inevitably decline with the development of industrial capitalist agriculture. The large capitalist farmer will replace the small landowner who must leave the future of viniculture to those better able to compete. In 1971, 18 percent of the active population in France was agricultural[7]. The government aimed to reduce the figure of about 1,550,000 agriculturalist to about 500,000, or 8 percent of the total active population by 1985. Although measures were taken to encourage producers to retire early, thereby reducing their number, government policies needed little adjustment. The market economy and free competition, acting on the infrastructure of the local economy based on class differences, would help achieve the 1985 goal. The following comparison of family monopolies and typical peasant farms analyzes how differences in class and production patterns were as fundamental to the evolution of the peasantry as the market or state action.

Most wealthier gentlemen had created agricultural estates as commercial enterprises after World War II and even as late as the 1960s. This gave them some economic advantages. Cooperatives produced mainly ordinary table wine. The family monopolies produced both ordinary and higher quality wines[8]. They had planted vineyards to capture a broader market. Large estates did not lose money re-adapting production to produce quality wines. But when cooperatives began the category of quality wines, VDQS, did not exist. Its appearance as an official category coincided with the entry of gentlemen winegrowers into commercial viniculture in the 1940s. In this region of Provence the larger winegrowers formed their VDQS wine syndicate, Coteaux d'Aix-en-Provence, in the 1950s. This organization helped family monopolies commercialize their wines for both a domestic and an international market.

When family monopolies began they had a two-fold basis of revenue – commerce and land. Large landowners were only slightly affected by the rural depression of the late nineteenth century. In the mid-twentieth century, the transfer of commercial capital into agricultural made the country estates models of industrial agriculture. These became commercial enterprises when viniculture was lucrative, and not, as in the case of peasantry, in the midst of economic disaster. Initially, then, greater affluence and diversity in capital resources complemented secure profits. In industrial viniculture the availability of capital was the main agricultural requirement for competitive power because viniculture was capital-intensive[9].

All land in the commune was irregular in moisture, soil type and exposure to winds[10]. Large estates were no exception. However, the land on large estates was unified. That a typical wine estate would have up to twenty times more land than a peasant farm was less significant than that the parcels were located in the same area. Consequently, large estates had lower depreciation of machinery (tractors wear out faster when parcels are farther apart), systematic planting (one patch of land planted with one plant variety), and the eventual possibility of using an American grape-picking machine which could only run on large plots of land[11]. The unity of the land also permitted winegrowers to coordinate a large number of workers at harvest with few overseers. In other words, large estates were able to be ordered, large-scale enterprises.

They were also often family affairs. The division of labor within family coincided with the three phases of viniculture: production, processing and marketing. Naturally this depended on the number of sons in the family, but the family monopoly was flexible. Each son took a specialized role. One son may have been in charge of production, another in handling marketing, another a wine technician (oenologue). A fourth son may have been placed as a distributive agent in a Paris branch. Likewise a son took on multiple functions if there were fewer children.

In the three communes under study there were a total of eight private wineries. Close by in neighboring communes were two more, equally large and successful. In all but one case the sons were to be fully integrated into the family wine business. Also, in all cases the sons were undergoing or received university-level training in agriculture and commerce. The family monopolies thereby made sons highly trained managers and experimenters. These sons would help bring in fresh ideas and strengthen the family estate.

Another important feature of this familial organization was the assured outlet for wines. Family monopolies had their own market networks which bypassed the middleman more successfully than cooperatives. More important, the unity of marketing and production allowed greater flexibility in two directions. If it was a poor year and production was mainly in ordinary wine, the estate could buy better wines and mix it with their own. Conversely, if the market required higher quality wines production could alter its patterns.

To emphasize how important this flexibility could be, let us consider the case of Chateau I. Two years prior to the actual opening of the common market a son in charge of marketing made trips to Italy to study the market and establish market networks. He learned of the potential export value of high quality rosé. Italy, on the other hand, was going to flood the French market with cheaper red and white wines. Another son (in charge of production) and his father bought the necessary winemaking equipment. Production was reorganized to produce rosé. By 1970 Chateau I's production was almost 80 percent quality rosé.

Both large and small winegrowers had the same basic equipment: tractor, rake, bin, and chemical products attachment. With these tools one person could work as much as fifteen hectares of land with hired labor only at harvest. Most peasant farms were based on unpaid labor. A man's wife and smaller children usually worked in the fields for harvest. Sons, on the other hand, might help their fathers with the tasks of tilling or sulphuring. Sometimes sons would work on weekends, holding other jobs during the week. Besides the family, the peasant relied upon friends and other landowners. Mislabelled 'individualist,' the peasant relied more on cooperation in production than his more affluent neighbors with private wineries. In the local private café in Rognes (le Cercle) men discussed daily agricultural problems. 'Michel's tractor broke down and Maurice lent him spare parts.' 'Pierre needs more land but can't afford to buy any. Does anyone know Madame Fourier who owns the parcel next to his? He wants to sharecrop the land'.[12] These kinds of conversations were important to the peasant's work. Free advice, mutual aid and exchange labor helped most small winegrowers to meet the scarcity of labor and capital.

When the peasants entered cooperatives ordinary table wines were selling well. Hybrid plants, while high in yields, were forbidden in quality wines. Yet these dominated peasant vineyards. Haphazard planting and harvesting were likewise adaptive to ordinary table wine. A small parcel of land looked like the shelf in a general store with VDQS plants such as Carignon or Ugni Blanc planted next to hybrids. In time, a son inherited land from his father and with it the pattern of land use[13]. Small producers needed to conserve what they had inherited. Replanting entire fields to meet new market conditions was not possible for all peasants given the problems left by the old planting pattern.

If large wine estates were ordered, the small landowner's production appeared chaotic. Peasants' lands were scattered in the uneven landscape[14]. Each winegrower had a tractor which wore down just going from one parcel to another sometimes twenty minutes apart. At harvest they would have lost precious time and money if they went from one parcel to another to pick up a homogeneous load with one plant variety. Separating and selecting plant varieties was the main prerequisite for the making of quality wines. But cooperatives which tried to enforce rigid selection rules often had difficulties.

Furthermore, given the location of parcels and their size it was doubtful that small landowning winegrowers could use the new grape-picking machine. Labor costs were climbing. Rise in costs of harvesters were the major complaint of small and large producers alike concerning costs of production[15]. When the grape-picking machine was demonstrated on a local estate peasants compared it to the first wheat harvester. They marvelled at its speed and at its price (over 50,000 dollars). The capital resources of a small producer came almost entirely from his lands[16]. As one peasant pointed out, his capital *was* his land. The land's value came from all the labor, money and dedication his forefathers could give. Almost none of his starting capital was in the form of money. And as all winegrowers knew, unless the land was cultivated it lost its value. By law in the 1970s cultivated land could not be sold to tourists. Given, then, the poverty of his capital resources the small producer attempted to balance the capital of larger landowners by pooling resources. Cooperatives were to give him a more equal competitive stance.

Production problems aside, there were other difficulties posed by the social organization of cooperatives. Unfortunately cooperatives were ill-adapted to changes in the market. One cooperative president said 'It takes twice as long for a group to make decisions. Private wineries adapt more efficiently.' The conflicts discussed previously had important economic consequences. The rigidity of the organizations made it difficult for the cooperatives to change processing to make higher quality wines. Decisions to change were blocked. What was possible and profitable for the larger landowning cooperative members was not necessarily advantageous for the smaller landowner. Thus the collectivity could not resolve the basic causes of tensions. That would have been contrary to the very basis of its existence. Instead the cooperatives achieved an end of ironic consequences: the perpetuation of political and economic differences by denying their relevance, which accentuated and therefore never resolved the social and class tensions within the organizations.

In sum, the success of the larger landowners under the same conditions of the common market spoke for the bankruptcy of small-scale farming. However unsatisfactory the state policies were, the possible end of peasant family farms could not be due to a government policy totally unfavorable to wine. Family monopolies in 1970 opened more of their wooded lands for vineyards. They were also adapting their vineyards for the grape-picking machine. While cooperatives felt threatened by the common market, larger landowners increased production of Coteaux d'Aix-en-Provence wines. In 1956 Coteaux d'Aix-en-Provence produced only 15,000 hectoliters. By 1971 production reached 50,000 hectoliters.

Cooperatives may see their life cycles end in the years to come. The village of Grimaud (Var) provides an example of the possibilities in the future. In 1970 only one-third of the Grimaud cooperative members were local producers. The remaining members were Swiss, German, Parisian or other 'foreigners.' With a decline in production levels one would anticipate a decline in the social and political importance of cooperatives. In a touristic village other organizations such as the tourist agency (*syndicat d'initiative*) may become centers of political or economic aspirations. The village winegrowers often spoke of their future in terms of their past. Even though change seemed inevitable, they had a history of hard struggles to protect their vineyards. Let their sons take a new direction, but why should they relent?

COALITION

Upper class winegrowers and small producers responded differently to the market. Still they found common cause for discontent. All producers had a 12 percent rise in costs of production from 1968–70 and taxes increased. Meanwhile within one year the buying power of one hectoliter of wine decreased 15.2 percent. Lower prices of ordinary table wines made large estate owners uneasy for they, too, had some production in VCC wines.

As it appeared the coalition seemed to be a rebellion in the wellknown 'red' belt of the midi, extending from the department of the Bouches-du-Rhones westward to Languedoc. From 1960–70 there were numerous protests: 1962, 1964, and 1968. These increased considerably in 1970–71. Five different demonstrations were organized that year. Demonstrations were not infrequent in winegrowing regions of France. The particular formation of the wine coalition was, however, an outgrowth of wine cooperatives in this region of Provence.

The two main characteristics of the ideology were expressed by the president of the Lambesc wine cooperative in 1956 when he was also vice national secretary of FNSEA (Féderation Nationale des

Syndicats d'Exploitants Agricoles). In a speech he pointed out that the ideological basis of the wine bloc was non-violent and that it purposely mixed social and political groups:

1. As a reformist philosophy, a non-violent strategy:
... I can only congratulate myself and all those responsible at various levels for the magnificent way in which order was understood and maintained.
Despite numerous barricades there was no such incident in our region. Nevertheless everywhere the leaflets were distributed and the grievances established; the demonstrations that were planned were carried out and we even had the pleasant surprise of seeing at this occasion some local syndicates whose activity seemed a bit sluggish, revive.

2. As an organization based upon the solidarity of a 'mixed' group, the distinctions again subrordinated to the structure:
This is the compensation for the syndicate leaders, this solidarity of even those who do not always adhere to syndicalism, the calm as well, and the dignity. Finally there is the mixed brotherhood at the barracks of producers and small agriculturalists, of workers and bosses, of rent-paying farmers and landowners, of young and old. This is a fine lesson for those dissenters who stupidly denounce, in this case, a manoeuvre of the 'big landowners' against the 'little ones' and of north against the south.

Both parts of the ideology fit a single scheme. The non-violent confrontation could only work if the mixed group were solidary. The unity of the wine bloc depended upon control over ultra-radical or conservative groups influencing the group. The coalition had to be unified as a political organization if it were to be mixed.
The brotherhood of many types of agriculturalists was established at the level of local cooperatives. To this set of organizations were attached others, each of which emphasized the interests of parti-cular groups. That is, the coalition at a supralocal level mixed groups by joining together organiza-tions which were dominated by particular groups – the cooperatives for the peasants, the Coteaux d'Aix-en-Provence syndicate and consumer cooperatives for the gentlemen, and FNSEA for all producers (not just winegrowers). These four organizations provided the core of the wine coalition. The leader of the department level cooperative organization, M. C—, called upon his identity as a peasant, winegrower, and cooperative administrator. FNSEA was headed by M. R— in 1970.
Peasants and gentlemen identities tended to be balanced in this organization. As for the wine syn-dicate, Coteaux d'Aix-en-Provence, the main identification was with the upper class winegrowers. In Coteaux d'Aix-en-Provence all of the founders had been from the upper class except the 1970 president, who was a former wine middleman. The organization also had its own society called the Confrérie du Roi René. The highest officer was a royalist, the Marquis de S—.
Finally, the agricultural consumer's cooperative, the Syndicat des Alpes et Provence, drew together peasants, aristocrats, and capitalist farmers under the leadership of the gentlemen class. The organi-zation was founded by the Marquis de Villeneuve. In 1970 the president was also an aristocrat whose father had been president just ten years before.
The cohesion of the coalition depended to a great extent upon the agreement of its leaders to particular alignments. In fact, in 1970 a rivalry between two leaders had led to a split between the cooperatives and FNSEA. The alliances were based upon more than ties of friendship between its leaders. There were also important interlocking officeholdings. This kept leaders in constant com-munication with one another. Even more significant, administrators were called upon to support the actions of each other's organizations. Taking each organization's key leaders one finds that they held key positions in as many as eight different organizations. These ranged from local cooperatives to national cooperative organizations. The network linked together banks, olive oil cooperatives,

technological advisory boards with the two main wine organizations – the cooperatives and Coteaux d'Aix-en-Provence.

Other organizations joined this coalition. In Tarascon, in 1970, Nicoud's shopkeeper organization backed the winegrowers. All of the stores in the town were closed in support of the wine coalition. The mayors and municipalities also showed their support by joining the demonstrations. Along with shopkeepers, mayors and municipal councils, the regional *ad hoc* committee for action (*Comité d'Action*) responded to the state policies through strikes, demonstrations, and occasional violence.

The leadership had to control the potentially volatile assembly of protestors. The wine bloc had taken an apolitical stand, but the events had to be planned to prevent politicization. Lack of discipline on the part of the demonstrators might have resulted in factions, violence, or deviation from the plan. The leaders stated they must prevent politically radical inspiration from within. They were also fearful of external 'agitators' or student leftist-Maoists from changing the course of an ordered and disciplined demonstration.

The most effective means by which congregations of thousands were controlled was by organizing a crowd according to communal and regional contingents. For example, in 1970 the winegrowers of Rognes and St. Cannat rode together in buses to Tarascon. Then the groups reorganized for the demonstration, each commune following its mayor, the presidents and cooperative administrators. Representatives from the same commune moved as a group and stayed that way in the main meeting place. An outsider was thus immediately identifiable. If there was a disturbance in the crowd, the members of each group would carry the person away themselves to the police paddy wagons. The leaders of the protests consciously had used this strategy to prevent incidents.

In sum, like other voluntary associations of the era, cooperatives eventually bureaucratized themselves, providing new channels to the state for locally ambitious leaders. Those leaders of local cooperatives who were able to move into regional and nationally influential positions then reconstructed the cooperative principles of a 'mixed brotherhood', apolitical wine politics in the *ad hoc* coalition as it appeared in the 1960s and 1970s.

The government's official response in almost all cases of confrontation was disappointing to winegrowers. In 1970, thirteen to fourteen million hectoliters of wine entered from Algeria and Italy. After each demonstration the government promised to control imports. However, in 1969 as in 1962, the government reversed the decision and allowed new imports of wine. The consistency with which the government maintained its set policy made the future of the wine coalition uncertain. The situation in 1970 according to one leader was volatile. The winegrowers were tired of busing to Beziers, Tarascon, Aix-en-Provence, then to Marseilles; demonstrations had become tedious rituals. The wine movement in his opinion could move in two opposite directions. It could die of disillusionment, or it could get completely out of control – anarchize.

CONCLUSION

For a period of time, Provençal wine cooperatives saved local economies and the peasant way of life. The surprising result of this study was that the class and political structure did not change fundamentally while the economic organization was undergoing a 'silent revolution.' Indeed, the conclusion is more explicit. Changes in the modes of production did not determine a different socio-political structure; the traditional structure survived not despite changes in the modes of production, but because of them. Economic success paved the way for the community to remain basically conservative. However, the end of peasants was also determined by the limitations of small-scale farming in a capitalist economy. The end of the replicate class and political structures would be inevitable if cooperatives should fail. And while the techno-economic conditions may ultimately determine the socio-political structure, *how* the two factors interact is often left to speculation. The history of cooperatives reveals a complex process, not easily explained by either orthodox materialist or structural-functionalist theories.

The factors examined in this study were at times outside the study of the cooperatives themselves. These other factors were the peasant and elite economic organizations, the class and municipal structure, peasant coalition, markets and the state policy. Of these, two were more significant than may have been expected, particularly if analyzed from the point of view of coalition leaders. The state policy and market changes influenced the economic crisis of the 1970s. Nevertheless, there were problems within the peasant economic organization and production. Also, the problems in the sociology of running cooperatives helped to set limitations on small-scale farming. Given the difficulties in both peasant production and contradictions in 'central,' 'vertical' cooperatives, it is relevant to ask: How did cooperatives succeed? This is, perhaps, a more basic question than why they would fail.

To understand how cooperatives succeeded, it was imperative that one examine the relationship between small communities and (supra) national processes. Provençal wine cooperatives modified the relationship between village and state. Economically, cooperatives were the means by which the local economy became integrated into a national and even international market network. Cooperatives centralized processing and marketing phases of viniculture. They mediated between small communities and the state. Through cooperatives, the state thus gained more control over local production. Politically, cooperatives modified the organizational basis of peasant unrest – from village to regional coalition. Cooperatives 'bureaucratized' into national-level organizations. They lay the foundations for the wine coalition under the common market. But in the process of national integration local communities rendered more economic and political power to the state. They could not resist the national forces which penetrated the traditional way of life. Peasants in the 1970s believe that in the future only the wealthy capitalist farmers will continue agriculture in this region of Provence. The large landowner's wine syndicate, Coteaux-d'Aix-Provence, rises like a Scorpio to the east at a time when the constellation of cooperatives is waning.

NOTES

[1] I would like to acknowledge The Ford Foundation which allowed the fieldwork for this study from 1969–71. Additional data came from written records of three wine cooperatives in Rognes (pop. in 1968, 1200), St. Cannat (pop. 1700) and Lambesc (pop. 2800), local histories, census data and interviews.

[2] For a discussion of 'horizontal' versus 'vertical' see Kerblay 1971:150.

[3] In the traditional markets, sellers and buyers would meet at various cities in order to discuss the prices of wine. Today the calendar of meetings for areas corresponds to the old market schedules:

        Monday – Nimes (*Comité de Cotisation*)
        Tuesday – Montpellier
        Wednesday – none
        Thursday – Narbonne
        Friday – Beziers
        Saturday – Avignon and Brignoles

[4] The main criteria for identification of peasant and elite are 'emic,' that is, according to the people's own self-identification. 'Peasants' is a glossing of the term *paysan*, used to identify those of

peasant origin engaged in agriculture. Elites are most often referred to as 'gentlemen,' a glossing of *gentilhomme.*

[5] Some figures on production and membership may help:

no. members at foundation	hl. one year after foundation	no. members 1968	hl. in 1968
Rognes 113	13,900	301	51,856
Lambesc 211	5,480	323	41,312
St. Cannat about 133	4,720	313	27,343

Figures on surface area planted in vineyards: Rognes in 1970 had 1,186.72 hectares in vineyards, more than twice the amount in 1913. Lambesc in the same year had 918.97 hectares, or more than one and one half times that in 1911.

[6] According to the *Journée Vinicole* (August 4, 1971) 89.3 percent of the imports into France were from Italy, and although the per capita incomes of French were generally higher than in Italy (2480 dollars in 1969 in France versus 1520 dollars in Italy), France also had the 17.65 percent value added tax (TVA).

[7] Mandel provides comparative figures for an earlier period. He indicated that in 1950–51, Italy had about 49 percent of her active population in agriculture. Germany had about 22 percent while France was second only to Italy with 36 percent (Mandel 1962:182).

[8] For example, on a large estate, out of a total of 7,276 hectoliters produced in 1968, 4,026 hectoliters were in ordinary table wine (VCC).

[9] Viniculture was not only capital intensive, vineyards required from four to five years before producers could harvest full crops. Capital requirements are rough estimates, but the Maison d'Agriculture of the Bouches-du-Rhone suggested the following to plant one hectare of vineyards (in *gobelet* pruning style, plants spaced from 2120 to 1 meter): The first year would cost 11,200 new francs. By the fourth year this should drop to fifteen francs. The accumulated investment at the end of the third year would be 15,140 francs per hectare. In addition the planting tax (*droit de plantation*) was 1,300 francs per hectare.

[10] An example of ecological diversity is found in Rognes. Within one square mile altitudes ranged from 254 meters to 471 meters. There were six major soil regions, each with a different soil type such as volcanic soil, limestone, clay and sand.

[11] The grape-picking machine (working on a Ford 4000 diesel motor) would do the work of seventy-five to eighty persons in one day. It was also equipped with special wheels to work in the rain and with lights for night.

[12] Sharecropping (*métayage*) was mainly a verbal agreement between laborer and landowner. Conditions of the agreement were as varied as the social relationships they involved. Sons sharecropped for fathers or widowed mothers, younger producers for retired friends or kinsmen living in cities. The agreement usually meant 2/3 of the produce's value for the producer who provided the

tools and part of the capital, with 1/3 for the landowner. Sharecropping was mainly between peasants and was a major adaptive mechanism to increased land fragmentation.

[13] Both upper classes and peasants in this region of Provence practiced equal, partible, bilateral inheritance. Peasant women usually transferred all property rights upon marriage to their husbands. Upper class women retained rights over their inheritance by contractual agreement (*mariage à contrat*).

[14] According to de Réparaz (1961), the fragmentation index for peasant lands ranged from twenty to fifty-two (*no. of parcels x 10*) total number of hectares.

[15] In 1971 the minimum wage was four francs an hour. Migrant workers had rights to social security which had to be paid by the landowner.

[16] There were some worker-peasants, but the study is based on those winegrowers whose main income came from agriculture in 1970.

[17] FNSEA – Féderation National des Syndicates d'Exploitants Agricoles.
la Fare – commune not far from Rognes.
CDCV – Conféderation Départmental des Cooperatives Vinicoles.
ITV – Institut Technique du Vin.
Eguilles – commune near Aix-en-Provence.
FNCV – Féderation National des Cooperative Vinicoles.
Alpes et Provence – agricultural consumer cooperative.
Chambre d'Agriculture – elected governing body of local agriculturalists.
AGPO – General organization of food oil producers.
CETA – Centre d'Etude Technique Agricole.

REFERENCES

Agulhon, Maruice
Pénitents et Francs-Maçons de l'Ancienne Provence. Paris: Fayard, 1968.

Anderson, R. T., and B. G. Anderson
Bus Stop for Paris. Garden City: Anchor Books, 1965.

Berger, Suzanne
Peasants Against Politics. Cambridge: Harvard University Press, 1972.

Dion-Salitot, Michele, and Michel Diot
La Crise d'une Societé villageoise. Paris: Editions Anthropos, 1972.

Hansen, Edward C.
The State and Land Tenure Conflicts in Rural Catelonia. *Anthropological Quarterly* 42:214–243, 1969.

Harris, Marvin
The Rise of Anthropological Theory. New York: Thomas Y. Crowell, 1968.

Kerblay, Basile
'Chayanov and the Theory of Peasantry as a Specific Type of Economy in *Peasants and Peasant Societies: Selected Readings*. Edited by T. Shanin. Middlesex: Penguin Books, 1971.

Mandel, Ernst
Traité d'Economic Marxiste, Vol. II. Paris: Union Générale d'Editions, 1962.

Mendras, Henri
Les Collectivités Rurales Françaises. Paris: Librairie Armand Colin, 1971.

Perceval, Louis
Avec les Paysans Pour une Agriculture Non-Capitaliste. Paris: Editions Sociales, 1969.

de Réparaz, G. A.
'Les Structures Agraires de Touloubre et Traveresse.' Aix-en-Provence: unpublished thesis of the Faculté des Lettres d'Aix, 1961.

Wolf, Eric R.
Peasants. Englewood Cliffs: Prentice-Hall, 1966.

8

Swiss Society and Part-Society: Organizing Cultural Pluralism

Daniela Weinberg
University of Nebraska-Lincoln

ABSTRACT

The acephalous non hierarchic political organization of the Swiss nation-state provides a striking contrast to other European states and offers a different perspective on the nature of community-state integration. History, ecology, and political ideology are the underpinnings of cultural continuity in the Swiss canton of Valais, where a 'nested' structure appears as a more viable and adaptive alternative to the prevalent model of 'encapsulation.'

The quickening pace of change throws into relief mechanisms of functioning and change that are usually obliterated by their slowness and the way in which they overlap within the general transition.

(Mendras 1970:15)

The modern nation-state appears to most Europeanists as a hierarchy in which the upper levels, through their sheer political and economic weight, inevitably crush the lower levels. For their part, the lower levels respond with desperate attempts to keep a toehold on the ladder by mimicking their superiors in a kind of prisoner-warden relationship. Historical and contemporary data are used to support this model. Scholars refer to the feudal lord-peasant relationship of domination and subjection, and to the subsequent development of the highly centralized, industrial, bureaucratic modern state. Anthropological theorists apply the model to contemporary rural societies and explain them in terms of the peasant's reaction to 'the demands and sanctions of power-holders outside his social stratum' (Wolf 1966:11) with first claims on his production. Such theories generate definitions of peasantry which either refine that of Kroeber-peasantries as 'part-societies with part-cultures' (1948:284) – or suggest that rural peoples today are no longer peasants at all but, if anything, 'post-peasants' (Foster 1967:7).

We do not deny that the centralized nation-state is the most typical form of modern political organization and that its bureaucratic core does exert enormous pressure on its periphery – that is, on all but the topmost levels of the hierarchy. We suggest, however, that certain inevitable biases growing out of anthropological method have contributed heavily to this model. Although anthropologists are beginning to accept the notion of regional, and even national, studies as being essential to the understanding of rural peoples, we are still burdened with our own history of and special competence in working with the small, relatively isolated rural community. In addition, the present moral climate of *mea culpa* in American anthropology, although it refers primarily to studies of our own indigenous peoples, must inevitably creep into other studies and lead us to anticipate oppression before becoming guilty parties to it. We are, after all, products of our own culture. One anthropologist has suggested, for instance, that we may be committing the genetic fallacy in our analyses of European feudalism, extrapolating our own capitalistic culture backward in time (John W. Cole 1973, personal communication).

But a more compelling reason to reexamine the prevailing model of the modern nation-state is the existence of Switzerland, in the very center of Western Europe – a modern, industrial, capitalist, democratic state with a long history of cultural deviance within the European community. The Swiss version of federalism is the antithesis of the centralized, hierarchic model of the state. Although at first glance one sees a state comparable to other European states, one soon discovers anomaly and paradox. For example, the Canton of Valais has more banks per capita than any other Swiss canton. Knowing that the Valais is an agricultural mountain canton, we might interpret this fact to mean that the proverbial Swiss Bankers have found perfect victims and are exploiting this more conservative and less sophisticated segment of the population. On closer examination, however, we discover that this impressive number of banks includes a large number of locally controlled, cooperative savings and loan associations (the Raiffeisen banks) as well as small, privately owned banks existing in only one community and not associated with any of the large, nation-wide banking corporations. Other examples would similarly reveal the peculiar combination of egalitarian individualism, of communitarian capitalism, that are basic to Swiss culture.

These apparent paradoxes – the modern transformations of Alpine political and social ideologies which created a chain of autonomous 'republics' in the Middle Ages – are supported structurally by the modern federalist system and are being threatened increasingly as the Swiss state is drawn more and more into the international system. By studying Swiss political organization, then, we are studying an acephalous, non-hierarchic state with a high degree of cultural continuity which is now struggling to maintain its identity in a rapidly changing environment.

In this paper, I will suggest that Swiss federalist ideology – a political abstraction from enormous cultural, ecological, and historical diversity – is, more than an ideology, an organizational principle and a frame of reference in which political behavior is played out. This paper is only a first step in a process which may ultimately lead toward a better understanding of European political systems. Here I will only delineate the fundamental and critical features of Swiss political organization and contrast them with those of centralized states. I will also suggest a theoretical framework which takes into account both political ideology and cultural-ecological necessity. My basic premise in this paper is cultural stability, and, for heuristic purposes, the emphasis will lie on the 'mechanisms of functioning and change that are usually obliterated by their slowness.'

COMMUNE AND CONFEDERATION

In the three-tiered Swiss political system – confederation, canton, and commune – the commune has temporal primacy. The 1291 Pact of the Forest States, which created the nucleus of the modern Confederation, was an agreement among autonomous local communities to surrender some of their sovereignty for purposes of defense and survival. The Pact formed a loose, essentially military alliance among the member communities. It stated:

In view of the troubled times, the men of the Valley of Uri, the moot of the Valley of Schwyz and the community of the Lower Valley of Unterwalden have, for the better protection and seemly preservation of them and theirs, most faithfully vowed: to stand by one another with help, advice and all favour, with their lives and worldly goods, within and without the Valleys, with might and main against all and every man that dare do them all, or any one of them ill, either by force, annoyance or injury done or intended to their life and goods. (Kümmerly and Frey 1972)

As additional members joined the Confederation – eventually larger agglomerations called 'cantons' – a second and complementary objective was added to the original one of preserving the autonomy of member 'states': to guarantee the free movement and residence of their citizens throughout the Confederation. This new political status of '*confédéré*' (citizen of the Confederation), formalized in the 1848 Constitution, was inspired by the French Revolutionary ideals of equality and fraternity. The cultural heterogeneity of the Swiss state made such personal guarantees essential, far beyond the dictates of humanism. Ultimately, these constitutional guarantees provided the necessary scale for a modern economy. Both principles of Confederation – the autonomy of member 'states' and the rights of '*confédérés*' – are embodied in the modern bicameral legislature: the Conseil National represents the people directly, its deputies elected by a system of proportional representation; the Conseil des Etats gives equal representation to each sovereign 'state' within the Confederation, its members elected by a method agreed upon locally in each canton.

The modern commune jealously guards its position as the keystone of the political structure. Politically and economically, it remains to a large extent the primary unit in the system. It has, for example, first authority over citizenship: every Swiss citizen, whether native or naturalized, must be accepted as a member of this fundamental community. Once a member, he and his male descendants remain members essentially forever, regardless of their actual residence. The Valaisan Commune of Bagnes, thus, officially consists of 11,000 *bourgeois* (commune citizens) – only 4800 of whom presently live on commune territory.

The *bourgeois* of a commune form a corporate territorial unit with a unique history founded on tradition, custom, and genealogical continuity. The contemporary witness to this history is the 'patrimony' of the commune – the ownership and management of its inviolate territory. While only the *bourgeois* actually own and manage the territory, all legal residents in the commune have use rights – at the pleasure and under the control of the *bourgeois*. The commune has its own financial resources – collecting revenues from its property, taxing all residents for specific services provided, and levying taxes in the form of cash payments or labor corvées.

The commune legislates and executes its own affairs. Ultimate legislative power rests in the hands of the residents who, in the larger communes, are represented by an elected council – called, in the Valais, the *conseil general*. This legislative council must, for example, approve the budget and the accounts presented to it by the executive body – called the *conseil communal* in the Valais. In case of non-approval, the canton intervenes as arbiter. Similarly, while the commune employs its own police force and elects its own magistrates to deal with minor breaches of civil law, the canton is responsible for major civil and criminal litigation and also provides courts of appeal. The essence of these cantonal functions, however, is the preservation of communal autonomy (in the realm of finance) and the protection of individual civil liberties (in the realm of justice) according to guidelines set by the federal constitution. In short, then, the commune, as a political and economic corporation,

has the right to administer itself freely, within the limits set by the Constitution and the law, or, often, by local traditions and precedents of jurisprudence... The commune provides, on a small scale, approximately the same public services as the state. Ordinarily, it has police to assure its territorial security; frequently, too, it organizes religious practice and public instruction; it maintains or subsidizes museums, libraries, theaters; through its rural employees, it surveys the maintenance of its land; it maintains public buildings, roads, lighting, fire prevention; in most cantons, the commune assists the indigent and ill; one of its principal prerogatives is the right to manage its own patrimony (Sauser-Hall 1965:177-8)

Within each canton, there is enormous diversity in the number, size, composition, and organization, and organization of its communes. In addition to the political commune described above, there may be other crosscutting units: the *commune bourgeoise*, consisting only of actueal citizens; the *commune scolaire*, specifically charged with public instruction; the *commune ecclésiastique* – essentially, the parish; the *commune d'assistance*, consisting of those citizens who have the right to public assistance. The political communes may range in size from 80 people living in a single village to 4000 or more – as in the case of Bagnes – occupying several villages and hamlets.

The political and the *bourgeoise* communes may coincide in their membership or they may be widely separated. In the Valaisan commune of Zermatt, for instance, only 200 of the 700 resident households are *bourgeois* and, therefore, exclusive owners of the territory which has become so valuable with the development of tourism. The commune may be primarily agricultural, touristic, or industrial. It may be urban or rural, and – within the rural category – a mountain or a lowland commune. The mountain commune of Bagnes, for instance, is economically a mixture of agriculture, tourism, and tourism-related industry.

Politically, the commune may be, by tradition, conservative, radical, or mixed. Some communes – especially in the Lower Valais – are famous for their support of the anticlerical movement in the mid-nineteenth century and for their receptiveness to church reformation even earlier. Others are known for their maintenance of family politics and their resistance to allying themselves with cantonally organized political parties. Still others are noticed because of a sudden wholesale switch in support from one major party to the other. Some communes threw off the yoke of feudal allegiance before the fourteenth century, while others remained subjects until the French Revolution. In Bagnes – as in other mountain communes – feudalism was weakly expressed. For the past century, the commune of Bagnes has been politically conservative but is also known for its history of anticlericalism and radicalism – both of which survive on the political scene in the form of a minority party.

There are also wide differences among communes with respect to their relative participation in the capitalist-bureaucratic system of the state. Some communes of peasant farming where the land allows for a high degree of mechanization have been readily transformed into large-scale industrial farming areas. At the other extreme, some mountain communes of marginal agriculture and no possibilities for tourism have become bedroom suburbs for nearby industrial cities.

Swiss federalism originated in and rests upon the combination of commune autonomy and the wide range of diversity among communes. The political power of the commune – its capacity for action – is restrained only insofar as an action might endanger either the existence of the commune or the constitutional liberties of its citizens. Restraint is usually applied by the canton – one of the member 'states' in the Confederation with whom it shares sovereignty.

The political and ideological environment of the commune is well expressed in the following discussion by an eminent Swiss jurist on the difference he draws between a 'nation' and a 'state'. Whereas a 'nation' may be formed of a population homogeneos in 'race, language, religion, customs or political traditions,'

none of these elements is sufficient by itself to make a nation. What is necessary above all is that the participating peoples have the desire to be unified, that they have the same hopes, the same memories, that their history has actually created a common soul. The nation is not, therefore, necessarily identical with the State; there are States formed of several nations: the most striking example for a long time was Austria-Hungary which counted among its citizens Germans, Magyars, Italians, Roumanians, and Slavs of various races – Poles, Czechs, Serbs, etc.; they formed a State, they did not constitute a nation. But there are also States consisting only of people having the same national sentiment: these are France, Italy, Belgium – although inhabited by Walloons and Flemish – and also Switzerland which – by bringing together three peoples of different race, language, and religion, but inspired by the same political ideal, the same sentiments of independence, and the same traditional will to remain unified – has truly given the nation its highest meaning: a voluntary grouping of populations with common aspirations. (Sauser-Hall 1965:18-9)

The author points out that a 'state' – but not a 'nation' – may be divided and destroyed by a multiplicity of ethnic, linguistic, and religious groups within its boundaries. He suggests the following tests for true 'nationhood':

We must look into the history, seek out above all the wishes of the population, examine their sentiments for independence, uncover their desire to escape the oppressive power of a State. The belief of a people— even a composite people – in its political unity, and its desire to live as a collectivity, are the best foundations for a nation. (Sauser-Hall 1965:19-20)

Sauser-Hall's distinction between 'nation' and 'state' highlights the unique Swiss formula for political organization: the dialectic between 'independence' and 'collectivity.' Even his double reference to 'state' is peculiarly Swiss: the 'oppressive power' of the 'state' may emanate from without – from a foreign state – or from within – from one's own political bureaucracy. Nor is it surprising to learn that the Swiss were inspired by American constitutionalists in framing their own modern constitution of 1848. One recalls, for instance, Jefferson's admonition: 'The price of liberty is eternal vigilance.'

But, in spite of a discomforting twinge of romanticism in this Swiss view of the state, we are impressed by the confrontation of a fundamental problem: how to organize cultural pluralism, how to exploit it to create a unified 'nation', how to prevent its degeneration into the kind of weak segmented society described by Moore:

Indian society, as many scholars have remarked, resembles some huge yet very simple invertebrate organism . . . Through much of Indian history down to modern times, there was no central authority imposing its will on the whole subcontinent. Indian society reminds one of the starfish whom fishermen used to shred angrily into bits, after which each fragment would grow into a new starfish. But the analogy is inexact. Indian society was even simpler and yet more differentiated. Climate, agricultural practices, taxation systems, religious beliefs, and many other social and cultural features differed markedly from one part of the country to another. Caste, on the other hand, was common to them all and provided the framework around which all of life was everywhere organized. It made possible these differences and a society where a territorial segment could be cut off from the rest without damage, or at least without fatal damage, to itself or the rest of the society. Far more important . . . is the reverse of this feature. Any attempt at innovation, any local variation, simply became the basis of another caste. (Moore 1966:458)

The Swiss Confederation, on the other hand, might be described as a simple *vertebrate* organism. It was formed by a process of accretion over a period of 500 years. Each new member was permitted to retain its own political and cultural forms as long as it submitted to the basic principles of respecting and defending the autonomy of other members and of permitting within its borders the free passage and residence of '*confédérés*' – citizens of other cantons. The cantons, thus, are the vertebrae of the organism, and the federalist principles the connective tissue – both together providing internal and external structure and strength. The analogy is even more striking when we recall that vertebrate organisms are distinguished from lower forms by their relative decentralization of control.

Administrative modernization and consolidation grew gradually. The administrative state was codified in the Constitution of 1848, which also expanded the political ideology to prescribe specifically democratic forms of government for all the cantons. Beyond that prescription, cantonal autonomy continued to be respected and supported. In India, a rigid hierarchy of political and social inequality – the caste system – was the common unifying feature in the enormous regional diversity. The Swiss state, however, rests on an egalitarian political ideology, an efficient and unobtrusive federal administration, diffuseness of political control, and concentration of executive power at the lowest possible level.

The problem of organizing cultural pluralism at the federal level is solved by inverting the normal chain of command and maintaining control at the lowest level: the culturally homogeneous commune. At this level, both opposition and innovation are handled in essentially face-to-face relations among equals. Local autonomy makes possible regional and national diversity.

95

Even within the commune – especially a large commune like Bagnes – there is a sense of the inter-play between uniformity and diversity. Residents of Bruson – one of the ten villages in Bagnes – refer to their canton as '*l'Etat*' and their commune as '*notre république bagnarde.*' Within the commune, however, they perceive regional differences based on geography, economy, language, political party affiliation, and a generalized category of '*mentalité.*' The different 'regions' have different interests and problems. These are represented in the *conseil communal* – the executive body of commune government. Significantly, it is only at the commune level that initiative and referendum do not exist – on the assumption that this is the level of 'pure' democracy, of the direct expression and implementation of the people's wishes. At this level, consensus is the preferred method of decision-making, and proportional representation the instituted method of electing officials.

PART-SOCIETY AND STATE

In this acephalous state with a high degree of distinctiveness of parts based on local power and autonomy, how can we describe the set of relationships, the product of the connections among parts, that is the 'state'? Is the part-society concept, as expressed in the following statement, a useful heuristic device for understanding the Swiss system?

What goes on in Gopalpur, India, or Alcalá de la Sierra in Spain cannot be explained in terms of that village alone; the explanation must include consideration both of the outside forces impinging on these villages and of the reactions of villagers to these forces. (Wolf 1966:1)

In spite of the Swiss inversion of the control hierarchy and the emphasis on local autonomy, the resulting distinctiveness of parts – whether political communes or ecological regions or social sectors – does indeed present a picture of 'outside forces impinging on' the village.

To paraphrase Wolf, 'what goes on in Bruson – a village in the Commune of Bagnes – cannot be explained in terms of that village alone.' What goes on in Bruson is, for instance, a function of what goes on in Verbier, another village in the commune: the peculiar combination of events in that international tourist resort that are 'good for' Bruson – tourist revenues for the commune coffers, and the overflow of skiers who find their way to the smaller development in Bruson – and 'bad for' Bruson – the enormous land speculation by outsiders that makes Brusonins wary of their own developing resort, and the danger to small shops represented by the advent of a national chain-supermarket in Verbier.

The Verbier boom has also given a boost to local industries such as construction and hotels, and thus has provided increased employment opportunities within the commune. But in this context we must also know something of what goes on in Bern, the federal capital. In 1972, as a consequence of the international monetary crisis, the federal government put a temporary ban on sales of land or real estate to non-Swiss. Though clearly a 'good thing' for the nation as a whole, the ban is a 'bad thing' for the promoters, real estate agents, builders, and construction workers – both in Verbier and in the commune as a whole.

An additional source of revenue for the commune, shared by all the villages, is the hydroelectric plant at the end of the valley. Since the plant and its water sources are on commune territory, all its customers pay the commune. During the immediate postwar years, the construction of the dam provided employment for local men; now the dam has become a tourist attraction, revitalizing the economy of the Upper Valley of Bagnes.

What goes on in Bruson is also a function of what goes on in several neighboring communes where small factories have been established with the help of federal and cantonal subsidies – providing an economic alternative to full-time agriculture. The watch factory in Vollèges has been employing women of Bagnes for several years now, and the more recent electrical appliance factory in Sembrancher will undoubtedly attract both men and women from Bagnes – as a similar factory has done in the mountain commune of Hereménce. At the same time, however, Bruson is one of several sites where federal experimental agricultural stations have been created in the commune – for the express purpose of improving the technology of mountain agriculture and dairying.

What goes on in Bruson is also a function of what goes on in Sion, the cantonal capital. The canton controls prices – for both producer and consumer – of staples like bread and dairy products. It encourages the formation of agricultural cooperatives – offering subsidies and experts for technological improvement, and chartering these cooperatives to maintain quality control. In the 1930s, when the canton drained the marshland of the Rhône Valley to create enormously productive garden land, what happened in Sion was the geginning of a schism between mountain and lowland agriculturalists. But, for a long time before that, what had been going on in the Rhône Valley had had its effects on Bruson. In the nineteenth century, the Rhône Valley was a market for the surplus crops of Bruson: apples, cherries, and pears were sold to the preserve factory in Saxon; honey, cheese, and grain to the people of Fully and other communes.

The distinctiveness of parts in the Swiss system and their functional interdependence are implicit in all these economic relations. The Brusonin is consumer of manufactured products; rural producer supplying food to the urban sector and raw materials to agricultural processing industries; mountain agriculturalist in competition with lowland farmers for economic and political support; owner and manager of recreational property for city dwellers; part-time laborer or craftsman supplying goods and services to tourists. Or we may choose our 'parts' in other ways. The Brusonin belongs to the 'state religion' of his canton; he is in the linguistic majority in his bilingual canton but minority in the confederation; he is a *bourgeois* of his commune and so participates in the political, social, and economic benefits that derive from the commune's autonomy in the larger political structure.

These data do indeed reveal that Bruson is a part-society which can be understood only by considering the 'outside forces impinging on' the village – whether those forces emanate from other villages in the commune, from other communes, from the cantonal or the federal level. How, then, can we argue that the Swiss political system is qualitatively different from that of a centralized hierarchic state? The difference lies in the *response* to these outside forces – a response predicated on the universal Swiss fear of growing centralization. To the extent that the Swiss state is itself a 'part-society' in the larger international 'whole', some unilateral federal decisions do penetrate the ideological fabric – for example, the federal regulation of land sales in 1972. In other cases, however – especially in domestic affairs – federalist ideology prevents or moderates such unilateral action. The recent controversy over land-use planning is an instructive example of dialogue and negotiation between various levels in the political structure.

In 1969 the Swiss people overwhelmingly voted for a constitutional amendment for the protection of the natural environment. Since the laws necessary for implementation of this amendment would not be ready for a popular vote until 1974, the federal government proposed a provisional ordinance to set aside certain lands as 'green zones,' forbidden for construction. Under certain conditions, however, a canton could make exceptions in particular cases. The people accepted this ordinance in 1971, and the government then presented its provisional plan to the cantons for approval or amendment. At that time, the government of the Canton of Valais objected to the magnitude of green zones proposed by the Confederation and created its own special commission to study the matter locally and propose an alternative plan. The commission, acting in the name of the Cantonal executive branch, requested that each commune submit a zoning plan for its own territory. Since very few communes responded, the commission drew up a comprehensive plan for the canton as a whole and submitted the appropriate portions to eadsch commune for study.

Any individual landowner had the right to appeal the zoning proposed for his lands, and the official appeal form was published in the daily newspaper. Over 14,000 appeals were received by the Valaisan government and many tens of thousands by cantonal governments throughout the country. The extent of opposition at the level of the citizenry transformed individual objections into a potential mass political response.

Opposition at the commune level, too, was expressed in political terms. Valaisan communes received the canton's zoning plan as a political affront, an infringement on their autonomy. It became clear that many of the communes that had not responded to the Canton's original request had been acting in defiance. Those few that had responded now claimed that their zoning plans had not been considered by the special commission. At bottom, of course, was the sudden realization on the part of individual citizens that the costs of enacting the ideal of environmental protection were to be their own out-of-pocket costs. Long-term plans to build a house for one's married son on land acquired gradually over the years, and short-term plans to build tourist chalets for income – these could be wiped out by the stroke of a drafting pen on a map, a stroke probably made by some urban planner who understood nothing of rural society.

The matter was aired in the cantonal legislature – the Grand Conseil, whose members are elected as representatives from local districts. The legislators raised serious and indignant questions about the actual powers of the Canton government vis-à-vis both the Confederation and the communes – suggesting that the Canton had not provided aggressive leadership. They also demanded to know the names of the members of the special commission – suggesting that these people were not truly representative of local commune interests. Finally, a large majority of the legislators openly renounced their own party colleagues in the executive branch, the Conseil d'Etat, and passed a motion to revoke the plan of the special commission on zoning.

The case is still pending resolution, but even at this point we can see certain important principles at work: formal and informal defiance of higher authority, conciliatory action on the part of these authorities, the unity and solidarity of the canton in the face of encroaching centralization of power, and the intra-cantonal 'federalism' expressed by the communes. The defense of federalism was put in modern terms by the Socialist press of the Valais:

The worst enemies of federalism are those who, by their immobility and their 'cantonism,' provoke the intervention of Bern. If we are not willing to put our own house in order, then others will do it for us, and in a manner that does not suit us. (Rosset 1973)

Considering that the Socialists are the only major party favoring federal centralization, one is all the more struck by this defense of federalist principles. The argument against 'immobility' and 'cantonism' is a plea to set aside a reactionary provincialism in favor of a more dynamic and offensive stance: in short, equal participation in the game of decision-making.

Although more research and analysis are required, dealing with specific cases like this one and comparing them with similar cases in other European states, we feel that the data strongly suggest that the Swiss situation diverges significantly from the model of the European nation-state. Although there are indeed 'outside forces impinging' on successively lower levels in the political structure, Swiss federalism – both as a legal and an ideological system – excludes the status of *absolute* power-holder. As we ascend in the structure, we find fewer politicians and more administrators. The federal executive itself is a group of seven men drawn from various non-political professions who rotate annually to serve as President of the Confederation.

Far from being an undifferentiated, top-heavy bureaucracy, the Swiss state is a complex and multifaceted set of shifting relationships. 'What goes on in Bruson' is a function of all the relationships – the most important of which are the closest. The village operates in the political environment of a national ideology of federalism, the idea of a voluntary grouping of autonomous units living in a collectivity. The political underpinnings of this collectivity are the diffuseness of executive control and the concentration of each type of power at the lowest possible level of the hierarchy. Cultural pluralism is sustained by political pluralism. The organic integration of this acephalous state is based on a historical tradition of federal heterogeneity and local homogeneity.

We saw how the Swiss Confederation grew from a military alliance among distinctive and autonomous political entities. These entities were not 'power-holders' in any sense but rather agro-pastoral mountain communities unified internally by their economic activities and kinship ties. The Forest States which made the original covenant of confederation probably conceived of themselves primarily as economic corporations *(Allmeinden)* exploiting a certain territory and marketing their surpluses in a central market. Political awareness probably came later, and the members of the *Allmeinde* became citizens participating in the political *Landsgemeinde*.

The Valaisan version of this history, although not well documented, was probably very similar. One of the oldest surviving institutions specific to Valaisan society is the *consortage* – an economic cooperative whose members have use-rights in *bourgeois*-owned summer pasturelands. In the Commune of Bagnes, the *consortages* existed at least as early as 1625, at which time the political commune entered into formal written agreement with the economic cooperative of each village to create a more equitable distribution of use-rights (Courthion 1907:266). The system of irrigation canals *(bisses)* is at least two centuries older *(Berard 1963:25)*. Economic historians hypothesize that these local economic associations predated the commune as a political entity (Bergier 1968:37).

The early Confederation, then, was composed of autonomous, economically integrated communities allied to preserve their autonomy and their distinctiveness. Napoleon imposed a French-style bureaucratic structure on this loose alliance – creating a 'Helvetian Republic.' The administrative hierarchy survived his defeat but became a Swiss-style bureaucratic structure with its major function being the continued preservation of local autonomy. In other words, this administrative hierarchy is simply a superimposed organization of underlying diversity.

The modern French hierarchy, on the other hand, was created from the top down, and power remains concentrated in the upper nodes. (See Figure 1.) The French 'tree' is easily collapsible into

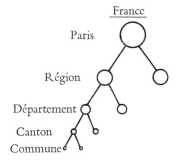

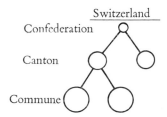

Figure 1

99

a simple two-level hierarchy with a wide branching ratio. That is, from the peasant's viewpoint, the set of relationships that constitute the 'state' reduce to a simple – and frustrating – relationship between 'we' (the peasantry) and 'they' (the state). (See Figure 2.)

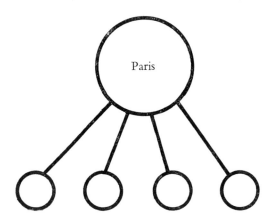

Peasantry   Figure 2

The Swiss system cannot be so reduced. I am reminded of a Swiss caricature of the French-style hierarchy that was presented to me in the form of a signature. A Bruson woman wrote out for me a recipe of a local food specialty, signed her name, and gave her address:

Ida B.	Bruson
Bagnes	Valais
	Suisse
	Europe

ENCAPSULATION VS. NESTING

The highly centralized and intermediated hierarchy that is the modern French state is a classic example of what Bailey has called 'encapsulation' (1969:146ff). Encapsulation is a political phenomenon which penetrates the economic and social life of the community. In Wissous, for example, (R. T. and G. Anderson 1962) the larger political structure was imitated in the bureaucratization of voluntary associations. What happens in Wissous cannot be understood without knowing what is happening in Paris. In Wissous the 'peasant dilemma' (Wolf 1966:12ff) has been resolved in favor of the non-peasant sector of the social order. Where there is no longer a peasantry, there can hardly be a peasant dilemma.

The Wissous 'solution' is characteristically French. In fact, any form of encapsulation – incorporation into the larger state structure – would be predictable in France. The Provençal village of Colpied, for instance, has been encapsulated through mono-culturization of its agriculture and the transfer of control to higher levels in the hierarchy (Reiter 1972). The Alpine village of St. Véran[2] has been encapsulated through transformation into a community of 'parkkeeper peasants' (Franklin 1969:220ff).

In all these cases of encapsulation, one common feature emerges: the simplification of the traditional community structure – economic, social, and political – so it may slide easily into a slot in the national hierarchy. The community's loss is the state's gain. The community contributes to the welfare of the state by reducing its internal variation to an absolute minimum. The process, of course, also reduces the adaptability of the community and renders it a dependent cog in the state machinery: the intermediated hierarchy collapses into a simple two-level hierarchy. The peasant dilemma of choosing between unsatisfactory alternatives is now reduced to one of maintaining a position at the lower level, of keeping up with the 'demands and sanctions' set by the higher level. There are no longer countervailing and sometimes contradictory internal requirements. Wissous is, simply, a Parisian suburb, Colpied a lavendar-growing village, St.-Véran a ski resort.

In the Swiss state, however – with its inverted political hierarchy – local diversity is not only preserved but also encouraged. The case of the commune of Hérémence[3] is instructive. Although traditionally an agro-pastoral commune, the terrain and steep slope of commune land made agriculture less profitable and less appealing as industry appeared in the Rhône Valley below. The danger of a wholesale 'rural exodus' was forestalled in the 1950s with the canton- and con-federation-subsidized construction of an important hydroelectric project on commune territory. For a decade, the dam construction employed a large proportion of the active male population of the commune, leaving the wives and daughters to maintain the farms. Having now removed men from agriculture, the commune faced the problem of losing them entirely upon completion of the dam. At this point, the canton assisted the commune in attracting an electrical appliance firm to establish a small assembly plant on commune territory – explicitly destined to offer employ-ment to local men after completion of the dam. Thus, rather than removing control from the local level, the state – canton and confederation – has helped to introduce new resources into the com-munal economic structure.

The concept of utilizing all possible local resources – even adding to the stock as necessary – is an economic expression of the political philosophy of communal autonomy and diversity. While the commune is a homogeneous cultural unit, it is integrated organically with other such units and can be differentiated from them along a number of dimensions common to all: historical, geographic and ecological, demographic, political, linguistic, religious, and occupational.

In the commune of Bagnes, this combination of cultural homogeneity and multidimensional differentiation is replicated at several levels. The commune maps cognitively into five regions – differentiated by their diversity of interests which arise from ecological, demographic, and occu-pational differences. The individual villages are further differentiated – along the same dimensions as the regions, as well as according to political and linguistic differences. Differentiation of a still finer grain takes place within the context of the village, with its various voluntary associations, and culminates in an ideology of individual uniqueness.

At each level of differentiation within the commune of Bagnes, there is also a replication of the philosophy behind the inverted state hierarchy: an analytic, problem-solving approach which identifies available resources and leaves their management in the hands of that particular level. Proceeds from the water rights in the dam – a commune-wide resource – are managed by the commune; proceeds from *bourgeoisie*-owned high pasturelands are managed by the village corpo-rations which have local usufructory rights; proceeds from the village dairy are managed by village members of the cooperative; the proceeds of an inheritance are managed by the heir and his or her household; and, ultimately, the benefits of having a particular reputation or expressive nickname are enjoyed and manipulated by the individual.

If encapsulation means thorough incorporation into a larger system, it also implies an ensuing loss of identity of the smaller subsystem. This is not the case in Switzerland. As we move *up* the hier-archy of administration, the 'whole' becomes more and more elusive and ephemeral. As we move *down*, however, the 'parts' become more distinct and vital. Rather than encapsulation, what we see is a kind of nesting of subsystems. The image we have in mind is a set of Russian Easter eggs –

painted wooden eggs of graduated size, each one nestled within another and simultaneously containing the next smaller. If the set is taken apart, each egg is complete unto itself – a separate integral unit. Put back together, the smallest eggs are most protected and the largest most vulnerable, most in direct contact with the environment. But removal of the largest egg – far from destroying the system – simply reveals the next layer. This system – although an intermediated hierarchy – does not depend for its survival on the largest egg but rather on the successive appearance of each egg. A larger egg does not encapsulate but is simply fitted around the next smaller.

This metaphor aptly describes the Swiss Confederation. There are at least three levels of nesting – the federal, the cantonal, and the communal. Beyond that, in certain cases, there may be even more levels. In a multivillage commune like Bagnes, the commune encases regions which contain villages. The village itself is a nesting of neighborhoods, households, and individuals. Further diversity is achieved within the village through the existence of kinship and voluntary associations which mediate between individual or household and the world outside the village.

The Russian Easter egg aggregate – although it does not reveal the great diversity among subsystems of the Swiss state – does express the common political philosophy which unifies the state: the highest possible degree of integrity and autonomy at each level. The historical primacy of the Swiss commune is also well modelled in the nested eggs, which are crafted from the inside out.

But the most important and interesting attribute of a nested state is the protective buffering it provides at each level of the system. Encapsulation negates identity; nesting promotes it. Encapsulation implies digestion; nesting precludes it. Encapsulation imposes monoculturization on the local community – suburbanization, tourism, or monocropping; nesting encourages the internal variety required for maintaining local autonomy. Recalling the uneasy feudal balance between lord and peasant, we may say that a nested system minimizes subjection and maximizes protection. In a nested system, therefore, we would expect to see the highest degree of cultural persistence at the lowest levels. Each level exists in its own micro-environment. Given some minimum population size and resource base, the local community should be able to deal with its micro-environment simply through regulation rather than through adaptation. The highest level in the system, however – the federal level – has, in a sense, *more* environment to deal with and so may be required to make certain adaptations in order to persist. The federal policy of neutrality is one such adaptation. It is a particularly clear example of Romer's Rule, since it effectively denies the existence of an environment.

The structural principle of nesting is not itself sufficiently explanatory. We must also take into account ecological factors. Although the smallest 'egg' in a nested set should be the most stable, it may lose some of its structural advantage for survival by being *too* small. We know, from evolutionary theory, that survival depends not only on stability but also on some minimum level of variety – a set of alternative responses to meet changes in the environment. We must, therefore, narrow our initial prediction that cultural persistence is best assured at the lowest levels of the nested system by adding the proviso that there is an ecological threshold below which the lowest level effectively drops out of the nest and can no longer benefit from the structural protection, offered by the system. Thus, a single-village commune with a small population and a limited resource base is at the greatest disadvantage. It lacks the requisite variety to servive in its micro-environment. Such a commune will tend to be drawn into the environment of the next higher level – perhaps the nearest city, or through geographic accident, the canton itself. The dangers of encapsulation and loss of identity are great, but only such a distinct adaptation will preserve the commune in any form.

The Valaisan commune of Vernamiège is an example of this disadvantaged situation (Berthoud 1967). The commune consists of a single village of about 250 inhabitants. It is located high up on a steep wall of the valley – too steep either for agriculture or for ski development. The commune has no other economic resources such as hydroelectric power. Its single major resource in human labor which it is exporting to the nearby cantonal capital of Sion. The commune has become a bedroom suburb, but even that seems to be only a stopgap adaptation, because the commune continues to depopulate rapidly (Berthoud 1967:70ff).

The commune of Trient[1], on the other hand, has long been a small summer resort area – a stop on the mountaineering route to Mt. Blanc, just over the border in France. Today, it also participates in the exploitation of local water power with the construction of the Emosson dam. The population of Trient has decreased from 130 to 90 over the past 50 years. About one-third of the present population is supported by dam-related employment, and a few of these families have actually moved into the commune from elsewhere. In addition, there has been some population exchange with the nearby city of Martigny – tending to make Trient a bedroom suburb.

Regulation of this type – hydroelectric construction, suburbanization – is too wide-ranging to be stable. When the micro-environment of such a small commune extends from the French tourist resort of Chamonix to the Valaisan market town of Martigny, adaptation will ultimately be forced on the commune, and it will be drawn into a larger orbit.

These examples reveal another aspect of Swiss nesting. Because of the federalist principle of an inverted chain of command which respects local autonomy, a non-viable unit at the lowest level will indeed become 'encapsulated' – not into the state but only into the next higher level in the nest. But size-dependence – whether demographic or ecological – may ultimately be superceded by the centralizing pressures which inevitably creep into any modern nation-state. As these pressures move down the chain of command – the nation-state's response to its international environment – they may destroy the concept of minimum viability at the lowest level. In effect, there may *always* be, by definition, a non-viable lowest level in the system, for centralization advocates 'efficiency' through the elimination of duplication. A centralized 'tree', as we saw in the French case, tends to reduce levels of intermediation, and ultimately collapses into a two-level hierarchy with a wide branching ratio – thereby focussing maximum control at the topmost level.

The contemporary Swiss response to centralizing pressures is, in effect, a move toward disintermediation which originates at the *bottom* levels of the structure. One of the forms this response takes is the creation of small, localized agglomerates – regional 'federations' of communes with similar interests which combine forces to meet outside threats to their existence, in much the same way as their ancestors did in 1291. No longer able to rely entirely on the protection offered by the vertical system of nesting, they are trying to broaden their resource base horizontally. These regional alliances are of a specific and limited nature, entailing a partial and voluntary yielding of commune autonomy: for example, associations for water purification, waste disposal, touristic development, and hydroelectric power. They present a challenge to centralization in the idiom of federalist philosophy: 'keeping one's own house in order,' in the words of the Socialist journalist.

ADAPTIVE DIVERSIFICATION: AN EXAMPLE

In the commune of Bagnes, environmental regulation has been greatly facilitated by the large population (about 4800) distributed among ten major villages, and the varied resource base. Although Switzerland did not participate in the two World Wars, their influence was nevertheless felt – in the form of partial mobilization for defense and, especially, the cutting off of food imports from other European countries. During World War I, the peasants, as one informant put it, 'tightened their belts.' By the time World War II began, strawberries had been introduced, the high summer pastures had been consolidated and improved, and a modern cooperative dairy had replaced several earlier ones in Bruson. The peasants, many of them now peasant-workers, met the national emergency by returning the strawberry fields to grain.

Shortly after World War II, the narrow-gauge railroad line was extended from the nearby city of Martigny to reach Le Châble – the commune seat and entrance to the valley. The railroad facilitated the rapid touristic development of Verbier as a ski resort, bringing revenue and employment to the commune as a whole. At the same time, dam construction began at the head of the valley– further increasing income and work. With expanded employment opportunities, young people prepared for non-agricultural careers and older people welcomed the opportunity for income to supplement their earnings from agriculture.

With this expansion of economic alternatives, a certain degree of regional and village specialization began to appear. Participating in a larger system, a particular village could afford to concentrate on its most productive resources. Le Chable – always somewhat specialized as the seat of commune government and the parish and market center – became, in addition, a gateway for tourism. Verbier and the neighboring villages on the north slope became the primary tourist center. Mauvoisin, at the end of the valley and always a modest summer resort, now capitalized on the tourist attraction of the dam, as well as those attractions based on its altitude, mountaineering tradition, and rare fauna and flora. Bruson and Lourtier, because of favorable topography, remained largely agricultural villages. Lourtier also became a center for small game hunting and the gateway to Mauvoisin and the 'High Valley of Bagnes,' while Bruson, too, became something of a tourist area through the winter exploitation of its fields and pastures. People from villages without solid resource potential found places in other commune activities – in construction, sawmilling, furniture making, hotels and cafés, and other tourism-related enterprises; in the commune administration, which grew increasingly complex with economic development; or even in teaching jobs in the commune schools, which maintained their enrollments because of the braking of the 'rural exodus.' Village specialization has been made possible and profitable because of the integration of villages within a larger cultural and political unit – the commune. At the same time, however, specialization has not produced occupational uniformity at the village level. Quite the contrary, specialization has enabled the continuation of the traditionally mixed economy necessitated by the micro-variability and marginality of Alpine ecology, and elevated from a principle of behavior to an article of faith.

The traditional mixed economy of Bruson always included agricultural and non-agricultural activities. In the past, the Brusonin was a part-time artisan, in addition to managing his agro-pastoral enterprise. To supplement his agricultural income, he might leave the commune – even the country itself – to work 'seasons' as a farm laborer or cowherd in the Savoie, or to find employment in hotels in Marseilles and on the Côte d'Azur. The agricultural activities of the contemporary Brusonin have been expanded through improved dairy technology and the addition of market crops, but he still operates a 'family farm' and subscribes to a 'family labor commitment' (Franklin 1969:15ff). To this extent, he is still a 'peasant' – someone who works the land.' He also retains the traditional 'peasant' characteristic of 'someone who does a little of everything'[5] – both agricultural and non-agricultural. Even those Brusonins who work fulltime at a skilled trade do so by choice, on an hourly-wage basis, and maintain their agricultural holding through a family labor force of wife and children supplemented by their own part-time efforts.

The *principle* of doing 'a little of everything' has remained operative, even though there has been some substitution of *content*. Thus, the Brusonin who used to work 'seasons' outside the commune may now be employed as the cheese maker in the village dairy. The Brusonin who in the past might have earned extra income as the village shoemaker, is now employed on an hourly-wage basis as a carpenter in a valley firm.

According to Franklin's typology of peasantry (1969:220), the contemporary Brusonin is neither a 'part-time farmer,' who retains his managerial functions, nor a 'worker-peasant,' who has given them up through participation in industry.

This distinction is not valid in Bruson, since every Brusonin with minimal resources of land and labor, whether or not he is employed outside or runs an additional business, completely retains both his commitments to and his managerial functions in his agricultural enterprise. In addition, most Brusonins who are employed outside their agricultural enterprises retain a high degree of control of their labor by working seasonally, for hourly wages, and by taking the time off necessary to maintain their farm holdings.

Indeed, some of their employment opportunities are especially and deliberately suited to maintaining this control. The nearby watch factory and electrical assembly plant, for example, although 'industrial' operations, are labor-intensive rather than capital-intensive. Since production does not depend on heavy machinery or special power supplies, work can proceed on a part-time, individually regulated basis and can even be done at home. Thus, the Brusonin is both 'worker-peasant' and 'part-time farmer.' His trade is simply another personal resource – along with a hayfield, a cow, a strawberry patch, a jeep, a vineyard, a healthy wife, a willing son-in-law, a widowed mother. For the Brusonin, the essential quality of 'peasantness' – the freedom to manipulate a diversity of resources – has been preserved as a fundamental principle of behavior and tenet of belief. This behavior and belief are enhanced by the special nature of the state in which he participates – the inverted nested hierarchy of autonomous societies in voluntary association with each other. It is paradoxical that, as Bruson has moved into the twentieth century and greatly expanded both its resource base and its autonomy – its 'peasantness' – it is ceasing to be a 'peasant' village. The economy is still largely a 'peasant economy,' based on familistic rather than capitalistic enterprise. But, although the Brusonin is more than ever in 'effective control [of his] land' (Redfield 1956:18) and other resources, he is less than ever 'subject to the demands and sanctions of power-holders outside his social stratum' (Wolf 1966:11). Although more than ever involved in the outside market through agriculture and through tourism, he is protected from over-dependence on the market by the nested political structure which allows him, more than ever, to broaden his local resource base.

It is remarkable that both kinds of political structure – the encapsulating bureaucratic 'tree' and the inverted nesting – ultimately transform the peasantry. While an encapsulated peasantry rapidly becomes a non-peasantry, the transformation of a nested peasantry is conservative, gradual, and subtle. In the Swiss case, because of the inverted chain of control this transformation also tends to be self-regulatory and more responsive to changes in the environment. Viewing such a system, one is more impressed with the force of cultural stability than with manifestations of culture change.

Future research should take the obvious – and difficult – direction of studying the nature of persistence in such societies. Traditionally, anthropology has studied the extraordinary to illuminate the ordinary. In modern European society, cultural continuity and stability are exotic and rare. In this paper, I have outlined the unique political system of Switzerland and suggested structural and evolutionary explanations for its persistence. The theoretical scheme proposed must be elaborated and tested in a comparative context, for the ultimate objective of this study is to develop generalized tools for the understanding of any modern European nation-state.

NOTES

[1] This paper is based on chapters from the writer's forthcoming book on the cultural adaptation of a Swiss Alpine village, Bruson (Weinberg 1975).

[2] I am indebted to Robert K. Burns, Jr. for recent information on St. Véran. The traditional village is described in Burns 1959.

[3] These data were generously provided by my students Ziporah Elstein and Douglas Barden.

[4] These data were generously provided by my student Roberta Zucker.

[5] These definitions of 'peasant' were elicited from mountain agriculturalists in Bruson ('someone who works the land') and Hérémence ('someone who does a little of everything').

REFERENCES

Anderson, Robert T. and Gallatin Anderson
The Replicate Social Structure. *Southwestern Journal of Anthropology* 18:365-370, 1962.

Bailey, F. G.
Stratagems and Spoils: A Social Anthropology of Politics. New York: Schocken Books, 1969.

Bérard, Clément
Bataille pour l'eau. Martigny: Pillet, 1963.

Bergier, Jean-Francois
Problèmes de l'histoire économique de la Suisse. Berne: Editions Francke, 1968.

Berthoud, Gérald
Changements Economiques et Sociaux de la Montagne. Vernamiège en Valais. Berne: Editions Francke, 1967.

Burns, Robert
Saint Véran, France's Highest Village. *National Geographic* 115:4:570-588, 1959.

Courthion, Louis
Bagnes-Entremont-Ferrex. Genève: A. Jullien, 1907.

Foster, George M.
'Introduction: What is a Peasant?' in *Peasant Society: A Reader*, 2-14. Edited by J. M. Potter, M. N. Diaz, and G. M. Foster. Boston: Little, Brown, 1967.

Franklin, S. H.
The European Peasantry. The Final Phase. London: Methuen, 1969.

Kroeber, A. L.
Anthropology. New York: Harcourt, Brace and World, 1948.

Kümmerly and Frey
Switzerland: Edition 1972. Translated by John McHale. Berne: Kümmerly and Frey, Geographical Publishers, 1972.

Mendras, Henri
The Vanishing Peasant: Innovation and Change in French Agriculture. Translated by Jean Lerner. Cambridge: MIT Press, 1970.

Moore, Barrington, Jr.
Social Origins of Dictatorship and Democracy. Lord and Peasant in the Making of the Modern World.
Boston: Beacon Press, 1966.

Redfield, Robert
Peasant Society and Culture. Chicago: University of Chacigo Press, 1956.

Reiter, Rayna R.
Modernization in the South of France: The Village and Beyond. *Anthropological Quarterly* 45:1:35-53, 1972.

Rosset, Lucien
Zones vertes: les députés voient rouge. *Le Peuple Valaisan*, July 6, 1973.

Sauser-Hall, Georges
Guide Politique Suisse. Lausanne: Payot, 1965.

Weinberg, Daniela
Peasant Wisdom: Cultural Apaptation in a Swiss Village.
Berkeley: University of California Press, 1975.

Wolf, Eric R.
Peasants. Englewood Cliffs, New Jersey: Prentice-Hall, 1966.

9

The Decline of Small-Scale Farming in a Dutch Village

Jojada Verrips
University of Amsterdam

ABSTRACT

This paper deals with the effects on a small-scale Dutch dairy farming community of three plans drawn up and implemented by the national government. The most important effects are the decline of small-scale farming and an increasing defunctionalization of the countryside. It is argued that one has to consider the plans not only as an answer of the central authorities to problems at the local level generated by large-scale international economic developments, but also as reflections at precisely that level of such processes as industrialization and increasing centralization pervading Dutch society at large.

The major problem of every farmer is no longer to preserve his property or the right to farm a particular plot, but rather to know whether his enterprise is condemned to disappear with him or will survive (Mendras 1970:225).

I INTRODUCTION

Anthropologists are human beings and as such they cannot have an omniscient view of society as a totality. They can be compared with an individual using a magnifying glass to decipher a certain passage from a badly written manuscript. As he concentrates on one passage, others lying at the edges of the magnifying glass seem to shade off into vagueness. They give the impression of being different. But a little movement of the glass will reveal their continuity within a single manuscript without whose context no particular passage makes any sense at all. I want to make it clear, by using this simile, that it is perfectly correct for an anthropologist to concentrate on local patterns of relationships and changes over time, as long as he is fully aware that he is considering only a specific part of a whole. Furthermore, he must make the relationships between the part and the whole clear. It is not only perfectly correct but also highly desirable. By working in local communities with such awareness, an anthropologist might be able to shed more light on what Tilly calls devolutionary processes, which are the counterpart of evolutionary processes at work in highly complex societies. In this paper the emphasis will be on ' . . . the devolutionary concomitants of increases in scale' (Tilly 1970:465) at the level of a small Dutch dairy-farming community. One could say that the theoretical *leitmotiv* underlying the approach consists of a view of society in which evolution in certain sectors is paralleled by devolution in certain others, especially the rural ones (cf. Tilly 1970).

2 THE PROBLEM

Muusland[1] is a small Dutch dairy farming community with approximately 750 inhabitants. It is situated between two rivers, the Lek and the Merwede, in the rural heart of central Holland. In January 1971, three small-scale farmers decided to sell their farms, as a result of a fall in output. At the same time at least 3,000 small farmers elsewhere in the Netherlands gave up farming. In Muusland, farmers were losing their influence on village affairs, of which they had been firmly in control up to World War II. In the postwar years their socio-economic position began to deteriorate. The halcyon days when they formed the village elite, with a dominant position in almost all spheres of social life following from their membership on the important councils and boards, are almost past. Although in the first half of the twentieth century the farmers still dominated the village scene, here as in other rural settlements, both in the region itself and in the Netherlands as a whole, the gradual decline of agriculture in Western Europe had already started by the mid-nineteenth century. A passage from Slicher van Bath's *Agrarian History* makes this quite clear:

... In the second half of that era (the nineteenth century) the industrial element in the economy of Western Europe was coming steadily to the fore. The west European need for agricultural products was being met to an increasing extent by non-European lands. This was made possible by the spectacular development of methods of transport. By about 1850 in most west European countries supremacy of agriculture was over (1963:5).

Several passages from Dovring point in the same direction. However, he emphasises that the decline in absolute numbers of the agricultural population in Western Europe only began in the twentieth century (1965:612). Here the radical fall in numbers of the agricultural labour force only occurred in the 1950s. Clout, for instance, gives for the Netherlands an annual rate of decrease of 2.4 per cent for the agricultural population in the period 1950–60 (1971:25). This decrease was mainly due to two developments: the first is that farmers' children no longer remained on their parents' farms; the second is that the number of hired hands in agriculture fell very sharply. Decisions by middle-aged farmers to abandon farming were a much less important factor. These developments have produced a number of adverse effects on the quality of the agricultural labour force. Clout, among others, stresses this fact (1971:22). The Mansholt Memorandum of 1968 devotes special sections to the problem of the aging farmers who stay on the land. Although most farmers in Muusland are fully aware of a gradual deterioration in their economic position and can understand why their children prefer to continue their education rather than enter farming, it is a shock to them to see a farm abandoned, in spite of their familiarity with the general line of development. At the same time they are left with the frightening question as to when they will also have to make the same decision, even more critical in the context of the community of which they are members. The farmers in Muusland not only have to cope with these tremendous economic problems but also with the effects of plans and programmes initiated at higher levels in response to developments at the local community level. Although these plans are intended to cure a worsening economic situation, they nonetheless constitute a threat to the position of influence which the farmers have held for such a long time within the village community. This effect is mainly due to the onesidedness and narrow economic scope of some of the plans. It may be no more than the irony of fate that the answers proposed by government officials to the problems inherent in the economic position of the small farmers will, once implemented, have a pronounced effect on the social structure of the village community.

The following questions must then be considered. Why is it that farmers are losing ground not only in Muusland, but also throughout the greater part of the Dutch countryside? Why are the farmers losing their positions of influence? One cannot find satisfactory answers to these and other related questions without considering at the same time both processes within Dutch society as a whole and developments at the international level. 'The rural community is no longer the semi-closed, restricted community of the past. It has been opened up to urban and supra-national influences by modern communications' (Franklin 1969:10). It would be incorrect, however, to assume that what goes on at the local level is only a consequence of national or international processes. Although empirically it may not be easy to separate local from national processes, one can still distinguish them for the sake of analysis. My approach will therefore consist of looking at the intricate social process constituted jointly by both kinds of development from a number of different angles. Furthermore, it is impossible to do full justice to the course of events (especially at the local level) without being aware that they have their roots in the past. My data therefore are placed in historical perspective wherever possible[2].

In the following sections I deal with: 1) the economic developments within the agrarian sector in general, i.e., at the national and the international levels and at the village level; 2) the implementation of a land consolidation scheme in the Muusland district; 3) the reorganization of the authorities in charge of water control; and 4) the administrative reorganization of municipalities within this region. We are here concerned with three specific plans drawn up and implemented by government authorities at both the national and provincial levels in response to the situation manifested at the regional and local levels. Furthermore, attention is given to the general economic trend which can be seen as the basis for these plans. Underlying these specifications is the theme of centralization. Two of these plans – the land consolidation scheme and the reorganization of the water control authorities – can be perceived as measures of structural reform taken by the government in order to counter the worsening economic situation of the farmers. I will describe how all three plans affect the farming population of Muusland and imply a restructuring of the patterns of social relationships, the power balance and the stratification system of the village. In the final paragraph I concentrate on what kind of perspective might be useful in dealing with the relationship between the local community and the national government. But first I will provide some background information on Muusland.

3 THE SETTING

The village of Muusland was founded in the Middle Ages. In the twelfth and thirteenth centuries feudal lords and clerics, looking forward to enlarging their revenues and expanding their power domains, began with the reclamation and the exploitation of the fens lying between the rivers Lek and Merwede, which until that time had been populated by people who for their livelihood relied on hunting and fishing. They gave out for reclamation small parcels of fenland to colonists and pioneers who, for the most part, came from those densely populated areas of the Netherlands where the possibility to establish farms was severely restricted by an unfavourable man-land ratio (Slicher van Bath 1963). Through purchase these people became the owners of the reclaimed fens. Nevertheless they had to pay tithes every year, a practice finally abolished in the mid-nineteenth century. After the reclamation was complete, the settlers relied on agriculture for their livelihood. Up to the early seventeenth century they grew crops for their own use and the market, while their cattle-holding served the same purpose.

In the course of the seventeenth and eighteenth centuries they intensified the growing of hemp for the market. The cultivation of this highly labour-intensive crop brought with it a marked increase in the scope of employment for the landless villagers as well as a reorganization of the existing field pattern. Many of the long strips of land lying behind the farmhouses were divided into numerous small plots marked off by deep ditches. The entire hemp production was sold to sailmakers. In the same period keeping livestock became important. Cattle dung was used as fertilizer for the hemplands. With the replacement of sailing vessels by steamships, however, the growing of hemp rapidly declined and then disappeared altogether by the mid-1880s. This was a serious blow to the farm labourers, who thus lost their main winter employment. The newly created field pattern, however, was not abolished, but remained in one way or another long after the cultivation of hemp had disappeared. Many of the small plots are now mainly in use as vegetable gardens and orchards, which can be seen as an additional factor contributing to the fragmentation of the lands surrounding the village. The practice of splitting up farms by bequeathing the land to more than one member of the family had already proved a hindrance to profitable farming earlier on. The division of the land into numerous small plots made this situation even worse. After the collapse of hemp cultivation, raising dairy cattle became increasingly important.

In 1970 all 54 farmers in Muusland were dairy farmers, and with a few exceptions they worked full time. Together they cultivated roughly 750 hectares of land within the municipality. The average holding has 20–25 cows, while the average amount of pasture that the farmers own and/or rent is about 15–20 hectares. The actual size of the farms has changed little since the nineteenth century. The number of dairy cows per farm has, however, increased significantly. One is confronted here with a trend towards an intensification of land use as a consequence of the steadily increasing use of chemical fertilizers, which improves the condition of the soil and the hay yield ratios. The situation with regard to farm size is not so bad when one takes into account that in the late 1960s 54 per cent of all farms in the Netherlands were under 10 hectares (Clout 1971:43). Before the introduction of dairy factories in the area (about 1900), farmers' wives made most of the milk into cheese and butter on the farms. They either sold their products to local entrepreneurs or transported them (frequently by boat) to nearby markets. At present the production of farm cheese and butter has almost totally disappeared from the village, since most farmers sell their milk directly to the dairy. Milk is their main source of income; they do not market crops. Although the number of farmers concentrating on raising pigs, cattle and poultry is increasing, especially among small farmers, one cannot say that these types of intensive farming are replacing dairy farming. Intensive farming is a highly risky business because it is very dependent on market fluctuations. A side effect of this increase of intensive farming is the construction of ugly barns for which it is not easy in this area to get a building license. The consequent clandestine building activities of some farmers, in turn, leads to conflicts with local administrative officials. Here one can see how a simple change in farming practices in a small village embedded in a nation-state with all sorts of national building regulations leads towards a worsening of social relationships. It is just this kind of effect which is not forecast in the planning of the central authorities in our highly complex society.

From 1900 to the beginning of World War II a high percentage (on the average 80 per cent) of the total working population was regularly engaged in agriculture in one form or another. After the war one can observe a sharp decline in this figure. In 1947 it was 60 per cent and in 1960 45 per cent, while it fell below 30 per cent in the period 1965–71. This rapid decrease is mainly due to the dwindling number of farm labourers, the unwillingness of many farmers' children to participate in farming activities, and the infiltration into the village of newcomers with nonfarming occupations. These newcomers, for the most part white- and blue-collar workers who work outside the village, could move in due to the development, in the mid-1960s, of a housing estate in the centre of the village. There is in fact little difference between the total number of full-time farmers immediately before and after the war. Only in the last few years can one see a decrease in the absolute sense. The designation 'typical farming' can no longer be used to describe the village population as a whole, but with little industry actually located in the center of the area, Muusland, like most villages of the area, still gives the impression of being a typical farming village. In this respect the seemingly unchanged character of the rural landscape, which disguises demographic and other changes, plays an important role (Franklin 1971:56). Over the past ten years, however, the character of the village has changed due to the construction of new houses and the implementation of the land consolidation scheme which will be discussed in section V.

4 INTERVENTIONIST GOVERNMENTAL POLICIES AFFECTING AGRICULTURE;
THE CAP OF THE COMMON MARKET

Since World War II national governments have intervened in the agricultural sector in almost every country in Western Europe. 'Initially the main aim was restarting production after the disruption of war. This was then modified to increase food supplies and end rationing. Now many governments are trying to tackle problems of agricultural overproduction' (Clout 1971:26). Although the governments in Western Europe and Eastern Europe were confronted with roughly the same problems in the field of agriculture, they differed in the way in which they intervened and attempted to make changes. 'In Western Europe these changes had been translated through price support measures and aid for technical development, but in Eastern Europe they had been associated with collectivisation' (Clout 1971:14). Until the formation of the EEC in 1958 there was little uniformity in the farm policies pursued by national governments. Each tried in its own way to support the farming population. After the signing of the Treaty of Rome by the six founding member countries, the road was open towards a common agricultural policy (CAP) and the gradual abolition of the often antagonistic national agricultural policies. In the 1960s particularly, problems of overproduction came increasingly into the open. One is confronted here with a very intricate phenomenon although after World War II the percentage of the working population in agriculture rapidly declined in Western Europe, this fact did not lead to a decrease in production. On the contrary, the ever-growing rate of agricultural production is directly connected with the introduction of new cultivation methods and the increasing use of farm machines.

The mechanization of agriculture in Muusland started in the mid 1950s. The most important machines which appeared on the farms were electric milking machines and tractors (an increase in the number of tractors was accompanied by a sharp decrease in the number of horses). The adoption of these labour-saving devices by the local farmers is directly related to the increasing costs of hiring farmhands and the decreasing number of children who participated in farming. Both developments, in their turn, cannot be seen apart from other developments in Dutch society, but I will not deal with them in this context. The market for agricultural products is, however, characterized by an inelastic demand, which explains the existence of huge surpluses of some products such as cheese and butter. The mounting supply of agricultural products has not been matched by a corresponding increase in demand-here one touches on a very problematic and delicate issue which the EEC now must cope with. In the 1960s it did this almost exclusively by price support and/or market regulating measures. 'Price support through the buying-in of certain products when prices fell below fixed levels was financed by the European Agricultural Guidance and Guarantee Fund (FEOGA) which ... was itself financed partly by national contributions and partly from the proceeds of external levies' (Clout 1971:50). During the same period, however, it was realized that the structural reorganization of agriculture was just as necessary as price support measures, which had as their primary aim a guaranteed and acceptable income for the farmer.

In 1968, Mansholt, the member of the European Commission concerned with EEC agricultural affairs, presented his famous Memorandum which contained several far-reaching and drastic proposals regarding a reorganization of farming in the EEC countries.

The general conclusion of the report was that at least 80 percent of West European farmers were marginal, given the technical and economic conditions of the late 1960s. Mansholt, therefore, proposed three objectives for West European farming by 1980: to accelerate the drift from the land, to change farm sizes radically, and to balance out the supply and demand for farm products. (Clout 1971:55)

A slightly modified form of his plan was accepted in 1970 by the council of agricultural ministers. This very important decision to accept Mansholt's suggestions boded a gloomy future for millions of so-called marginal farmers within the EEC countries. Although the national governments of the member countries did not receive concrete instructions on how to implement the proposals, they were nevertheless obliged to develop measures in accordance with the aims stated in the resolution. This case is a good illustration of how a transfer of power from the national to the supra-national level becomes a necessity for nation-states embedded in a highly complex international market economy, if they want to rescue a category of producers from a certain economic downfall. No matter how high the level on which the decisions are taken, their effects can be clearly observed at the lowest levels, e.g., that of village communities where, in a remote sense, they originate. Despite the price support measures, small-scale farmers are still not able to work their farms profitably as a result of ever-increasing production costs involved in profitable (dairy) farming. The internationally agreed minimum prices for dairy products do not increase in proportion to the rise in production costs and the rise in the standard of living in the Netherlands. The gap in incomes remains and, moreover, is widening.

At the village level one can observe many phenomena which are a direct reflection and expression of the deteriorating economic position of the small-scale farmers, despite and/or owing to[3] the government's interventionist policy based on international agreements intended to improve the situation. There is, for example, the already mentioned gradual decrease in the absolute number of small dairy farmers in the village and the low standard of living of the remaining farmers who desperately try to earn a decent living by intensification and in some cases diversification of their farming activities. Many small farmers in the area have had to liquidate their farms and find jobs elsewhere outside agriculture. They often move to nearby towns and work as unskilled labourers. The possibility for them to find jobs is helped by the fact that industrialization and urbanization have already made heavy inroads into several towns on the borders of the region along the rivers Lek, Noord, and Merwede. There are many regions in Europe, such as the Massif Central in France and the Southern parts of Italy, to mention but a few, where there is a total lack of such alternative employment, seriously hampering an outward flow of marginal farmers. The small farmers in Muusland who struggle to survive take refuge in particular solutions to their problems. As a consequence of their bad financial situation and their lack of sufficient capital to invest in machinery other than tractors and electric milking machines, two or three of them (frequently neighbours and/or kinsmen) buy farm machinery on a cooperative basis (Franklin 1971:30)[4]. These adaptations generate new patterns of relationships and can involve new sources of conflict. Another consequence of the deteriorating agrarian situation is a decreasing interest in farming among heirs to farms. Some prefer to train to be teachers, clerks, or administrators, and their fathers pay for them to attend schools in order to gain the appropriate qualifications. It is no longer attractive for the heirs to go into farming if they run the risk of heavy mortgage due to the high costs involved in buying the siblings' shares of the inheritance, particularly when there are many siblings. Farming is also not attractive to them because it is a heavy job which allows no vacations and offers no promise of a relatively high income. The son who does go into farming is usually the sole heir to his father's farm. But even then, in spite of this favourable position, he might be reluctant when he compares his own situation with that of his peers who have decided to find a job outside agriculture. Formerly farmers' children usually stayed in the village, but now on completing school they frequently leave. Only the big farmers with relatively modern farm equipment and enough capital to invest are nowadays able to earn a decent living. It is this category of farmers, in fact, which profits most by the price-support measures within the EEC, while they have lower production costs per unit of output[5]. Owing to these 'protective' measures, the farmer in a sense loses his independence, while the state enhances its power to influence the former's situation by taking still further 'protective' measures[6]. In the next section I will pay attention to just such a measure: the implementation of a land consolidation scheme in the area of Muusland.

5 LAND CONSOLIDATION

Redistribution of land is by no means a new phenomenon in the Netherlands, although it appeared here relatively late in comparison with other countries in Western Europe where land consolidation schemes were already implemented in the eighteenth and nineteenth centuries (see Dovring 1965: 628-9). Except for a lone voice advocating its necessity in the mid-nineteenth century, it was not until the turn of the twentieth century that some surveyors emphasized the agricultural necessity of reallotment. These people even designed a bill which they brought before the magistrates, however, it was not accepted at that time. In 1924 the national government enacted the first Land Consolidation Act. This LCA enabled the government to implement reparcelling plans in rural areas where a majority of the farmers requested it. Until World War II there was only a limited implementation of reallotment plans[7]. During and after the war there was an increase in reallotment activities in rural areas which had a fragmented pattern of landownership. Since 1924 several revisions of the LCA have been enacted by Parliament, the last one in 1954 enabling the government to combine the reparcelling with the enlargement of farms too small for modern standards[8]. Since the war the area around Muusland was known as a problem area with regard to land fragmentation and farm size. Both these factors form tremendous obstacles to the rationalizing of farm practices within this particular region. In the late 1940s officials of the National Board for Land and Water Use (Cultuurtechnische Dienst) had already listed it as an area where land consolidation was necessary in order to revitalize agriculture. It was not until the mid 1960s that these officials could begin implementing what was called at the time the largest land consolidation programme ever accomplished in Western Europe (roughly 23,000 hectares of land were involved in the area as a whole). One of the reasons behind this significant delay was the hostile attitude of many farmers towards the plan. In 1964 11% of the farmers in the area, owning together 30% of the total land, voted against it[9]. One of their major objections was the high cost involved in an implementation of the reallotment plans[10]. The foremost goal of reallotment was to make farming in the region a more profitable enterprise by radically reorganizing the old pattern of land distribution (amalgamation of scattered plots) and by enlarging the existing farms into more viable units (holdings with 25 hectares of land)[11], which inevitably included the abolition of numerous small-scale farms. The implementation of the plan involved the construction of new roads to enable the farmers to reach their newly consolidated plots without losing too much time and to use modern farm machinery without seriously damaging the watery peat surface of the fields next to large-scale drainage works (see next section). It further involved building modern farms along these roads as well as the repair of suitable farm buildings still in use. These and other structural rearrangements were directly triggered by the deteriorating economic situation of the (small) farmers in the area, whose position in turn was closely related to the economic developments outlined above (see section IV).

At the village level the implementation of the reallotment plan was felt in many ways. Farmers with enough capital and courage left their old homes to start afresh on newly built farms. Very often they sold their old farms to well-to-do people from urban centers who were looking for peace and quiet in rural areas where water and air are less polluted (cf. Franklin 1971:115). In many cases the gradual inflow of this type of newcomer has a disruptive effect on the old patterns of social relationships. All sorts of conflicts arise between the new settlers and the established ones who see their old way of life threatened. In Muusland the native villagers, especially the members of the Dutch Reformed Church with their rather strict way of life, often criticize the newcomers' 'deviant' life-styles. Negative remarks are frequently made about the refusal of the newcomers to adapt themselves to community life. An additional distorting effect has been the rearrangement of the settlement pattern involved in the building of new farms in the polders outside the village.

Farmers who are unable to afford new farms try to modernize their enterprise with whatever means they have. Since many of the farmhouses were built in the nineteenth century, such attempts are for the most part unsuccessful, often resulting in a further shrinking of capital and an increase in personal debts. Therefore farmers of this type often prefer to invest whatever capital they have in the construction of special barns in which they can raise pigs, cattle, and battery chickens, instead of modernizing their dairy enterprise. Others continue to farm in the traditional way, while still others have had to sell their farms immediately. The latter must find jobs in sectors with which they are unfamiliar, and consequently they often experience a loss in status and prestige. The 'stayers' gossip about their being bad farmers after all, even though they acknowledge that the decision to quit was a wise one given the circumstances[13].

In short, the implementation of the land consolidation scheme for purely economic reasons has the effect of reinforcing a relatively autonomous process – the decline of small-scale farming in industrializing and urbanizing societies of Western Europe. It upsets the social structure of the village at large and it disorients the farmers, who are confronted with measures which they hardly understand. They are unable to trace the social origins of these measures or their connection with national and international developments, especially in the worldwide market for agricultural products. In order to find an outlet for their uneasiness with their daily situation they blame the government and the European Commission (EC) for their misfortune – for destroying their way of life. In their opinion they are the victims of those in power at the national and the international levels, who do not care what happens to the small-scale farmers. 'They kill you in order to fill their own pockets,' a farmer once declared to me[14].

In Muusland as well as in other villages in the region some farmers did voice their protest against the implementation of the land consolidation scheme and they continue to do so (although not all of them). But they have no hope of being heard. Their main objection is the financial burden consolidation places on them, which they find impossible in their circumstances. There are, however, variations in the way the farmers view the reallotment, ranging from rejection to acceptance. It is the small farmers who generally tend to reject it, while the bigger ones are inclined to favour it[15]. This fits in with the trend towards big farmers with capitalist enterprises, a trend brought about by land consolidation and other measures.

6 THE REORGANIZATION OF THE SYSTEM OF WATER CONTROL

At the end of the 1960s the provincial government, in cooperation with officials of other government departments, designed a plan to reorganize the intricate administrative system concerned with the drainage of the polders[16]. As we have seen, this system developed following the Middle Ages in connection with land reclamation (see section III). It has remained virtually unchanged for centuries, at least in so far as the types of administrative bodies included in it are concerned. To make agriculture possible in the watery fenlands between the rivers, ditches and canals as well as small dikes were necessary in order to ensure adequate drainage and an appropriate ground-water level (Slicher van Bath 1963:151ff). In this way several polders were created and as their number increased, the drainage system became increasingly complex. When thirteenth century feudal lords began constructing dikes along the banks of the rivers to protect the newly cultivated lands against flooding, it became a problem to get rid of the surplus water. Formerly, it could flow away naturally to the rivers, however, dike construction and the sinking of the soil (a consequence of the shrinking of the peat surface after reclamation) made this impossible. In order to cope with these increasingly complex problems the feudal lords dug large canals to function as reservoirs, and sluices were built through which the accumulated waters could flow into the rivers at low tide. Until the introduction of the watermill in the second half of the fifteenth century, this was no mean affair. A consequence of dike construction was a higher water level in the rivers, which complicated the emptying of the reservoirs. It occurred frequently that they could not contain all the water, especially in autumn and winter, and the reclaimed fenlands were flooded. Here we have a clear example of how the solving of problems connected with the exploitation of certain natural environments may create other, sometimes larger, problems.

With the introduction of the watermill things subsequently became better. This does not mean, however, that the struggle against water was over. In every century this region was afflicted by floods. Between 1350 and 1953, 33 floods occurred (Schakel 1954). In the nineteenth century wind power was replaced by steam power for use in draining the reservoirs into the rivers, and in the 1950s steam engines were replaced by electric motors.

In the thirteenth century the feudal lords, who had until then worked relatively independently, joined forces to cope with the problems posed by the natural environment[17]. Convinced of the necessity of a central administrative system for controlling the water level and maintaining the dikes, they gradually developed an organization for this purpose (Goudsblom 1968:141-2).

At the end of the 1960s the provincial authorities decided for the sake of efficiency to replace the old system with a less complicated and more centralized one[18]. In their opinion a marked reduction in the number of administrative units (Water Boards), and the establishment of a strongly centralized administrative apparatus, would make it possible to cope more adequately with the ever-increasing problems connected with water pollution, the use of the canals for recreational purposes, the maintenance of old and new roads, and the drainage of the more than thirty polders lying in the region. These problems are a consequence of a number of developments in specific sectors of society at large, of which the rapid industrialization and urbanization of the Dutch Conurbation (*Randstad Holland*) and the seeming lack of these processes elsewhere are examples. For generations the local farmers had provided (often in an almost hereditary fashion) the membership of the Water Boards (e.g., the polder committees). They protested vehemently against the reorganization. Their objections against the proposals were, in most cases, of a purely technical nature, although reorganization would mean for them a serious loss of power and prestige at the village level. Until then they themselves had been responsible for the polders – they decided on the water level in the ditches and the canals. With the reorganization, these affairs would be in the hands of full-time specialists assisted by a small number of farmers democratically elected for that purpose. The reorganization brought with it the abolition of many positions of power and prestige in the local setting. Despite the protests of the farmers this reorganization was begun in 1972. With that came an end to the strife between what were known as the 'low water' and 'high water' farmers in the village. This strife was directly related to the gradual mechanization of farming, which began in the mid-1950s (see section IV). 'Low water' farmers are those who possess low-lying plots of land and who transport manure, milk, hay, etc. overland on wagons drawn by tractors. For them a high water level in the ditches and trenches meant a high ground-water level and thus difficulties with transport. 'High water' farmers, still using boats for transport, have problems when the water level is too low. Before the reorganization the two categories were often in conflict at the meetings of the local polder committees. With the steady increase in mechanization, however, 'high water' farmers were already on the decrease in Muusland. In other words, the reorganization merely accelerated a process that was already taking place.

7 GOVERNMENT POLICY CONCERNING THE ADMINISTRATIVE AUTONOMY OF MUNICIPALITIES

The national government has developed a plan aimed at transforming municipalities in areas which have a population of fewer than 3,000 inhabitants into larger administrative units, which should be implemented within the next few years. In a development plan for the region in which Muusland is situated, accepted by the provincial government in 1969, the provincial authorities emphasized the need for such a reorganization. Elsewhere in the Netherlands similar plans had already been carried out. Every Dutch city, town and village has its own municipal council, with a high degree of independent authority in matters regarding local schools, housing, public health, and so on. Every council has a chairman, mayor or burgomaster, but not every village or town has its own mayor, since some burgomasters serve two or three municipalities at the same time.

... Many of these municipalities with fewer than 1,000 inhabitants have been separate political units since the Middle Ages. In order to curtail the autonomy the cities had enjoyed during the Republic, equal legal powers were, in the early nineteenth century, given to all municipalities, large and small. Today, the small municipalities are, by and large, poorly equipped to fulfill the differentiated tasks of modern administration. A programme of amalgamations has, therefore, been drafted, and it is slowly being put into effect, often against strong local resistance. Between 1950 and 1964 the total number of municipalities dropped from 1,014 to 967 (Goudsblom 1968:140).

Government authorities believe that the formation of administrative units serving the interests of at least 5,000 people is required in the area of Muusland. Only when the small, politically independent municipalities disappear will a balanced development of the area become possible. Whereas municipal councils of neighbouring villages frequently argue with each other over 'village interests,' an amalgamation would rule out such quarreling. At the same time it would enhance the possibility of controlling adequately the processes of industrialization and urbanization, particularly along the banks of the rivers. The suggestion from above that several municipalities should disappear worries the members of the village and town councils, as well as the members of the local branches of the political parties. They all try to find suitable solutions before the government officials impose their own solution. In fact, many villagers have mixed feelings concerning the reorganization. They want to preserve their local autonomy or, rather, what remains of it. Why should their village become part of a larger administrative unit? Why should the distance between them and the administrators be increased? A fusion for them, in a certain sense, would imply the loss of a reference point, and also a loss of power. If the reorganization is implemented, this will be just another blow for the farmers, because they, on the whole, are the municipal council members, at least in the dairy-farming villages. Another realm in which they were once the men of power will be closed to them, or made almost inaccessible. With their positions of power already lost in other spheres of activity, they face a gloomy future. The only place where they can still exert some influence is in church affairs, but even here they are under attack (cf. Verrips 1973).

In almost every way farmers, particularly small farmers, are experiencing hard times. They are losing their positions, power and prestige, and, at worst, their farms as well. Their whole way of life is at stake. The small farmers have to sacrifice themselves for the big ones, who will produce more than ever before, which means that a number of them may also disappear within the near future. For centuries the farmer has been the cornerstone of Dutch society. In Muusland and elsewhere in the region a rapid disintegration is taking place of the full-time farming industry. I have attempted to show this by indicating how the farmers' affairs are affected by (inter)national economic developments and plans and programmes initiated by the national and provincial governments in response to regional and local developments.

The social class of farmers in Muusland is splintering and shriveling, while that of white- and blue-collar workers is increasing. The farmers have ceased to be the upper stratum of the community. Positions held by them in several important local institutions are gradually being taken over by nonfarmers, or are ceasing to exist. The times are over in which a farmer could treat his fellow villagers, farm labourers in particular, as if they were serfs. In the old days a well-to-do farmer could, with a gift of cheese, buy the votes of local farm hands and artisans in order to get himself elected as a village councillor, or force a labourer to change his church affiliation in exchange for employment. With the decline in the number of rural labourers as a consequence of the mechanization of farming and their increased wages such practices belong to the past. The labourers became, for the most part, industrial workers earning wages significantly higher than the income of the farmers. Whereas formerly the farmers impressed the nonfarming village population with their lifestyle and conspicuous leisure, the roles are rapidly reversing. Nowadays it is no longer the labourers who look with envy at the farmers, but the other way around – the farmers see the labourers possessing the economic security which they themselves lack[19]. The deterioration of the socio-economic situation of the farmers and the much improved situation of the white- and blue-collar workers in Muusland has resulted in a change in the previous existing class structure[20], as well as in the prevailing patterns of interpersonal relationships. It has also given rise to new patterns of behaviour. These local-level processes are directly related to – or form part of – large-scale developments in society as a whole. The ever-increasing 'influence' of the central government in the Netherlands on the local level has diminished the relatively autonomous socio-political position of the local community, in which the farmers were once the dominant powerholders[21]. I cannot but see in this development a strong confirmation of the following general statement made by Tilly:

This could well be the general pattern: evolution to a larger scale, devolution at the smaller scale. If this is the case, it probably means that the roles which have their chief significance at the smaller scale ... shrivel with the expansion of scale, and persons who have their chief investments in those roles begin to lose their social identities (1970:453).

In the final section of this paper I will deal in summary form with the perspective underlying my approach, the relationship between local community and society at large, and the contribution of community research towards a better insight into the workings of highly complex societies.

8 LOCAL COMMUNITIES AND SOCIETY AT LARGE: SOME CONCLUDING REMARKS

Traditionally anthropologists have taken as their unit of research a small-scale community, a tribe or a village. I did this also when, in 1970, I started my fieldwork in the Netherlands. Although I realized that Muusland was far from isolated, and that it was obviously a part of Dutch society as a whole, I did not at first concern myself too much with the nature and significance of this part-whole relationship. Instead, I concentrated on the patterns of interpersonal relationships and their dynamics within several local institutions and spheres of activity in this territorially bounded unit. Gradually I began to realize that these patterns and their dynamics could not be understood properly in isolation from their anchorage in the past. Furthermore, it was necessary to take into consideration the way they were affected by several large-scale societal developments and how, moreover, these developments found a specific expression at the local level. We are concerned here with the problem Pitt-Rivers describes in *The People of the Sierra* as '... one of the hoariest problems in social anthropology ...' by which he means the question: Why should a system of social relationships that defines a community stop at its spatial boundaries? This problem

turns out on closer examination to be a pseudo-problem. One delimits the area of one's data according to the techniques which one intends to use. In studying any society one must face two problems: What is the system of social relations within the community? and how is it affected by being a part of the larger structure of the country, or of the continent (Pitt-Rivers 1961:208)?

This observation and orientation of research is of great importance to anthropologists doing fieldwork in small-scale communities in complex societies. It justifies the search for patterns of interpersonal relationships in spatially bounded communities as well as the change in these patterns over time. At the same time, it contains the warning not to neglect the way these patterns are affected by their being part of much larger configurations and the way the latter change over time. This perspective is in my opinion clearly implied by Pitt-Rivers: 'Being part of a larger structure ... the community is subject to the powers of provincial and central government and of persons allied to those powers, whose nonmembership of the community enables them to escape the sanctions whereby its values are maintained...' (1961:209).

In this paper I have attempted to demonstrate how small-scale farmers in a Dutch community were, and still are, subjected to exactly the powers Pitt-Rivers mentions, as well as to the persons allied with those powers. What is needed in our studies of local communities and central government is not so much new concepts, but a new perspective to work from. We have to put such concepts as micro and macro, part and whole, and so forth in another perspective if we want to avoid false polarizations and reifications. We have to use them against the background of clearly formulated ideas about how local communities are 'distinct' instead of 'separate' parts of that vast complex we call society, about how the members of these communities are also members of other 'units,' and about how processes generated by individuals on the levels of both the local community and central government form, in fact, one total process[22]. Social scientists like Elias, Tilly, and Wolf already demonstrated how we can move in that direction. If we decide to travel along the roads they sketched, there is no need to look for another unit of research. On the contrary, by doing fieldwork in small communities within complex nation-states based on the works and insights of the scholars just mentioned, the anthropologist still has an immense but interesting and rewarding task ahead of him.

NOTES

[1] A pseudonym for the village in which I conducted fieldwork during 1970–71. The research was supported by a grant from the Netherlands Organization for the Advancement of Pure Research (Z.W.O.). I am most grateful to Anton Blok and Dick van den Bosch for their valuable comments on an earlier version of this paper. I wish to thank Rod Aya, Jeremy Boissevain, Mary C. Jetten and Edward H. C. Jetten, who were kind enough to correct my English.

[2] I follow in this context the statement of C. Wright Mills: 'Our chance to understand how smaller milieux and larger structures interact and our chance to understand the larger cause at work in these limited milieux does require us to deal with historical materials' (1958:149). See also Ger Harmsen (1968:80).

[3] I use this expression because the measures of the government are ambiguous or contradictory. The economic measures are in many respects insufficient to solve entirely the small dairy farmers' problems, but they at least enable them to continue their unprofitable pursuit. The structural reform measures, however, aim at their accelerated drift from the land, which is seriously constrained by just these economic measures. One has to perceive this ambivalent character of the governmental approach to agrarian problems as a rather curious mixture of a legacy from the postwar past (i.e. interventionist policy on a national scale) which was continued by the EEC countries on an international scale, and recent economic developments (i.e. surplus production) which call for a drastic reduction of the agricultural labour force.

[4] See Dovring (1965) for a very thorough analysis of the motivation for farmers to invest in machinery.

[5] This fact is explicitly acknowledged in the Mansholt Memorandum (cf. paragraph 38, page 20). See also Franklin (1971:21).

[6] 'To have the State as partner, or provider of capital; to have it also as protector, not only in the old sense, but exercising monopoly powers on his behalf so as to protect him from the fluctuations of the market; when these services are provided for him, the problems of the 'independent' farmer, which have vexed him for so long, may appear to be solved. Yet how much, then, is left of his independence? It is by his political weight that he has attained this favoured position, and that could prove to be a wasting asset' (Hicks 1969:120).

[7] The most spectacular one was accomplished in Staphorst in the mid-1930s. In this rural community in the eastern part of the Netherlands the pulverisation of farmland as a consequence of the existing inheritance system had reached incredible proportions. Almost 1830 hectares were fragmented into 1300 plots belonging to roughly 1700 owners.

[8] For a detailed exposé on land consolidation in the Netherlands, see the country chapter on the Netherlands (pp. 143–187) in *Structural Reform Measures in Agriculture*, 1972, Paris: OECD.

[9] The voting procedure is very much resented by the full-time farmers because everyone with a piece of land has the right to vote, i.e. many nonfarmers, part-time farmers, etc. Furthermore, those who stay at home on the day of the voting are deemed to have voted 'yes.'

[10] While the state pays 65% of all the costs involved, the farmers together have to pay the remaining 35%.

[11] The criteria for what can be considered a viable unit are constantly changing. What was deemed to be a viable unit in the mid-1960s turns out to be a nonviable one in the 1970s. Holdings with 25 hectares are a far cry from the units envisaged in the Mansholt Memorandum. Land consolidation schemes often are already outdated by the time they are implemented.

[12] See Dovring (1965), who sketches the cyclical pattern in the arrangements of rural villages in Western Europe since the Middle Ages.

[13] In this context it is relevant to know that since the mid-1960s the Dutch government has been experimenting with termination schemes, in addition to land consolidation schemes, for the purpose of revitalizing agriculture. The first scheme (1964), which under certain specified conditions provided for termination of payments to low-income or marginal farmers with unviable farms, was replaced by another in 1966. From then on, farmers of every age and income could apply, but the compensation paid under this scheme was rather low. The effect has been a significant decrease in the number of farmers applying. Therefore another scheme was enacted with more favourable conditions in 1968. When in 1971 the government decided to pay an extra premium for vacated land, the number of farmers who applied increased rapidly. (For a detailed exposé on the governmental termination schemes, see the above-mentioned report of the OECD.) However, it is not only the indemnity payments offered by the government which play a role in the decision of farmers to liquidate or sell their farms; it is also the perception they have of the economic situation in society as a whole. They are very much influenced by what happens in the industrial sectors, for example. As soon as they hear of an economic recession, their willingness to give up farming decreases. The decision of the three Muusland farmers mentioned in the first sentences of this article must be seen in the context of these governmental measures. At least two of them asked for indem-

nity payments from the Development and Rationalization Fund *(Het Ontwikkelings- en Sanerings-fonds voor de Landbouw)*, nicknamed by the local farmers as the funeral fund. These farmers were, however, highly dissatisfied with the rather slow procedures of the officials - one of them did not hear for months about his application. Just this kind of governmental delay creates the impression among the farmers that they are to an increasing degree manipulated by forces beyond their control and vision. It heightens their feelings of insecurity in an already insecure situation.

[14] The sudden rise in the Netherlands in the 1960s of the Farmers' Party, which vehemently opposed the agricultural policy of the government, has to be related to the feeling existing among many small farmers that they are betrayed by the authorities. See A. T. J. Nooij (1969), who made an extensive study on disorientation and radicalism among Dutch farmers.

[15] With one particular detail many farmers are relatively content, i.e. the construction of the new roads. Before the reallotment, many plots could only be reached by crossing the plots of other farmers – one of the most important sources of conflict among farmers in Muusland in the past. Some cases were even fought out in the courtroom, while others were dealt with by the local church councils. The construction of several new roads ended many of the longstanding conflicts.

[16] There exists a close connection between this reorganization plan and the implementation of land consolidation in the area. The construction of new roads and canals has direct effects on matters of water control.

[17] I consider this to be a good example of how control of a specific environment by human beings has direct consequences for previously existing or lacking patterns of relationship among them. From relatively independent operators the feudal lords became more and more interdependent/dependent on each other. See Norbert Elias (1970:173), who deals in a very lucid way with these levels of control and their interconnectedness.

[18] The administrative system became more and more entangled within the national government system as it took its shape in the seventeenth, eighteenth and nineteenth centuries. Now the administrative organization falls directly under the authority of the provincial government and the office of the Secretary of State in charge of traffic and water affairs.

[19] A host of writers have pointed to just this feature of external income disparity and its consequences. See van Lierde (1967), Clout (1971), and Franklin (1971), to mention only a few. For example, take this statement of Franklin: 'In previous eras the peasant was the most representative member of society in most continental European countries. Today it is the factory worker. His standard of living sets the social norm' (1971:18).

[20] See Thorns (1968), who reaches similar conclusions for several English rural communities.

[21] See Norbert Elias (1974), who speaks of the defunctionalization of village communities in more differentiated or highly complex societies.

[22] 'Communities which form parts of a complex society can ... be viewed no longer as self-contained and integrated systems in their own right. It is more appropriate to view them as the local termini of a web of group relations which extend through intermediate levels from the level of the community to that of the nation.' (Wolf 1956:1065).

REFERENCES

Clout, Hugh D.
Agriculture. Studies in Contemporary Europe. London: MacMillan, 1971.

Dovring, F.
'The Transformation of European Agriculture,' in *The Cambridge Economic History of Europe*, Vol. VI (2), Ch. VI. Edited by H. J. Habakkuk and M. Postan, 1965.

Elias, Norbert
Was ist Soziologie? München: Juventa Verlag, 1970.
'Community and State. Towards a Theory,' in *The Sociology of Community. A Collection of Readings*, Foreword. Edited by Colin Bell and Howard Newby. London: Frank Cass, 1974.

Franklin, S. H.
The European Peasantry. The Final Phase. London: Methuen, 1969.
Rural Societies. Studies in Contemporary Europe. London: MacMillan, 1971.

Goudsblom, J.
Dutch Society. New York: Random House, 1968.

Harmsen, Ger
Inleiding tot de Geschiedenis. Bilthoven: Uitgeverij Ambo N.V., 1968.

Hicks, J.
A Theory of Economic History. London: Oxford University Press., 1969.

Lierde, J. van
Europese landbouwproblemen en Europese landbouwpolitiek. Antwerpen: Standaard Wetenschappelijke Uitgeverij, 1967.

Memorandum
Memorandum inzake de hervorming van de landbouw in de Europese Economische Gemeenschap (voorgelegd door de Commissie aan de Raad op 21 december 1968). Supplement van het Bulletin nr. 1/1969 van de Europese Gemeenschappen. Secretariaat-Generaal van de Commissie, 1969.

Mendras, H.
The Vanishing Peasant. Innovation and Change in French Agriculture. Cambridge, Mass.: MIT Press, 1970.

Mills, C. Wright
The Sociological Imagination. London: Oxford University Press, 1959.

Nooij, A. T. J.
De Boerenpartij. Desorientatie en radikalisme onder de boeren. Meppel: J. A. Boom en Zoon, 1969.

OECD
Structural Reform Measures in Agriculture. Agricultural Policy Reports. Paris: Organisation for Economic Co-operation and Development, 1972.

Pitt-Rivers, J. A.
The People of the Sierra. Chicago: University of Chicago Press, 1961.

Schakel, M. W.
De waterwolf slaat toe. Noordeloos, 1954.

Slicher van Bath, B. H.
The Agrarian History of Western Europe. A. D. 500–1850. London: Edward Arnold Ltd, 1963.

Thorns, David C.
The Changing System of Rural Stratification. *Sociologia Ruralis* 8:161–179. 1968.

Tilly, Charles
'Clio and Minerva,' in *Theoretical Sociology: Perspectives and Developments*, 433–467. Edited by John C. McKinney and Edward A. Tiryakian. New York: Meredith Corporation, 1970.

Verrips, J.
The Preacher and the Farmers: The Church as Political Arena in a Dutch Community. *American Anthropologist* 75:3:852–868, 1973.

Wolf, Eric R.
Aspects of Group Relations in a Complex Society: Mexico. *American Anthropologist* 58:6:1065–1078, 1956.

10

Social Change in a Dutch Village [1]

Lodewijk Brunt
University of Utrecht

ABSTRACT

Since the mid-1960s, many people are trying to escape the congested cities, especially in the heavily indus-trialised and urbanised western part of the Netherlands. Thanks to private transport, it is no longer necessary to live where you work. Thousands of urbanites are buying houses in small villages in the countryside, many of them becoming involved in local politics. Although some of these newcomers to the villages are quite willing to adapt themselves to the local way of life, others try to change it. The confrontation between urban newcomers and the local population in Stroomkerken, a small Dutch village, is the subject of this paper.

INTRODUCTION

In this paper I analyse how the power structure of a small Dutch village is affected by the settlement of new residents, mostly people pushed from big cities by bad housing conditions, traffic conges-tion and pollution. This is a process in which all parties concerned, in the village as well as at higher levels, are to a great extent being confronted with unintended and unforeseen consequences of technical developments determined by a capitalist economic system essentially international in its orientation.

This may seem to be a rather abstract statement, however, it is based on my perception of major changes in Dutch society as a consequence of the growing importance of the automobile as a means of private transportation and the infrastructure being adapted to this means. In 1960 there were 800,000 automobiles in the Netherlands, compared to well over 3,000,000 today; in this same period the Dutch population increased only from about 12,000,000 to 13,000,000.

This process has changed the economic geography of the country radically. Like its predecessors, the steam engine and the railway, the automobile changed the whole way of living (Baran and Sweezy 1968). Thanks to the automobile, people are no longer forced to live near their places of work. The western part of the Netherlands has become a vast area of cities and suburbs, 'a desert of stone and glass' as it is sometimes called. The urbanisation of the Dutch countryside has received new impetus as a consequence of the large numbers of urbanites settling there. The 'massive internal migration' which has been taking place in the U.S.A. (Baran and Sweezy 1968:300; also Sweezy 1973) is also taking place in the Netherlands and, of course, almost everywhere in western Europe. The population of large Dutch cities such as Amsterdam, Rotterdam and The Hague is decreasing, whereas many small towns and villages are growing rapidly (and often suddenly).

How these macro-economic and sociological processes affect the living conditions of people on a local level is the question which underlies this paper. I sought the answer to this question during my fieldwork in Stroomkerken, a small agrarian Dutch village of 4,000 inhabitants. About one-third of Stroomkerken's population consists of people who were not born there. A considerable number of these 'newcomers', moreover, have moved in since 1965. This immigration of urbanites threatens the relative autonomy of the village, by changing the relationship between the local communities and the state in the Netherlands. (This same process is analysed from a different point of view by Jojada Verrips in his contribution to this volume.) The local power structure not only is affected by the decreasing importance of small farming, but also by the establishment of competing power groups.

In dealing with the newcomers' reaction to their new environment and the way they were confronted with different groups of the settled population, it will be necessary first to dwell upon the nature of the local social structure. A distinctive feature of this structure is its division into two mutually antagonistic ideological blocs. As a consequence the village lacks (normative) unity and consensus, for these groups reacted differently to the newcomers.

In anthropological jargon it can be said that major changes in Dutch society amount to changes in the environment of the local political arena. On the village level, new political capital becomes available, i.e. new voters. The competing political parties recruit representatives of the urban migrants in order to capture their votes, although they differ remarkably in the degree to which they are open or closed (bounded) to the newcomers. In the following historical analysis I suggest a link between this difference in boundedness and the power structure.

THE INTERNAL DIVISIVENESS OF STROOMKERKEN

A most striking aspect of Stroomkerken's social structure is its 'pillarized' nature. In this paper I cannot go deeply into this phenomenon, but must restrict myself to a rather global outline. At the end of the nineteenth century the Dutch orthodox Calvinists and Roman Catholics began to organise themselves socially, politically and economically against the dominant conservative bourgeoisie, the 'liberals'. One of the main issues of conflict between the confessionals (right) and the liberals (left) concerned the nature of education. The confessionals wanted 'free schools' in which children could be educated on the basis of religious dogmas without interference from the 'neutral' government. These free schools had to be subsidized on exactly the same terms as the state schools, in which no particular religious education was given. The preferential treatment of these latter schools by the liberal bourgeoisie was considered one aspect of a systematic discrimination against the religious groups concerned. Both groups developed into 'emancipation movements', which, as a consequence of striving for 'strength in isolation', emerged as real pillars during the first decades of this century. A pillar (*zuil*) is defined as a more or less isolated social group, based on differences in world view or ideology. These differences are expressed in separate organizations, such as political parties, trade unions, and schools. These pillars have divided Dutch society. Religious pillars were followed by a 'quasi-religious' socialist one, and some observers also discern a fourth, liberal or 'general' (*algemene*) one.

Pillars are mostly seen as vertically organised, ideologically homogeneous blocs. They have been compared to pyramids between the tops of which (the respective elites) some form of communication existed. This communication has been brilliantly analysed by Arend Lijphart (1968). He calls it the 'politics of accommodation' or the 'pacification politics': a conscious effort of the Dutch political elite to pacify the potentially explosive opposition between fundamentally antagonistic ideological-organizational systems.

In Stroomkerken, situated in a predominantly Protestant region, where Roman Catholics have been almost completely absent since the Reformation, the pillarization has taken the form of a bipartite system. The division is between various orthodox Calvinist groups on the one hand and liberals and socialists on the other – in local terminology between right and left. Political parties are perhaps the best example of pillars. Because they constitute an important context for interaction between right and left in Stroomkerken, being responsible for the distribution of scarce resources, I shall focus on party politics here, as it is the briefest and clearest way to come to grips with the si-uation.

Of the five Stroomkerken political parties, three are confessional and belong to the right. The *Anti-revolutionaire Partij* (Anti-Revolutionary Party) is the oldest and largest. Together with a second confessional party it occupies four of the eleven seats on the municipal council, including an alderman. The third confessional party occupies two seats. Ever since the 1930s, the right has had an absolute majority in the council. The parties of the left are the *Volkspartij voor Vrijheid en Democratie* (People's Party for Freedom and Democracy: V.V.D.; this is the liberals' party. In Dutch political life, the liberals are one of the most conservative political groups, and the V.V.D. is the party of the employers and the well-to-do) and the *Partij van de Arbeid* (P.v.d.A., Labour Party). The second alderman belongs to the V.V.D., although the party obtained only two seats in the 1970 municipal elections. The P.v.d.A. obtained three seats but lost one of them within a year, when one of the councillors resigned from the party. He now occupies his seat as an Independent. The right pillar forms an almost self-sufficient bloc. It has its own schools, its own corporate life, its own 'industrial complex' (dairy factory, bank, insurance company), and, of course, its own political parties. Ideologically there are internal differences, mainly based on different interpreta-tions of religious dogmas, ranging from an extremely strict observance of certain orthodox prin-ciples to a relatively more easy-going attitude. Nevertheless, the region of which Stroomkerken is a part is known in the Netherlands as very orthodox (Brunt 1972).

These internal differences, however, are negligible in comparison to the differences in world view between right and left. By their very name, the Anti-Revolutionaries express their disapproving attitude towards the 'Principles of the French Revolution'. 'Against the Revolution, the Gospel' was their party's motto in the nineteenth century and it still is today. Political and social life should be ruled by biblical norms – the humanistic-oriented ideologies of liberalism and socialism are rejected as essentially in conflict with God's Will.

By closing their ranks and excluding so-called 'worldly influences', the Stroomkerken orthodox Calvinists have forced the local liberals and socialists into the left pillar. However, one of the few institutional forms of cooperation between liberals and socialists is the local state school. The inter-nal ideological differences within the left pillar, i.e. between liberals and socialists, are matched by definite social structural differences. In the corporate life and the industrial activities of the left the liberals are clearly pulling the strings. In a certain sense, then, it is misleading to speak of the 'left pillar'. Yet, during my fieldwork I witnessed numerous political issues of great importance in which the left stood firmly united against the confessionals. In contrast to the right, membership in one of the left political parties does not necessarily imply membership in other organizations, especially since the Second World War. A person's political conviction is not dependent upon his religion. To qualify as a full member of a left party, a 'minimal involvement' is in principle suffi-cient. Thus, Stroomkerken consists of two different political communities, only one of which – the right – is firmly bounded. There are no general or uniform rules to mark off members from outsiders (Bailey 1969:23) which apply to the entire village.

The Stroomkerken pillarization is still rather pronounced. The difference between right and left is for many people a most important principle to judge people's and parties' behavior. In Dutch society as a whole, however, the sharp edges are gradually disappearing. In the national political arena both liberals and socialists are stressing the 'polarization' between owning classes and the working classes as the only significant basis for political organization. The once crucial power of the confessional political parties is crumbling. Their formerly very efficient mechanisms of social control are losing their impact as social mobility increases. Especially in the cities and among broad layers of the middle class, people are now hardly ever confronted by 'pillarized' phenomena in many spheres of everyday social life.

THE URBAN MIGRANTS IN STROOMKERKEN: CONSEQUENCES OF MACRO-SOCIOLOGICAL CHANGES IN DUTCH SOCIETY

The Stroomkerken newcomers belong largely to a category of so-called *noodforensen* (emergency migrants; Saal 1972). They did not move to the village because they are particularly fond of living in the countryside, but primarily because they were more or less pushed from the city. They are trying to retain an urban way of life and, in general, they are not very much interested in the local political and social affairs of the village. A second category consists of the 'pragmatic dualists' (I borrow this designation also from Saal). These are people who deliberately moved to the village, sometimes from small towns or other villages. To a large extent they come to work in Stroomkerken, as higher employees of local firms, as schoolteachers or as professionals of some regional organisation. Although some are moderately critical of village life, they are willing to adapt themselves to it and even defend it against attacks from outsiders. They are acquainted with pacification politics.

During my fieldwork in Stroomkerken (1970–71), I was able to observe how some of the urban migrants got involved in the local political arena. In my analysis of this process I shall restrict myself mainly to the relationships of these newcomers with two different political parties, the P.v.d.A. and the A.R.P. With reference to these relationships two different newcomers' political careers might be distinguished. A relatively small group of newcomers – at the time of my fieldwork about 20 to 25 – is characterised by a confrontation-career. Among these there were some six or seven who penetrated the P.v.d.A. and took over the party. These newcomers are typical representatives of the *noodforensen*. A somewhat larger group of newcomers belonging to the pragmatic dualists pursued an assimilation-career. This group was mainly being encapsulated by the right pillar. The A.R.P. recruited members from this category.

By whichever career the newcomers might be distinguished, from the standpoint of the Stroomkerken political parties all newcomers are potential voters. In 1970 municipal elections were held. The new voters – since the last elections in 1966 – could have had a decisive influence on the local political power structure. Voting as one bloc, they could have obtained one or two of the eleven seats in the council. Three of the five political parties – A.R.P., P.v.d.A. and V.V.D. – entered the elections with at least one newcomer in an eligible place. Both left and right (i.e. the A.R.P.) were obviously interested in profiting from the changes in the environment (the increasing population) by enlarging their political capital (number of votes). The way in which they tried to attract these votes, however, differed markedly. I shall describe this difference by contrasting in succession the relationships between newcomers and the P.v.d.A. and the A.R.P. The V.V.D. took a more ambivalent course. Its leaders did not oppose newcomers per se, but selected those who were members of the party before they moved to Stroomkerken, and, in general, those who were better off socially and economically, more educated, and in short, more *bourgeois*.

CONFRONTATION-CAREERS: THE NEWCOMERS AND THE P.V.D.A.

Especially among the newcomers who moved to Stroomkerken in 1969 (more than 50 families during several months), a definite group of neighbours and acquaintances took shape. This was characterized by a shared dissatisfaction with the village's facilities and general social atmosphere. From this circle, a coalition came into existence to attempt to do something about it. After considering the creation of a new political party oriented exclusively to what was called 'The Newcomers' Interests', it was decided to join one of the existing political parties.

All but one or two of the members of this newcomers' coalition had no outspoken political preferences; in the cities they had never participated in political activities apart from voting.

After visiting the Stroomkerken municipal council meetings several times, some members of the coalition decided to contact the councillor for the P.v.d.A., who had made a favorable impression upon the visiting newcomers by opposing several proposals of the burgomaster. They thought all other councillors did nothing but nod assent to everything the burgomaster or one of the aldermen said. The P.v.d.A. councillor reacted positively on hearing the newcomers' complaints, saying: 'You have come to the right place. If there is any party in Stroomkerken willing to help you, it is ours!'. The councillor promised to present their case to some prominent party members. His friendly behavior, however, led the newcomers to consider ever-increasing demands. They decided that they would offer to register as party members in exchange for the guarantee that at least one of them would be given an eligible place on the list of candidates for the coming elections.

In the negotiations that followed, not all members of the party's executive committee agreed with the newcomers' demands, but the majority were clearly in favour. Some stressed the party's need for 'fresh boood', as several of the party's leaders were planning to withdraw because of their age. In the spring of 1970, several months before the elections, the list of candidates was published. There were three newcomers among the first five candidates, one of them in second place. Moreover, in the elections for a new party executive committee, the chairman and the treasurer were replaced by newcomers. The P.v.d.A. obtained three seats in the council, one more than it had, so that this party came to be represented by a councillor who had lived less than one year in the village.

Within the P.v.d.A., a 'working consensus' (Goffman 1959:9-10) was found between the Stroomkerken members and the newcomers. This appeared to leave ample room for the latter to use the party as a vehicle for their own interests, notably a policy directed to the creation of typical urban facilities in the village. Moreover, old positions within the party were vacated and completely new ones were created to be occupied by newcomers. Within less than a year after the first contact, the newcomers occupied more than half of the 29 party positions. While it is normal for any party official to occupy more than one position in the party structure, the eight officials of Stroomkerken origin occupied an average of about one and one half positions, whereas the newcomers secured an average of four!

The newcomers justified their dominant position within the party by arguing that the lack of urban facilities in the village was just one reflection of the profound backwardness, stubbornness and dullness of the local population. They tended to see themselves as sophisticated men of the world, with a kind of natural right to 'shake up' the village. They did not hesitate to bring forward these feelings of superiority in demanding positions of power and whatever they strove for, both within the party and in the village as a whole. From their point of view, then, there were in fact no boundaries of any importance around the political arena. The first party they came in contact with received them very generously, despite some weak opposition. In other words, the party's frontiers were not guarded, tresspassers were not checked. They could not offer anything more valuable than a number of complaints about the way they felt they were being treated by the Stroomkerken authorities and inhabitants and some vague promises about their trying to secure part of the newcomers' votes in het municipal elections. Obviously this was sufficient for the P.v.d.A.

ASSIMILATION-CAREERS: THE A.R.P. AND THE NEWCOMERS

While the P.v.d.A. offered eligible places to what in fact could be called 'strangers', the newcomer who figured high on the list of A.R.P. candidates was no stranger at all. Though he came from Rotterdam, in 1970 he had already lived in the village for five years. In contrast to the newcomers in the P.v.d.A., this man had built up a social career in the Christian corporate life, had been a loyal churchgoer and showed a positive attitude towards the Christian part of the population. This does not imply that he did not complain about the difficulties of adapting himself to the people and the living conditions in the village. Neither had he gained full confidence of the party leaders. Indeed, after his first performance as a councillor, some of the latter more or less openly regretted having chosen him as their party's representative.

He told me more than once that he had been very surprised to have been invited to be one of the party's eligible candidates. He himself did not approach the party, and he was singled out on the party's conditions, not on his own. The special interests stressed by the P.v.d.A. newcomers were not recognised as legitimate by the A.R.P. In this party's view, newcomers ought to adjust them-selves to existing local relationships, and they were not expected to feel superior. A newcomer might participate only after having lived in the village long enough to know the local 'rules of the game'. The A.R.P. newcomer met this condition, more or less. He frequently commented upon the behavior of his fellow newcomers in the village as follows:

When I came to live in this village I understood little of the way it was put together. I was shocked by some things, attracted to other things. I kept quiet for some years to look around and learn. Gradually I managed to get the feel of the situation. For three years now I have been the leader of my church's youth club and now I understand things much better ... I am against the negativistic attitude of the Rotterdammers (i.e. 'people from Rotterdam', a usual way of designating the Stroomkerken newcomers). They seem to think they can step on everything here. They have no positive offers to make ... They are destructive and they shit on the church ... In the council people with experience and wisdom are needed. Not only technical know-how is needed, but especially political know-how, which is just the thing these Rotterdammers do not have. They have no insight in the political atmosphere of a small village...

In this comment the difference in attitudes between the *noodforensen* and the pragmatic dualists is clearly demonstrated.

For the majority of the P.v.d.A. leaders, anyone willing to be a member of the party can in prin-ciple become one. Certain personal characteristics – such as style, education, manner of speech – are generally sufficient to qualify as a representative of the party. In contrast, the A.R.P. is rather exclusive. Certainly people cannot be prevented from voting for the party (if there should be anyone willing to prevent this), and it is rather difficult not to allow people to become members of the party after they have formally declared approval of the party's principles. But to qualify as a representative, a councillor, member of the executive board or some committee, one has to be religious, join and be active in Christian associations, have one's children educated in 'Schools with the Bible', and show a sound knowledge of local political relationships, including sufficient detailed background information about people and places.

This contrast was reflected also in the styles of behavior of the respective newcomers. The one associated with the A.R.P. met with much criticism from his fellow party members. Both in the council and outside, his style was rather uncertain. The P.v.d.A. newcomers, on the other hand, met almost no overt criticism in their party and behaved rather free and easy.

Insight into the specific nature of the differential boundedness in the village might be gained by comparing the respective resources – power position and organisational strength – of both parties concerned. In the following comparison I analyse the parties' power positions by pointing out some important features of the history of the village as a whole and of each party in particular.

THE ANTI-REVOLUTIONARIES

At the end of the last century (1890) a local branch of the A.R.P. was established in the village. Its purpose was, among others, to organise the opposition against the powerful liberals, both in the village and in the region. Until universal suffrage was realised in 1917, the struggle between the Calvinists and the liberals in the village was mainly a struggle between two factions of big farmers. Particularistic interests seemed more important than ideological contrasts. After 1917 the A.R.P. succeeded in developing into a strong party. Thanks to the intimate links between the party, the church and the gradually developing Christian corporate life, it included a considerable number of agricultural labourers, small shopkeepers and artisans. In the 1930s, the liberals were forced definitively into a minority position.

The A.R.P. can be seen as a strong and powerful core, held together by a common ideology multiplex relations and many overlapping memberships. Although the A.R.P. was forced to accommodate other political parties in the village, since then it has been able to put its stamp on the Stroomkerken political structure. As a result of its dominant position, many members of the party tend to see Stroomkerken as 'their' village. All accomplishments are theirs, each initiative, decision or measure concerning the whole village must have their approval.

Mainly due to the impetus of a very ambitious burgomaster in the 1950s and 1960s, Stroomkerken began offering attractive building sites both to individuals and contractors. At the same time the whole region, which always had been rather isolated geographically, was made more accessible for traffic through the construction of new roads and highways. This made it possible for the contractors in the village to attract people from the big cities, offering 'nice dwellings' in the countryside. Both party and church have tried to see that the contractors' advertisements were published in orthodox Calvinist newspapers and journals in order to reach only 'decent, Christian people' – a good example of 'pillarized thinking'. Some of the contractors, however, paid no attention to this pressure. The recruitment of new villagers appeared to be more dependent on the principles of the free market than on the orthodox Calvinists' preferences. The control of the A.R.P. did not reach beyond the village. It had to be accepted that urban migrants were not always the 'decent, Christian people', the loyal clients of the local orthodox Calvinist patrons, that had been expected. As already mentioned, most urban immigrants prefer not to become involved in village life, be it of the right or of the left. They have no economic, political or social links with the village. In general, even the religious people among them are not used to the rather strict orthodoxy of the local churches. They are not inclined to let themselves be restricted by the demands of the local confessional elite. Indeed, the newcomers who align themselves with the right are frequently dependent on it in one way or another: schoolteachers, workers in the factory, clerks in the municipal administration, etc.

The party clearly has its reservations about the admission of newcomers. Ideological purity and maintenance of power position are given priority. The party, in cooperation with the church, disposes of effective means of social control. The general increase of indifference towards the church in the Netherlands will unquestionably undermine these. With regard to the newcomers it is trying to avoid taking risks. It carries out close screening of its leaders, although some people think it is not close enough. Thus, it is not easy for an ordinary member to become the party's representative. Some people, however, are willing to pay the costs – it can be very rewarding to be a leader of the orthodox Calvinist core, to be paid respect, to belong to the notables. This is especially attractive to urbanites, used to the relative anonymity of the big city.

THE SOCIALISTS

It was only in the late 1920s that the socialist movement acquired serious adherents in the region. The specific working conditions of agricultural labourers, working and often living in close proximity to their employers with little opportunity to come into contact with other labourers, frustrated early attempts to organise them. Moreover, big farmers generally did not tolerate expressions of political consciousness by their labourers. They were allowed to vote for the employer's party, and that was all. The big farmers, both Calvinists and liberals, formed a solid bloc in these matters. Agricultural labourers, as well as labourers in the dairy factories, were repressed. In the case of both employer and employee being Calvinists, this repression might have been obscured by their common ideology and membership in the same church, whereas in the case of the employer being liberal and the employee being Calvinist or socialist or whatever, the repression might have been harsh and crude. In both cases, however, the employers pulled the strings, supported by the church and municipal authorities. A labourer who showed any 'revolutionary' tendencies – such as asking for higher wages – was fired. Once fired it was very hard to get another job, or even to benefit from governmental or church relief measures, since decisions about which persons were entitled to relief were made almost exclusively by big farmers. The church, moreover, interfered extensively in matters of politics. In orthodox Calvinist circles, socialism to a greater extent than liberalism was considered as an almost satanic ideology.

In the beginning, then, people who openly expressed socialist thoughts were ostracized and, if 'their' farmers or the church did not get them back into harness, they were practically forced to leave the village. Nevertheless, a very small socialist movement developed in Stroomkerken, supported by a handful of agricultural labourers. However, it was not until after the Second World War that a relatively full-grown branch of the P.v.d.A. emerged.

The socialists always have had a lack of proper leadership. Many agricultural labourers tried to find a job in industry outside the region. Moreover, especially after 1950, the number of farmers employing labourers has also been steadily decreasing.

Seen from the standpoint of the Stroomkerken socialists, the village is not really theirs. In a way they are strangers, hardly motivated to identify themselves positively with their social environment. Until recently it was customary for the farmers living in a certain quarter of the village to refuse to allow the building of labourers' houses there. As a party, the P.v.d.A. has few institutional links with other networks in the village.

The arrival of urbanites in the village did not prompt the party to close its ranks: there was nothing to lose. For the majority of the party members it seemed only natural for 'strangers' to align themselves with other strangers. The party was not much worried about the newcomers' claims that the village was backward and the inhabitants dull and ignorant, and that modern, urban facilities were badly needed. The lack of identification with the village's political structure made it possible for the P.v.d.A. to make capital out of the newcomers' needs for accommodation in the village. The number of party adherents increased and it was the only party which gained a seat in the 1970 elections (the A.R.P. lost one!).

This lack of boundaries, however, points to a lack of available leadership and power too. It is remarkable that there were some definitely undesirable persons among the newcomers who took over the party. As a consequence of all kinds of troubles among the newcomers, the party lost the very seat it had gained: the elected newcomer resigned his party membership, but retained his seat. There was nothing that could be done about it. After some time many Stroomkerken party members regretted their lack of resources to erect effective boundaries.

Nevertheless, among some of the newcomers a keen insight into the local political power structure is gradually developing. For the first time in their lives they have become politically involved. Thanks to their membership in the P.v.d.A. (which in the Netherlands as a whole is very powerful), they can gain the know-how of a specialised party bureaucracy. They follow courses that make them politically conscious and read books and pamphlets to educate themselves politically. Through these people, acting as brokers, the local branch of the P.v.d.A. may gain confidence and strength. The younger members of the party, recruited mainly through the efforts of these newcomers. are considering attacking the foundations of the local political system instead of trying to adapt to it.

CONCLUSION

Stroomkerken consists of social groups which have fundamental antagonistic interests, ideological (left vs. right) and economic or political (labourers vs. employers). During my fieldwork I was constantly reminded of this (Brunt 1973). I have analyzed the way the power structure of this small Dutch village is affected as a consequence of macro-economic and political change in the society as a whole. In order to explain this process at the local level, I thought it necessary to show the relative power positions of the various groups in the village from an historical perspective, making it possible to gain insight into the differential reactions to the urban newcomers of two Stroomkerken political parties. I have chosen these parties because they represent respectively the most powerful and the least powerful group in the village.

Stroomkerken is changing rapidly. This change, ultimately, is the result of the changing technical basis of an international capitalist system. In the whole of Western Europe this kind of supranational process is taking place. Like many other villages, Stroomkerken is losing its agrarian character, and is increasingly becoming a reservoir of a mobile labour force which is socially and economically no longer linked to it.

In small communities like Stroomkerken, with limited facilities for local economic development, the proportion of *noodforensen* among the newcomers will increase, provided, of course, that the village continues to expand. For them the complicated rules of the local pacification politics are meaningless. These rules do not correspond with their urbanoriented daily experiences. They were pushed from the city, not pulled to the village. Their dissatisfaction over the lack of urban facilities in the countryside will probably keep at least some of them politically active, though. If this dissatisfaction is channeled by the local socialists in the way I have described, the position of the groups which hold on to the pacification politics will increasingly be threatened.

Pillarization has been used by both confessionals and liberals to defend their privileged positions. Before the Second World War it was used by the big farmers to keep the socialists out of the decision-making structures. Now it is used to keep the *noodforensen* out, and to defend the status quo. A strong coalition of *noodforensen* and socialists, however, will force pillarization to give way to polarization.

NOTES

[1] My fieldwork was financed by the Netherlands Organization for the Advancement of Pure Research. An earlier draft of my paper was kindly commented upon by several participants of the conference. To the following persons I feel especially indepted: Jeremy Boissevain, Emmy Brunt, Thomas Crump, John Davis, Soon Young Song Yoon and Daniela Weinberg. They are not to blame for any shortcomings. In this article I present the Stroomkerken situation as it was until the municipal elections of May, 1974.

REFERENCES

Bailey, F. G.
Stratagems and Spoils. Oxford: Blackwell, 1969.

Baran, P. A. and P. M. Sweezy
Monopoly Capital. New York and London: Monthly Review Press, 1968.

Brunt, L.
The 'kleine luyden' as a disturbing factor in the emancipation of the orthodox Calvinists in the Netherlands. *Sociologia Neerlandica* 8:2::89–102, 1972.
Anthropological fieldwork in the Netherlands. *Current Anthropology* 22:2:311-14, 1973.

Goffman, E.
The Presentation of Self in Everyday Life. New York: Doubleday, 1959.

Lijphart, A.
Verzuiling, pacificatie en kentering in de Nederlandse politiek. Amsterdam: De Bussy, 1968.

Saal, C.D.
Dorp en Route, Waartoe en Waarheen? *De Gids* 4:279–286; 1972.

Sweezy, P.
Cars and Cities. *Monthly Review* 24:11:1-18, 1973.

II

On the Increasing Importance
of the Small Community
in the Irish Political Process

Mart Bax
Free University, Amsterdam

ABSTRACT

By means of data from the Irish Republic, this essay attempts to challenge the established view that the small community in modern European countries is declining politically. In Ireland, politics at the local level has been increasing; indeed, the small community has obtained more power in the national political process. This is mainly the result of the increasing importance of political brokerage. The paper describes the processes that led to this increase, and demonstrates this at the local level. Parallels are drawn with other European countries, and comments are given on the relation between brokerage and development.

INTRODUCTION

It is widely held that small communities in European countries are decreasing in importance. Demographically they are declining, and many of their functions have been taken over by regional and central institutions. Consequently, it is argued, they become an almost negligible factor in the national political process. Usually this is regarded as a normal process, as a necessary stage in the development of modernizing societies.

The present essay is an attempt to challenge this established view. It demonstrates that the small rural community in the Irish Republic has become an evermore important political arena over the past fifty years. Indeed, national politics has become to a great extent 'parochial' politics. The main determinant of this process is the increasing importance of political brokerage.[1] The Irish political elite changed from nationally oriented leaders into parochially oriented power brokers who intensify politics at the level of the parish or some slightly larger area.

The paper consists of two parts. Part One describes the main Irish national factors and processes that led to the increase of political brokerage. Part Two recounts the emergence of local power brokers in a rural parish, here called Patricksville, and the consequent intensification and parochialization of the political process. The main line of the argument is as follows: When ideological controversies decreased, politicians were no longer able to attract voters on a predominantly moral (ideological) basis. They were forced to do so on a more transactional basis, and therewith they became brokers[2]. Communication and more general management problems generated local intermediaries who act as links between the population and the politicians. These local brokers occupy a powerful position *vis-à-vis* the ordinary people and the politicians, for each is dependent upon the broker for communation with the other. In their attempts to expand and consolidate their power, these local brokers increase politics at the local level.

PART ONE: FROM NATIONAL HEROES TO GRASS-ROOTS BROKERS

The Irish Republic is a rather young independent nation. In 1921, after a five years' war against England, which had dominated Eire for some seven centuries, the southern part of the country became a Free State and founded its own government. In 1949 it became a republic.

During this period and the subsequent civil war (1922–23) and its turbulent aftermath, Ireland became strongly divided into two opposing camps. These camps constituted the basis for the newly founded political parties, *Fianna Fail* and *Fine Gael*, which have been dominating Ireland up to the present day. The basic issue in the political game of those years was Ireland's position *vis à vis* Britain. Fianna Fail, still called the republican party, propagated complete independence from England. It attracted the lower-middle and lower classes of the population. Fine Gael's stand in this turbulent period was more complicated. On the one hand, as the party of the establishment, it wanted to remain on good terms with England, for its members were economically strongly dependent upon Britain. On the other hand, it aimed at some form of self-government which the country had lost in 1800.

The first representatives of these parties who entered the *Dail* (2nd Chamber) and the county council (the main Irish form of local government) were born and bred in the country and of middle and lower-middle class. Most of them were 'true gaels'; they participated actively in the war against England, the civil war, and in other nationalistic organizations such as the Gaelic League and the Gaelic Athletic Association (GAA). They are popularly referred to as freedom fighters[3].

Not all these freedom fighters were true national heroes, and not all occupied a similar position in the political field of those days. The men with the best national records, the 'brass' of the fighters, entered the Dail, whereas the 'gunmen' in the lower echelons obtained seats in the county councils. The members of the Dail, *Teachtai Dala*, TDs for short, were almost automatically elected, and for some time reelected, on their national records. Their primary tasks consisted of making laws for the country and putting their party programme into practice. They were true national leaders. The members of the county councils (MCCs), on the other hand, were not only forced to render favours in order to obtain voters because of their less distinguished records, they were often consulted by the electorate because the majority of the voters' problems were county council matters. They were also in a favourable position to obtain prizes for their voters, as policy making and administration were to a great extent in their hands. In short, the MCCs played a brokerage role and occupied a strong position as patrons.

Thus, during the first decade of independence, one part of the political field was characterized by nationally oriented leaders who attracted supporters on a moral basis, while the other part consisted of locally oriented politicians who tied their followers more transactionally. We now consider the main factors and processes that increased political brokerage, and therewith parochialism and transactionalism.

EXPANSION OF LOCAL GOVERNMENT SERVICES: COMPETING REVOLUTIONARY ELITE

In the early 1930s, when the country settled down to more tranquil and constitutional politics, the government's tasks increased rapidly. Especially county government expanded its services with a notable speed. Local welfare services were improved and expanded, and the war-damaged infrastructure was repaired. As a result of this expansion the influence of the MCCs increased. They became powerful patrons in the countryside. With this expanded power many attempted to climb the political ladder to the Dail. They called on influential persons in the area, soliciting their help. They renewed old bonds and promises and they showed by their calls that the recipients were men of influence whose help was needed and who might expect the best services of the candidate if elected. The TDs, on the other hand, who had entered the Dail on their national records, observed that ideology and heroworship were no longer enough for a safe seat. They realized that a councillorship was a very effective means for attracting support. Consequently, they threw themselves into the 'rat race' of local government elections. They also approached locally influential persons for rallying supporters. The result of this competition between TDs and MCCs was threefold. Firstly, the need for supporters forced the increased number of candidates to compete with one another to create larger clienteles. Consequently, the bargaining power of many voters increased. Secondly, a pattern emerged which is typical today; that is, increasingly TDs began to occupy seats in the county councils, and started considering these as the basis for their power. Thirdly, local power brokers, intermediaries between TDs and electors, began to manifest themselves. Thus parochialism, transactionalism and brokerage began to dominate the whole political field.

THE PASSING OF THE REVOLUTIONARY ELITE

The increasing transactional content in the relationship between leaders and supporters, and parochialism in general, was strengthened even further when the revolutionary elite disappeared. These national figures have almost been eliminated from the scene by the passage of time[4]. The successors, the elite of today, belong to the same socioeconomic categories, but they lack a national record with which to attract voters. Therefore, they ,more than their predecessors, are compelled to build up a following by rendering as many services as possible. But since the power base of today's TD, like that of the MCC ,is predominantly located in the sphere of local government, the TD is in fact compelled to poach in the preserves of many MCCs. To do this, and to keep his very large flock together, he creates a circle of quasi-professional intermediaries. This, however, has generated a third competitor in the arena, which not only threatens the MCC's position but also the TD's. As the intermediary creates his own small following, he is thus also a broker. He may at any time hive off from his boss, start an independent life, and try to obtain a seat in the county council. If he succeeds, the TD loses part of his following and must look for ways to make up for the loss. He generates new brokers or takes them over from other TDs. Moreover, the ex-local broker replaces a sitting MCC who therewith loses his seat. Thus, creating local brokers has generated a chain of reactions in the political field, and has increased the transactional element and parochialism in politics.

THE ELECTORAL SYSTEM

The results of the processes described so far are underpinned and even further stimulated by the nature and functioning of the electoral system. Elsewhere I have described this system in detail; thus some general remarks will suffice here (Bax 1971, 1973). The system, known as proportional representation by means of the single transferable vote, PR for short, is conducted in multi-member districts. It is used for both central and local government elections. With this system the voter is given considerable power over the election of individual candidates. He has one vote, but with this single vote he can give as many preferences as there are candidates in his constituency, and express these preferences on his ballot paper. It is he – and not the party executive – who decides that order. Thus he primarily votes *not* for a party but for individual candidates. This system may promote party multiplication and independent candidates. However, the peculiar historical circumstances of Ireland indicated above have militated against this tendency and have produced a specific pattern of competition. As a result of the war against England and its aftermath, only two big parties emerged and have dominated the scene eversince. These parties have always been able to attract a stable support. Indeed, the Irish electorate has almost always voted predominantly along party lines[5]. Given these peculiar circumstances, it will be clear that competition for votes is very much confined to candidates of the same party. These persons, of course, cannot compete against each other over differences in ideology; they must do so by rendering as many services as possible to the electorate. In short, the electoral system and the political climate foster the development of brokerage and therewith of political parochialism.

REVISIONS OF ELECTORAL DISTRICTS

A final process has to be mentioned which keeps brokerage going. This is the regular remapping of the constituencies, branded by the opposition as gerrymandering. The Irish constitution requires the constituencies to be revised at least every twelve years so that the ratio between the number of seats and the electorate stays roughly the same. This rule of the political game provides the governing party with a splendid opportunity for systematically revising the boundaries in accordance with its own interests. The Fianna Fail party, which was in power for all but six years from 1932 to 1973, made ample use of this opportunity[6]. Since its foundation in 1926, Fianna Fail's strongholds have been the poor western areas. These areas, however, have been steadily losing population through emigration. In contrast, the population of Dublin and its surroundings has been increasing rather rapidly. In order to keep its power, Fianna Fail has been carving up the central and eastern areas. Although primarily intended to weaken opponents, Fianna Fail politicians have also been victims of these tactics. As a result of these revisions politicians regularly lose parts of their domains, and to make up for these losses they must infiltrate new areas. The most efficient way to do this is by creating a circle of local brokers who build up credit for their boss and subvert other politicians. This credit can be 'harvested' during the elections.

In the preceding pages the main processes have been described which changed the political elite from national heroes, who were morally tied to their voters, into locally oriented brokers who attract voters more transactionally. The rural Irish politicians of today are centrally located in country life and live and work in their constituencies. They have a strongly particularistic attitude and parochial outlook and they shrewdly manipulate their environment for their own benefit and that of their equally parochially oriented clients[7]. The pages that follow recount the emergence of local brokers in the rural parish of Patricksville and the consequent intensification of its parochial political process.

PART TWO: POLITICAL PAROCHIALIZATION IN PATRICKSVILLE

Background and Setting

Patricksville is a parish of about 1,500 inhabitants. The town, with some 900 people, is the centre of the surrounding region which consists almost exclusively of scattered farms and a few villas. The parish is the basic unit of the Catholic church, but it is also the organizational basis of many social, economic and recreational activities for which the town is the institutional centre. Like most rural Irish parishes, Patricksville has no government of its own. The administration is conducted from the capital of the county (for local government), and from Dublin for central government. Politically the population is articulated with central and local government through TDs and MCCs, who are elected from large and smaller electoral districts respectively.

Traditionally the parish is divided into two opposing camps, roughly running parallel to the town versus the rural part of the parish. These differences are the outcome of national social, economic demographic and political processes. Today, town and countryside differ in almost every respect. The countryside, the farmers' domain, is clean, prosperous and industrious, whereas the town exhibits many features of social and economic decay, characteristic of the majority of today's Irish small towns. This difference has not always existed. The town was once a flourishing centre. Up to about 1920 it was an English garrison town, and the 'barracks' constituted the basis of its prosperity. This economic boom ended abruptly, however, when Ireland became independent (1921) and the military left the town. Subsequent national processes, such as emigration, mechanization and extensivation in the agricultural sector, and the increasing influence of supermarkets and cattle fairs in nearby big towns, have caused further deterioration. Today, the town consists of old and rather poor people who can barely live on their income because the old-age pensions are low and employment is scarce.

The situation in the rural part of the parish, the farming community, stands in sharp contrast to this decay. Its population declined also, but mainly because farm labourers left. Although the farmers of this parish have never been poor, they have improved their position considerably since the Second World War. They pick the fruits of a protectionist policy which is actually intended for the agricultural problem areas in the west and south. The townspeople envy the farmers and frequently compare them with the former English and Anglo-Irish landlords, the 'ascendancy.'

The contrasts between town and countryside are also found in the sphere of party policial affiliation. The countryside is almost exclusively Fine Gael, whereas Fianna Fail dominates the town. This division is the result of a slow but often very rough process of polarization which started long before the two parties came into being. Several times people were killed during the clashes that took place between 1900 and 1935, and each camp blames the national political leaders of the other for what has happened. The outcome of this turbulent process has bedevilled parochial life up to the present day.

In spite of its small size and its rural character the parish presents clear differences in prestige, status and power. Indeed, the inhabitants are very class conscious, and they quickly provide the outsider with a status scale and a picture of the community's 'socializing circles' or cliques. The three circles that concern us here are the farmers, the 'bastard aristocracy,' and the 'Joe Soaps.' The farmers occupy the highest rung of the ladder. They are the backbone of Irish society. Today, most of them are not much involved in local activities, though there was a time when they were. (I come to that shortly.) The farmers numerically form a large category, and their power base is considerable, though previously it was more important. These days, some 40 townspeople earn their living as farm labourers, and they can of course be fired. The farmers also patronize the three big shopkeepers in town, though increasingly they run their errands in the larger towns nearby. Furthermore, the farmers also form an ideologically closely connected group; they are all Fine Gael voters. This ties them together and enables them to close ranks and form a strong coalition. Another important circle that stands closer to the ordinary townspeople is the 'bastard aristocracy.' It includes the bank clerk, the creamery manager, some local government officials, the three big shopkeepers, the teachers, the midwife, the home assistance officer cum registrar ad interim. Although almost all are of local stock they feel a cut above the rest through their better education, work and income. They occupy a hybrid position in the community and are not popular with the local folk. On the one hand, they are community oriented and active in many voluntary associations. On the other hand, they try to socialize with the farmers' circle where they are, however, not completely accepted. The bastard aristocracy, though numerically weak, have a very strong power base. Many townspeople are dependent upon them for work and other prizes. Another factor that strengthens their position in the local arena is their close relationship with the farmers. Almost all of them are of farming background, born and bred in the parish, and eight out of a total of twelve share party affiliations with the farmers. The remaining four joined Fianna Fail to protect and continue their jobs. The local population, however, does not regard them as 'true gaels' and therefore looks down upon them. Despite this division, however, the bastard aristocracy form a fairly coherent group and will constitute a united front against the ordinary townspeople.

Finally, there is the ordinary population of the town, usually referred to as the 'Joe Soaps.' They are looked down upon by farmers and bastard aristocrats. Their power base is very limited. Indeed, many are dependent upon members of the other circles. Yet for three reasons they are a potentially strong grouping. First, their strength lies in their numbers, for they outnumber farmers and bastard aristocrats even if these join forces. Second, they are tightly connected by a common ideology. Almost all are Fianna Fail supporters, and either their parents or they themselves were active in the IRA. Third, a high degree of interaction exists between them. They meet in the pubs and the streets, they are members of the Gaelic Athletic Association (GAA), and as the poorest category of the community they are tied by relations of mutual help. These factors bind them together into a tightly united group, and provided that personal interests are not damaged, they will join forces against their common enemies, the farmers and the bastard aristocrats.

THE EMERGENCE OF LOCAL BROKERS

These three groupings dominated parish politics for a long time. The most important and long-lasting parochial political game in which they were involved took place between 1948 and 1956. Since it forms the background of another game in which local brokerage manifested itself, a short sketch of that antagonistic period must be given. The central issue in this game was: Who is going to govern the town's recreational activities? Up to 1948, the main activities (the horse fair and the carnival week) had been organized by the leading members of the GAA, all Joe Soaps who had been active in the IRA. In 1948, their power position was threatened by parish priest canon O'Toole, who introduced *Muintir na Tire*, a community development organization, and appointed some farmers and bastard aristocrats as members of its governing body, the council. The GAA core did not like this new organization, but they became violently opposed to it when the canon declared that from now on all communal activities should be organized by Muintir's council. The years that followed were characterized by a series of antagonistic interactions between the council and the GAA core. The council, supported by the bastard aristocracy and the farmers, attempted to consolidate its position. The GAA core tried to rally the support of the Joe Soaps with whom they were closely connected. But they were seriously handicapped: many of the townspeople were tied trans actionally to farmers and bastard aristocrats. About 1952, however, the tide turned in the GAA's favour when most of the farmers left the scene. This was the result of both a clash with the canon and the bastard aristocracy and the more general process of the increase of scale. Increasingly the farmers went to the nearby bigger towns to meet their economic and recreational needs. Finally, in 1955, the GAA, regained its power position and dominated Muintir's council.

This period of GAA domination came to an end after 1957. In that year, Kevin Shaughnessy, a bastard aristocrat and a leading member of the former Muintir council, obtained an important asset that was to change the balance of power. During the 1957 general elections, Con Doherty from the big town of Clonferry obtained a seat in the Dail. Doherty took advantage of the declining power of the former national freedom fighter Sean Pearse of Streamtown, and replaced this Fianna Fail politician in the Dail. However, Doherty had to expand his support and consolidate his power, for not much had been heard of him in several areas. To show his influence, or 'pull' as this is popularly called, in the area of Patricksville he selected his nephew Kevin Shaughnessy and asked to inform him of everything that turned up and might improve his position there. For Shaughnessy this was a unique opportunity for strengthening his own position in the local power struggle and that of the old council of Muintir. Through his connections with his uncle he could bring many new prizes into the community. By means of these prizes, and with the help of farmers and bastard aristocrats, upon whose services many townspeople depended and with whom he was closely connected, Shaughnessy was able to build up a clientele and put many GAA supporters on half pay.

With the introduction of this new role into the community, parochial politics changed. New ways to win support and new external resources were added to this game and turned it eventually into a party political game.

The years that followed were characterized by expansive activities from Shaughnessy and the results were remarkable. In 1960, a large part of the ordinary townspeople was in one way or another dependent upon his prizes and services. Since they knew that the continuation of their favours, or those of their close relatives and friends, were in Shaughnessy's hands, they dared not go against his wishes in Muintir. Some stayed away from the meetings, while others joined him openly to curry favour with him. The GAA camp thus saw its support crumble to a few. 'We were utterly bewildered, we felt spoofed, and we did not know how to hit back,' a member of the GAA core told me. Moreover, four pro-GAA representatives on the council of Muintir were forced to renounce their allegiance to that camp because they were patronized by Shaughnessy. By the end of 1960, the old council camp and its moral supporters had won back their power position and ruled Muintir again. Thus, it became widely known that Shaughnessy was *the* man for 'good pull.' Although Doherty was the official national representative for the area, the population looked primarily to Shaughnessy for help and they acted according to his parochial wishes. Thus 'Fianna Fail politics had turned into Shaughnessy politics,' as an informant put it clearly. The following example illustrates how Shaughnessy got many Joe Soaps into his toils:

THE CONSTRUCTION OF ST. BREANDAN'S PLACE

Early in 1959, Kevin Shaughnessy informed a general meeting of Muintir that he had good news from Con Doherty. Their TD had told him that the county council had ratified a plan for the construction of 20 new cottages in town. This was indeed good news for the community. It meant not only new housing facilities but also work for local craftsmen and labourers, since the county council usually selects a tender from a contractor of the area concerned. For Shaughnessy this scheme was a unique opportunity to subvert the GAA camp. Indeed, it might enable him to restore the power of the old council camp. In order to obtain maximal results he undertook a very shrewd course of action which is now widely known and called a public scandal. First, he went to the local builder cum contractor and told this man that he, Shaughnessy, might be able to obtain the contract on certain terms. The two made a deal. Shaughnessy would do his best to obtain the contract, and if he succeeded he was entitled to select the craftsmen and labourers for the work. Moreover, our local broker would also receive £100 for 'services rendered.' Shaughnessy's next step consisted of a chat with his uncle. He explained to the TD that the builder was anxious to obtain the contract, and the terms Shaughnessy had stated. He said that this was *the* opportunity for Doherty to increase his 'pull' in Patricksville. Doherty found it an attractive plan and promised to see what he could do in the county offices.

Two months later, Shaughnessy was informed that the builder's tender had been accepted by the county council. Now he could take a third and most effective step. At a fireside chat of Muintir he told them that their local contractor had been selected. This would provide work for the community. To give each applicant a fair chance, however, the builder had asked Shaughnessy to constitute a small selection committee. This consisted of the builder, himself, and the home-assistance officer. Shaughnessy invited those who were interested in a job to register with one of the three, where upon the committee would decide.

During the weeks that followed, the committee members were besieged with candidates. Shaughnessy, however, had figured out who had to be selected, and he made sure that his proposals were accepted. Eventually more than 40 persons were selected.

BROKERAGE IN FULL SWING

Early 1961, the game that has been described so far took an abrupt turn. This was the result of the death of the Labour MCC from a nearby small town. Although his seat was filled by coopting his former running mate, a vacuum in the regional balance of power remained. The successor was weak and rather unknown, whereas his predecessor had always attracted many personal votes, even from Patricksville which is predominantly Fianna Fail. During the years that the old Labour MCC represented the area, Patricksville had not attempted to nominate a local Fianna Fail candidate. His chances would have been too small with a powerful Labourman on the doorstep. In this new situation, however, and with local government elections in the near future (1962), a popular and or influential inhabitant might well have a chance.

Shaughnessy was the first one to discern the implications of the recent events. He thought them highly favourable for converting his local credit into political office. To that end, however, he needed the support of the local Fianna Fail club, for the club nominates its candidate. But the number of his supporters was small; the majority, consisting of leading GAA members, was violently against him. Furthermore, he needed the support of other political clubs in the area who together nominate the candidates at the nomination convention. And in this regional field Shaughnessy's position was also weak, for he had only a few connections in the area. However, he started working for the realization of his goal and therewith the battle scene changed from Muintir to the local political club. In the following months he changed the power balance in his favour by bringing new members (clients) into the club, and by putting two influential club officers on halfpay. In the regional arena, however, he was not fortunate. Here his opponents were stronger. Under the leadership of Tadgh O'Sullivan, the local shoemaker, journalist and electricity meter reader, the opposing camp went along to all the clubs in the area and canvassed against Shaughnessy's nomination.

By the end of 1961, when this regional competition was in full swing, new obstacles turned up which were to be fatal for Shaughnessy. These were the result of changes in the regional balance of power. During the 1961 Dail elections, Shaughnessy's boss Con Doherty lost his seat in the Dail. A main reason for his defeat was the revision of the constituencies through which Doherty lost a number of votes. A fellow party TD had infiltrated his area with the vigorous help of Sean Dwane from Streamtown, who now wanted to gain a seat in the county council. Dwane has a widely ramified network of contacts, and with the help of O'Sullivan and his friends he was able to give Shaughnessy a showdown. In the local government elections of 1962 Dwane won the seat and Shaughnessy was defeated. This was a tremendous victory for Shaughnessy's local opponents, though his power was not yet destroyed, as we see shortly.

COMPETITION BETWEEN LOCAL BROKERS

With Sean Dwane's election in 1962 as the Fianna Fail MCC for the area, the political game entered a new and for this description the final stage. Although major clashes between the two camps did not take place during the next few years, the balance of power began to change. This was the result of Shaughnessy losing much power and of O'Sullivan's offensive. The star of local broker Shaughnessy was decending for a combination of reasons. To begin with, when his boss Con Doherty lost his seat in the Dail, Shaughnessy's prestige received a serious setback. Indeed, it was decreased even further by O'Sullivan and his friends, who told the population that Doherty was no longer interested in Patricksville. Doherty, now an ordinary MCC, would only work for the people of his own area, which was far away from Patricksville. Shaughnessy did his utmost to prove the opposite[8]. But since Doherty spend most of his time on other areas and their problems, it seemed as if O'Sullivan was right. Thus, fewer prizes were given to Patricksville with the result that Shaughnessy's credit decreased.

Another reason for Shaughnessy's declining influence was the election of Sean Dwane. Dwane, now the official local government representative for the area, regularly visited Patricksville. This made Shaughnessy's role of local broker almost redundant and decreased his 'pull.'

These changes in the power balance took place almost without any purposive actions of the GAA camp. As O'Sullivan put it: 'Things simply straightened out for themselves.' After 1965, however, regional political changes brought the GAA camp new opportunities for more effective attacks. In that year Sean Dwane was elected as the Fianna Fail TD for the western part of the constituency. His improved position on the political ladder, however, created communication problems. Dwane had to live in Dublin for some days of the week, and his area had now become very large. These two factors made it impossible to make regular and frequent tours along all his local clubs. During his absence somebody had to look after his interests which might be harmed by Doherty or his local man Shaughnessy. He selected Tadgh O'Sullivan for this job because Tadgh was an influential member of the local club and a leader of many in the community. O'Sullivan accepted the job enthusiastically, for it provided a splendid means for attacking Shaughnessy. Indeed, it might even enable him to make a bid for a seat in the county council. The period that followed was thus characterized as a competition between local brokers for supporters. My neighbour in Patricksville, a small shopkeeper, described those years very vividly. His phrase illustrates also clearly who was the strong man and why. He said: 'It was like them saints in the chapel. You prayed to saint Tadgh for the grub, but you promised saint Kevin (Shaughnessy) a candle when he helped you out'.

With the experience that he had acquired in previous situations, O'Sullivan started attacking Shaughnessy and his supporters wherever possible. His first attacks took place in the arena of Muintir. He agitated publicly and criticized Doherty for having failed to provide some local amenities asked for. 'If there was pull in that man,' he proclaimed, 'he should come out and show it.' To illustrate that there was real pull in the area, O'Sullivan would take up the matters with Dwane, and see that the amenities would come. A month later, he produced a letter from the county offices stating that the amenities would come shortly. Similarly, he started opposing the parish priest.

To many people it became clear that Dwane was *the* politician for the area, and that O'Sullivan was his right-hand man. Thus Tadgh built up his political credit. His star rose very quickly, however, when he announced that a long desired industry would be established in town. Boss Dwane had obtained a grant from the government for establishing a knitting industry which provided full-time employment for some 25 persons. This was of course splendid news for the community. More importantly, it strenghtened the basis of O'Sullivan's power *vis-à-vis* the local people, for *he* in fact could select who would obtain a job. The population realized this and O'Sullivan made use of it. From that date our local broker has been hearing many 'confessions.'

The results of O'Sullivan's activities for the local power balance were remarkable. Before he had started his actions, the balance had already tilted in his favour as a result of Doherty's defeat. But when he began to establish his name as local broker this process accelerated. Many persons who had supported Shaughnessy now disappeared, whereas others simply crossed the floor and followed O'Sullivan. And after 1965, when Con Doherty openly declared that he would no longer stand as a Dail candidate, O'Sullivan got rid of opponent Shaughnessy, who now definitively lost his power base.

CONCLUSIONS

In the previous pages I attempted to disprove the widely held notion that the small community in modern European countries is on its decline. I did this by means of data from the Irish Republic. In that country politics at the local level has been increasing. Indeed, the small community has obtained more power. This is clearly illustrated in the nature of today's national political process and in the role of the public representative. Small parochial and regional issues dominate the debates in the national arena, the Dail. The main task of today's Irish politician consists of looking after personal and local problems. The emergence of local intermediaries, powerful links between the politician and the local electorate, has intensified this trend.

It may be objected, however, that this development is unique for Ireland. I think it is not. Although rather specific factors intensify politics in the Irish small communities and give it more power in the national political process, similar developments are to be found in many European countries. People start turning back to life in the countryside and attempt to defend their small communities against the power of the centre. Locally and regionally based groupings are organized and demonstrate, boycott, or take more violent action against the centre's directives. Indeed, their actions seem to be successful. In Ireland a part of a politician's constituency (a political machine) is capable of preventing the government from closing a regional hospital; in Holland a rural town organizes a pressure group against the government for the preservation of an old windmill, and succeeds; in Germany a combination of villages successfully opposes the government's plan for a speedway through their area. In short, in all these countries a change in the balance of power is taking place which is in the advantage of the small communities. This change, of course, has to do with the development of the welfare state policy. This policy, developed to bridge the gap between the centre and periphery, now almost automatically leads to a decrease of the centre's power. Thus, in the national power process the small community is on its way to becoming a factor of importance. Another conclusion can be drawn from the previous description concerning the relationship between brokerage and development. Many scholars regard brokerage as a function of a society's stage of development. When dealing with this topic they refer particularly to the government's policy of centralization by means of a rapidly expanding bureaucratic apparatus. Roughly they argue as follows: When the centre plants out its bureaucratic units throughout the country, it thereby creates the channels for the population to communicate directly with it. In that case, they argue, brokerage will disappear, or at best continue to play only a minor role[9]. From my description it is clear that this argument does not hold for Ireland. In that country increasing centralization and bureaucratization has not led to a decrease of brokerage; indeed, the phenomenon has been increasing[10]. By means of the centre's general development policy ever more fields are created in which brokers can operate.

Why then is there no direct connection between centralization, bureaucratization and the fortunes of brokerage? This question can be answered if one realizes that centralization and bureaucratization are elements of a larger process of increasing communication between a centre and other parts of the society. It is a twoway process, between at least two parties, and with two communication paths. The centre of any developing country attempts to infiltrate the lives of the population *directly*, by means of its expanding bureaucratic apparatus. Ideally the other side of the process is that the population makes *more direct* use of these communication channels. These two aspects of the process must be distinguished and dealt with separately, for they need not go hand in hand. The centre may well increase its direct influence on the rest of the country through an ever-widening formal system of bureaucratic organization. At the same time, however, the population may continue to communicate with that centre through informal, face-to-face contacts of brokers. Put differently, increasing communication from the top need not correspond with similar initiatives from the bottom. Factors specific for each country may be at work which encourage resistance from the bottom to straight communication with the top and help to maintain brokerage. For Ireland this is the strong particularism and parochialism of politicians, bureaucrats and voters. These cultural traits are kept alive because Ireland is basically still a preindustrial society of small farmers. Indeed, the mechanics and implication of the electoral system support these cultural traits. Thus, there is an interplay between the working of the electoral system and the population's particularistic world view; the two reinforce each other. The population expects the politicians to act as brokers, and the electoral system reinforces these expectations, because it compels the latter to play this role. Finally some remarks about the methodological relevance of studying small communities for understanding larger processes. It is a commonplace among Dutch sociologists that even if we investigated a thousand communities we still would not understand Dutch society. Similar remarks can be made regarding all complex western societies. Clearly, the small community is no small replica of the larger society, no microcosm in which everything of society is reflected and thus can be investigated. This statement, however, illustrates a widely held idea about the nature of society and its constituent parts. The small community and the larger society are usually presented as polar concepts. This polarization has given rise to different specializations: anthropology studies the small community and sociology the larger whole. It is time that we abandon this polarization, for the small community and the larger whole are not separate things, but mutually dependent elements of the same total configuration. Each influences the other and each generates processes that are relevant at the level of the other. This interdependency has been illustrated above for Ireland. The generation of local brokers was the result of processes at the national level, but their activities in the grass roots greatly contributed to the nature and intensity of the political process at a higher level. It is time that we as anthropologists abandon our preoccupation with village and village-outward studies and focus on this interdependency, for only then will our knowledge of *society* increase. In this view the small community is no more than a convenient starting point for analyzing *societal* processes.

NOTES

[1] Brokerage is described here as any process, activated by a person or a group of persons (the broker), through which communication is brought about, either directly or indirectly, between two or more social aggregates which are located at different points in the power hierarchy.

[2] These polar concepts of moral and transactional are derived from Bailey (1963, 1969). Followers are mobilized on a transactional basis when their motive is calculation of profit and advantage. Supporters are recruited on a moral basis when this transactional element is absent.

[3] More information on these revolutionary elites is given in Cohan (1970) and Bax (1973).

[4] In 1965, only 15 TDs out of 144 were still in this category, and after the general elections of 1969 their numbers decreased even further.

[5] The party loyalty during Dail elections is clearly illustrated by Chubb (1971:157). This author observes: 'Throughout the history of the state never fewer than six and usually seven or eight out of ten of all electors have supported one or the other of the two major parties and another has supported the Labour Party. Moreover, analysis of the results of the elections of 1957, 1961 and 1965 show that almost all electors who gave their first preferences to major party candidates gave their second preferences to other candidates of the same party.'

[6] Constituencies were revised in 1923, 1935, 1947, 1959, 1961, 1968.

[7] More details on the elite are given in Bax (1973).

[8] The allegations of O'Sullivan were not true. Doherty was determined to enter the ring again in the 1965 general elections.

[9] Cf. e.g. Barth, 1963; Bailey, 1969; Blok, 1969; Scott, 1972; Silverman, 1965; Weingrod, 1968; Wolf, 1956.

[10] Chubb (1971:222) observes that the bureaucratic apparatus more than doubled in personnel between 1945 and 1965. For more details on centralization and bureaucratization see also Bax (1973).

REFERENCES

Bailey, F. G.
Politics and Social Change. Orissa in 1959. London: Oxford University Press, 1963.
Stratagems and Spoils. A Social Anthropology of Politics. Oxford: Basil Blackwell, Pavilion Series, 1969.

Barth, F. (Ed)
The Role of the Entrepreneur in Social Change in Northern Norway. Bergen-Oslo: Norwegian Universities Press, 1963.

Bax, M.
Kiesstelsel en leider-volgeling relaties in Ierland. (Electoral System and Leader-Follower Relations in Ireland) *Mens en Maatschappeij*, 46:366–375, 1971.
Integration, Forms of Communication, and Development: Centre-Periphery Relations in Ireland, Past and Present. *Sociologische Gids*, 19:137–144, 1972.
Harpstrings and Confessions. An Anthropological Study of Politics in Rural Ireland. Amsterdam: University of Amsterdam Press, 1973.

Blok, A.
Variations in Patronage. *Sociologische Gids* 16:365–379, 1969.

Chubb, B.
The Government and Politics of Ireland. London: Oxford University Press, 1971.

Cohan, A. S.
'Revolutionary and Non-Revolutionary Elites: The Irish Political Elite in Transition; 1919–1969.' Unpublished Ph. D. thesis, University of Georgia, Athens, 1970.

Scott, J. C.
Comparative Political Corruption. Englewood Cliffs, N. J.: Prentice-Hall, 1972.

Silverman, S. F.
Patronage and Community-Nation Relationships in Central Italy. *Ethnology* 4:172–189, 1965.

Weingrod, A.
Patrons, Patronage, and Political Parties. *Comparative Studies in Society and History* 10:377-400, 1968.

Wolf, E. R.
Aspects of Group Relations in a Complex Society: Mexico. *American Anthropologist* 58:1065-1078, 1956.

12

Ethnic Identity, Resource Management and Nation Building in Northern Norway

Waling T. Gorter
University of Amsterdam

ABSTRACT

This paper discusses some of the problems which arise when ethnic minority groups in northern Norway come into contact with Norwegians, the dominant ethnic group in the country. One of the responses is to establish formal organizations. As long as these are multi-ethnic they assist peripheral communities to benefit from national resources. Ethnic revitalization movements, however, fail to exploit national resources for these communities because they are manipulated to serve only the interests of their leaders.

INTRODUCTION

When examining the meaning of small communities in the context of (supra) national processes in Europe, one ought first of all to pay attention to the main ideological backbone of the nation (or state, country, policy) in question. Typical of many European states, since the time of the Enlightenment at least, are administrative systems which do not recognize ethnicity. The constitutional laws of these states reflect the Platonic principle that all men should be treated as equals, whether they are equal or not. As long as an 'administrative system' is based on the non-recognition of ethnicity and equal treatment of all citizens, it is an easy task to show the system as proof of impartiality and equal opportunity. But it is in fact the culture of the dominant ethnic group that is reflected in the 'administrative system'.

In Europe the nation-state emerged as part of the historical process of integration. Integration brought about (and was partly brought about by) a reduction of relative power differentials (Elias 1972). One result was the extension of the administrative system to the periphery of Norway. In northern Scandinavia various ethnic groups increasingly come into contact as the process of integration continues. The accurate delineation of national borders there is recent, and they have not coincided with the cultural borders, but rather with the balance of power of the nations. The last border adjustment occured at the end of the Second World War.

In this paper I discuss some problems that are likely to arise when ethnic minority groups increasingly come into contact with the ethnic majority group dominating the administrative system of the state. This discussion focuses on Laxefoss,[2] a small immigrant community in northern Norway, a result of supra-national processes. One of the consequences of nationism (the expansion of the nation-state) is the Norwegianization of the community.

I will at the same time discuss the two-way relationship of Laxefoss with the outside world. As Laxefoss is inhabited by individuals belonging to various ethnic groups (a common situation in many small communities in this part of Norway), the problem will amount to *why* these people got together and *how* a sense of belongingness and cooperation developed among them. I will argue that such development was made possible by formal organizations that were not based on ethnicity. All formal organizations are branches or copies of organizations already present in Norwegian society. Through these Laxefoss articulates with the larger Norwegian society and people defend their interests. The way people in Laxefoss have developed a sense of belongingness and cooperation by activities in formal organizations is unusual for a multi-ethnic village in this part of Norway. I will explain why people in Laxefoss were able and willing to make use of formal organizations. The integration of various ethnic groups in these formal organizations in Laxefoss allows the community as a whole to integrate on a national level. This paper therefore deals with *two* types of integration.

NORTHERN NORWAY AND LAXEFOSS

Today most of Laxefoss' 206 inhabitants endure the cross-pressures of multiple ethnic identity. Norwegian citizenship is becoming the basis for identity management by the people. This in itself is a result of pressure for cultural unification and uniformity. Pressures like these both cause and result from increasing integration in the Norwegian society[3]. Most inhabitants, however, also acknowledge Finnish ethnic identity; a minority accepts Skolt identity, and a few Same identity[4]. In fact, only the school teachers and their families and some other inhabitants can claim exclusive Norwegian identity. They experience the advantages of not having to toil with cross-pressures and language problems and of belonging to the ethnic majority group in the township, the province and the state, advantages which can work against them in contacts with people who can manipulate multiple identity. The 'pure' Norwegians also rank highest economically. In most households today Finnish is used for colloquial communication, the so-called 'kitchen-Finnish' (*kjökkenfinsk*), although everyone can converse in Norwegian.

In line with other studies of small communities whose inhabitants belong to ethnic minority groups, we may expect that crises of ethnic identity and interethnic tensions develop. Disintegration of local ethnicity and community feeling may result when such a community comes under the increasing impact of external pressures and tensions.

The comparatively stable population in Laxefoss and its smaller turnover compared to overwhelmingly 'Norwegian' communities in the same township[5], would rather seem to be due to failure to adapt to 'Norwegian' ways (partly due to the stigmatization of non-Norwegian ethnic identity), than to stable relations inside such a community or its good economic prospects. But in this respect Laxefoss is an example that contrasts with what other authors have observed. Integration does not necessarily have a disruptive effect on small communities in the periphery.

The small community on which I focus is a positive case. It offers an example of how national and international processes can cause the birth, growth and maintenance (or eventually the breakdown) of a small community. It appears that in Laxefoss factionalism resulting from external pressures can be coped with in terms of local formal organizations. These formal organizations were invariably instituted by a few Norwegians who migrated to Laxefoss. The rules, written in Norwegian, on which these organizations are based correspond to the notion of justice and equality before the law that is fundamental in Norwegian governmental actions also. Formal organizations are often not present in ethnically non-Norwegian villages. In such cases external pressures often cannot be coped with and massive emigration into larger Norwegian society results. Formal organizations can in this context be seen as tools to fight the 'enemy of integration' with its own weapons. This often turns the tables to the advantage of such a community. Laxefoss is an example of just this. I do not, in other words, believe that 'ethnic identity differences' or 'social stigma' alone can explain the continued existence of some of these communities, nor can relative distance from a larger center. There are too many exceptions to confirm such rules. In my conclusion I come back to this argument and its theoretical implications.

After World War II a social and economic enlightenment took place. In Norway the functions of the Welfare State were greatly extended to its far corners. In northern Norway there has always been a feeling of being exploited by southern Norway. (Northern Norway still imports more from southern Norway than it exports, although its international trade balances.) The social horizons of the inhabitants of northern Norway were broadened both by the two World Wars and their aftermaths. The Welfare State was born and economic funds were (in principle) indiscriminately put at the disposal of applicants. But there remains much to be done. Most important was the aid to build new houses, as many old ones had been burned or bombed by Germans and Russians or were of very poor quality.

Differences in economic and social development led to a social gap between small and large communities (or region versus center) which, due to language problems and the lagging behind of social values (so-called lagging emulation, see Friedl 1964), could not easily be bridged by formal organizations. Many people, of non-Norwegian identity in particular, did not know how to benefit from aid programs provided by the state. Unequal ability to make use of these new resources disadvantaged many small communities. It also delayed the emancipation of such small communities in Norwegian society, by creating a general feeling that they were inferior. Laestadianism, a Lutheran prophetic movement from the middle of the last century, proved no longer an alternative for social organization[6].

Integration of northern Norway in the Norwegian state and society has had rather disruptive effects on its small communities. This was the more so in communities which house a sizable number of inhabitants of non-Norwegian identity. In such communities Laestadianism had been strong. The books with prayers and sermons used are printed in Finnish, as is often the Bible (most Lapps understand Finnish, as Lappish is also a Finno-Ugrian language). Laestadianist congregationalists disapprove of formal organizations for ideological reasons, as they are against a hierarchy of persons and delegation of authority. Paine was the first one to describe the negative effects of Laestadianism on activities of formal organizations necessary for social and economic development in ethnically non-Norwegian communities in today's northern Norway[7].

But there are telling and interesting exceptions. Analysis of *why* these exceptions exist can be illuminating and help us understand the meaning of small communities as part of larger societies. It can also help understand what should be done in small communities which until now react negatively to the process of integration. Socially strong, small communities could very well change the rather one-sided contact between center and periphery, the more so as continued economic and social growth has made the peripheral areas indispensable to economic and social centers. This holds both on a national and an international level.

LAXEFOSS

During the 19th century Laxefoss was still part of the migration routes of some Skolt families. Under the impact of Finnish immigration to Laxefoss, the Skolts settled permanently by the end of the century. By 1891 immigration to Laxefoss from Finland had come to an end and a Norwegian schoolmaster established the first formal organization: the Salmon Fishers' Association. Formal organizations, at that time unknown in this area of Norway, were introduced by Norwegians, who were used to such organizations in their 'social landscape' in southern Norway. Approximately ten other formal organizations followed in due course, all introduced by Norwegians. Most of these still function. Below I shall argue that Laxefoss as a small community developed a sense of identity and cooperation of its own *thanks to* these organizations.

These organizations were introduced by people of Norwegian identity. They were not recruiting membership on the basis of ethnicity (as the existing informal activities did), but on the basis of place of cohabitation (a river valley) and or work activity. Their meetings came to function as a setting for contact between people who hardly met or spoke to each other. Still today the various clubs recruit their members from the inhabited part of the valley which is about fourteen kilometers long. Most neighbourhoods are represented in all clubs. It should be pointed out that this is different from the situation in most solidly Norwegian villages. In such villages the local clubs are often the institutionalizations of existing rivalries. This helps explain the peculiar function of formal organizations here, and also why rivalries between individuals and their allies and between neighbourhoods with different ecological interests exist *in* rather than *between* the clubs. The facts show that such rivalries are often contained (but not always!) and that external pulls and pushes are a factor, as indicated in the examples below.

Laxefoss came into being and was shaped by immigration from Finland. It was mainly an immigrant village; emigration has never threatened the existence of the community, though it may sometimes have exceeded the emigration flow from certain Lappish communities (for comparison see Eidheim 1958 and 1971a:70u) .Not all immigrants planned to stay in Laxefoss; some went on to the United States.

Due to contact with Norwegians (especially schoolteachers) in the past, the Laxefoss population has not had as many difficulties as many other ethnically non-Norwegian communities in getting the most out of the formal organizations and knowing how to manipulate them in the face of the larger Norwegian society. Even the State has lost court cases against Laxefoss-based organizations, and vice versa. As a judge is reported to have said some years ago on such an occasion: 'Do you people think that you are your own little kingdom?' *(Tror dere at dere er et lite kongdömme for dere sjöl?)* Such bits of history are codified: they become part of the local code. This small community does not show disturbing signs of disintegration under the impact of the external pressures of increasing integration. Laxefoss residents have been able to keep quite a few of their original non-Norwegian habits, such as having a sauna once a week, cooking certain dishes, speaking Finnish and Lappish or practicing a particular method of salmon fishing.

The township in which Laxefoss is situated is an administrative unit, consisting of a center and peripheral areas. The center is heavily dependent on a mining company and other firms working for this company. The local civil service is concentrated there, as are many shops and various schools. As for the different ethnic identities, the main trends in comparative numbers can be calculated from population counts and church registers.

Figures for 1801 and 1825 show the situation before the waves of Finnish and Norwegian immigrants reached the area which today is a township of its own. In 1825 of the 320 inhabitants of the township area 12% were Skolts, 78% Samer, and 10% 'mixed' (people with at least one parent of 'pure' descent). There were 320 inhabitants. Figures for 1870 and 1891 show the results of Finnish immigration to the township. In 1891, of the 1,965 inhabitants, 1% were Skolts, 37% Samer, 46% Finns, and 17% Norwegians. Figures for 1910 and 1930 give an impression of the immigration of Norwegians due to new activities of the big mining company. In 1930 there were 0.1% Skolts, 10.9% Samer, 15% Finns, 72% Norwegians and 2% 'mixed', with the population increased to 7,590. For 1971 no such figures are available, but the trend has continued. There are now 10,600 inhabitants.

For Laxefoss the development has been different. In 1825 the population of Laxefoss consisted of 97% seminomadic Skolts and 3% Finns. There were 30 inhabitants. By 1891 there were 218 inhabitants: 9% Skolts and 91% Finns. 1930 shows 9% Skolts, 86% Finns, and 5% Norwegians. In 1971, my own census of the 206 inhabitants indicates 2% Skolts, 2% Samer, 44% Finns, 11% Norwegians, and 41% 'mixed'.

In Laxefoss, integration is also reflected in the heavy increase in people of 'mixed' descent. This is borne out by collected life histories, and by a kinship table which traces everybody's kindred back to the moment of immigration. In the center of the township (about 7000 inhabitants), Norwegians dominate heavily in numbers. The processof Norwegianization continued for the center, but less for Laxefoss. To Norwegianize and populate this township has been a conscious state policy for over a century. The mining industry was founded in 1905 after other efforts to Norwegianize the area, such as stimulating farmers from southern Norway to establish themselves in the north, had failed.

The current pattern of migration to and from the township as a whole can be calculated from figures of the provincial authorities. In 1969, immigrants included 44% from northern Norway (28.2% from the same province), 25.6% from Oslo and vicinity, and 29.4% from other areas and abroad. The number coming from other parts of northern Norway and from the same province has increased. Emigrants in 1969 included 31% to northern Norway (15.9% to the same province), 42.4% to Oslo and environment, and 26.5% to other areas and abroad. The number going to the same province or to other parts of northern Norway has decreased more sharp. On the basis of these figures and others we conclude that since 1967–1968 the center has been accumulating migrants from the province, who after a few years migrate to southern Norway. Emigration exceeds immigration, but the number of inhabitants is highly stable because of a rather high birth rate (about 23%, twice as high as in Oslo). This is partly due to the youth of the people who move to the center from the periphery of the township, from the same province and from other parts of northern Norway. Labour conditions, the social and natural climate, and an air route to southern Norway can help explain migration. The opening of a civil airfield in the township in the mid-1960s has led to a dramatic increase in contact with southern Norway, as indicated by the S.A.S. transportation figures. Since 1971 there are even regular DC 9 flights every day. Finnair has weekly flights to and from Finland. In 1973 SAS alone handled 56,000 passengers at the township's civil airfield.

Compared to the center of the township, Laxefoss has quite a stable population, although emigration and immigration occur. Low immigration has contributed to the stability of the local value system, as it implies less interference by outsiders. The high population turnover in the center is another factor which helps Laxefoss keep its identity. The annual population turnover in the center is at least 7%, while it is almost nil for some peripheral areas. This high population turnover hampers contacts of small, comparatively stable peripheral communities like Laxefoss with the center, the municipal administration and thereby the wider Norwegian nation.

Improved communications and southern Norway-oriented mass media have worked in the opposite direction, however. On the basis of the population count of 1891 and my own census of 1971 I constructed population pyramids for Laxefoss, which show that the population has grown older. In 1891, 39.8% of the inhabitants were 1–14 years old, while in 1971 this number was 20.9%. People over 61 years old comprised 6.4% of the population in 1891 and 23.4% in 1971. It should be kept in mind that 1891 shows a rather young population due to a 'push' from Finland, while 1971 shows a rather old population due to 'pulls' from the township center and from the southern Norwegian center (Oslo and environment). In 1891, 94 inhabitants claimed Norwegian nationality, 111 Finnish and 13 Russian (218 inhabitants). In 1971 20 were Norwegian, and 2 were Finnish (205 inhabitants), clearly illustrating the integration which has taken place in this part of the state.

WHY, OVER TIME, HAVE PEOPLE IN LAXEFOSS GOT TOGETHER?

Let me sum up some of the main reasons why people belonging to different ethnic groups got together. It is important to note that the perception of the situation in which people found themselves differed according to ethnic group. These differences are remembered and sometimes activated in quarrels along ethnic lines. Such quarrels can cut right through the local clubs which, on the other hand, help to keep people on speaking terms with each other. Why and how these formal organizations have fulfilled these functions will be clarified later. Quarreling along ethnic lines can happen in spite of the fact that now nearly all inhabitants are Norwegian citizens. Below I sketch the main reasons for immigration to Laxefoss for each of the ethnic groups separately.

SKOLTS

Until the 1820s the only people who used the valley of Laxefoss were Skolts who had a summer salmon fishing station close to one of the waterfalls in the river. Here they had a Russian Orthodox chapel. The Skolts were half nomads; dimensions of time and place were aspects of one and the same thing[8]. Laxefoss was an in-between station. In the winter the Skolts resided more inland, in a Finnish (Russian) area where they also had a chapel and a marketplace. In the spring they moved to the mouth of a Norwegian fjord, mainly to fish for cod, their cash crop. The whole migration area belonged officially to this group of Skolts. They paid tax to both Russia and Norway (i.e. Denmark and later Sweden), each of whom disputed the right of the other to tax. Old decrees (issued by Czar Ivan the Terrible in the sixteenth century and Czar Boris Gudonov in the seventeenth century) granted them the rights to the land. In 1826 Norway and Russia came to an agreement over the disputed area and divided it between them. All former agreements, rights and privileges were abolished unless otherwise stated. The Skolts' area became divided and the Skolts *had to choose* their citizenship. Most of them chose to become Norwegian, because their salmon fishing station and cod fishing grounds were located within the Norwegian borders. The fisheries were their main source of cash income. With it they had to pay tax, buy flour, tobacco, some strong drink and fishing nets. For some time the Skolts considered the old territory as theirs: until at least 1891 some of them lived part of the year in Finland (Russian) in two family areas, where they still maintained a chapel. In the valley of Laxefoss this perception of the migration territory as theirs led to a claim on all salmon fishing and land. Not only has this resulted in conflicts with non-Skolt inhabitants, but also with State authorities. Until about 1917, a Russian priest came to say mass in the Laxefoss chapel at least once a year. Laxefoss was part of a Russian *kapellani*, and some Skolts were educated at Russian monasteries. The religious and national border did not yet coincide. Both Norway and Russia had by that time state churches.

SAMER

Until about 1870, Samer were a majority in the township, but they did not live in the valley of Laxefoss. Many of them are so-called Coast-Lapps. They were not nomadic; most nomadic Lapps of the township moved by the end of last century to another part of the province because of bad reindeer pastures and orders of the provincial authorities, while some nomadic Lapps ('reindeer Lapps') settled down. Some of these were immigrants from Finland, and a few came to Laxefoss. Descendants may refer to themselves as Finns, Samer, or Norwegians as it suits them. Coast-Lapps traditionally lived from a combination of farming, fishing, hunting and reindeer breeding. They had very few reindeer, which – as was a general habit in the area – often were used as draught animals. A number of Finnish immigrants used oxen instead.

As for most inhabitants of the periphery of the township, farming, state pensions, road labour, some fishing and work in the center of the township provide sources of income. Quite a few Samer have moved to the center and live there. Recently most of the population of Laxefoss has had an open conflict with Samer from the area around Laxefoss over the ownership of reindeer and grazing rights. Ethnic identities were (and are) manipulated in this conflict.

FINNS

Some of the reasons for Finnish immigration have to be made clear in order to show how factors outside the valley helped generate Laxefoss. Economic and demographic trends and differing legal systems on either side of national borders explain a lot. Borders in the area were not made clear until the nineteenth century, and therefore hardly had any meaning before. The province of Finnmark in northern Norway was by then the only area in northern Scandinavia where state land was distributed and settlement stimulated. Norway itself had heavy emigration from the south, but did not manage to move more than a few to migrate to the north of their own country. Many inhabitants of Finland (and some of Russia and Sweden as well) were attracted by differences in rules as to land ownership and taxation. Others were simply forced to migrate so as not to die of starvation. During the nineteenth century it happened several times that crops failed year after year in Finland. This was no new phenomenon, but the population increase was, and the combination of the two made for critical years. Given the level of technology and infrastructure, the countryside was overpopulated in such years, even in the most sparsely settled regions.

Some Finns came because they fled the Russian or Finnish police for inability to pay their taxes or debts or because they had committed crimes. Many Finns came to take part in the rewarding cod fisheries or as miners in an English copper mine in the province. At first they came as migrant labourers, and only for a season. There is some correlation between peak years in cod fishing and the migration flow from Finland. Last but not least, the province was also a migration route for Finns planning to sail to the United States, though not all of them made it that far.

In other words, the Finnish migration was part of a larger process of migration which integrated countries and continents and helped widen people's social horizons. This larger process often had far-reaching local consequences, which can only be clarified with the help of history.

In Laxefoss the Finnish immigrants disagreed with the Skolts, then among themselves, over rights to fish salmon in the river. In 1849 this resulted in a major court case in which the state ruled that all inhabitants in the valley should have the same rights. What happened has been formulated in general by Barth:

Where two or more interspersed groups are in fact in at least partial competition within the same niche ... one would ... (with time) ... expect one such group to displace the other, or an accommodation involving increasing complementarity and interdependence to develop (Barth 1969.20).

In fact both things happened. Finns became the dominant group in Laxefoss. The lingua franca was Finnish. Cooperation and interdependence between the members of different ethnic groups developed. Skolts were employed to herd the reindeer of the Finns in addition to their own.

In the beginning of the twentieth century when the mining center in the township started up, reindeer meat gained value as a commodity since there was now a market for it. The number of reindeer increased steadily, and by the end of the 1920s there were thousands of reindeer in this 'Skolt herd'. The economic crisis of the time seems to have stimulated local Norwegian teachers, a Norwegian customs officer and some Finns to oust the Skolt herders to get better control over the herd. The Skolts were even forbidden (in the renewed statutes of the Reindeer Breeders' Association in 1928) to look after their own animals. Afterwards some Samer from outside Laxefoss were employed as herders.

Likewise the prices of salmon rose sharply and caused keen competition, which somehow had to be contained to prevent total anarchy in the valley. Quarreling over land continued as dairy farming became attractive due to the mining center and the fact that the government still had not handed out all land in the valley. Lately, speculation in tourist huts has added to this problem.

NORWEGIANS

The state policy to populate northern Norway with Norwegians did not always meet with success. During the nineteenth century there were only a few Norwegian teachers, some shopowners, one clergyman, one doctor and a number of Norwegian fisherman and farmers in the township. Norwegian traders had established a hacienda type debt relationship with many inhabitants of this township. Russian traders competed with the trade of the Norwegians and broke their monopoly, and the Norwegian traders upon whom the township depended were nonresidents.

Immigration waves of Finns were at first stimulated, but Norwegianization of the area became a grave concern to the state. There was even international pressure to do so. The English government, for example, asserted that Russia deliberately Finnicized the area as an excuse for annexation. Norwegianization thus became part of an international policy intended to keep the number of Russian harbors to a minimum. Concern for the area increased during the 1920s when Finland became independent and showed expansionist tendencies, and even more so when it joined forces with Germany.

In 1902 the state built a Lutheran church in Laxefoss, facing the Russian Orthodox chapel across the river. In 1903 the state built a big school and boarding house for the area, the first one of its kind in the province. The latter was necessary to get children to school at all. A post office and a customs station were opened and a telegraph installed. The Norwegians there divided the offices among themselves. But this peaceful situation changed when in 1910 a conflict between right and left wing oriented Norwegians broke out in Laxefoss, reflecting a social struggle which raged through the whole country. A Norwegian caretaker of the boarding house made himself into an alternative leader of the Skolts and Finns. A conflict between him and the Norwegian teachers on the spot was fought out along a left-right division and both sides ended up competing for a following. The local Labour Party Association and the 'Middle-Class Village Club' were established. The right wing club lost the competition, despite much money from ruling parties, and it was not even reestablished after the Second World War. This lack of a local opponent helped to deactivate the local Labour Party Association politically. Before the last war two of its members made their way to the Norwegian Parliament in Oslo, both of them Finns. As early as 1911 a famous May day banner in the township center read 'Down with the King, the Altar and Capitalism' *(Ned med Kongen, Alteret og Pengeveldet)*. This banner and the subsequent discussion about freedom of opinion nearly brought down the government. It illustrates nicely the influence even a most peripheral township can exert.

Party activity in Laxefoss echoed a stage of integration in the larger society, but not in the township[9]. Integration in the township hardly occured until after the Second World War, when the functions of the township were extended by the Welfare State (see also Kjellberg 1965). After the Second World War center-periphery polarizations became more important than old party lines, as reflected both in regional planning and in the split within existing parties. The EEC vote in 1972 made this painfully known to some parties.

In Laxefoss, Norwegians have always been umpires, not only because of their fluency in the official language in which all requests have to be made, but also because they often had the best contacts (or best possibilities to come into contact) with authorities on the township, provincial or state level. When Norwegians founded all the formal organizations, self interest as well as idealism played a role. They found it strange to live in a place without formal organizations. Seen from this point of view, their efforts were aimed at making Laxefoss more 'Norwegian'. To this extent their aims converged with those of the state, which (in most cases) paid their salaries. These activities have – at least in the long run – had a favourable effect on the whole community, as they have helped to 'translate' conflicts along ethnic lines into conflicts where ethnicity differences are sought not to be made relevant at all (see note 3).

RESOURCE MANAGEMENT

Cooperation and a sense of belongingness in this multi-ethnic community were made possible because people could join in activities of formal organizations that were not based on ethnicity. At present there are seven local organizations which are socially important. They fall in two categories: organizations which help manage local resources, and organizations which are local branches of national organizations.

The Salmon Fishers' Association and the Reindeer Breeders' Association are organizations founded to help manage local resources. The same applies to the Agricultural Association, which falls in between resource management organizations and politico-cultural organizations.

The Salmon Fishers' Association was founded by the first Norwegian schoolteacher in Laxefoss, to create law and order in fishing affairs[10]. In order to understand the meaning of the organization for Laxefoss one must know the history behind its statutes. This also applies to other organizations and explains the lengthiness of my historical presentation.

In the 1880s many new Finnish immigrants had come and not all of them kept to the old rules for fishing in the river. They started to fish individually from their own plots of land, making the traditional practice of joint fishing impossible. There had also been ethnic problems, which, added to the manipulations by nonresident Norwegian merchants who tried to get control over Salmon fishing by establishing debt relationships, made it necessary to state explicitly that fishing rights must follow people in Laxefoss and not the land bordering on the river. In 1891 the rule was stated as follows:

Salmon fishing in the Laxefoss River shall be common privilege for all the people settled in Laxefoss who own or use land which has a registry number and who are living on that land[11].

Forty years later when defense against the new center of the township was needed, it was added that each participant in the fishing must have five dekar of tilled land (598 square yards) in use or ownership. This way the local population prevented people in the center from buying land and thereby gaining the right to fish in the river. In 1891, 29 people (households) signed the rules, along with the schoolmaster who did not yet live in the community but who had written the documents. Hardly any of those who signed could read or write Finnish, let alone Norwegian, the language used in the agreement.

By channeling collective action through the Salmon Fishers' Association it has been possible to get control over long stretches of the river bordered on both sides by state owned land. According to the law the state disposes over the fishing rights in such cases. The Association has gained control over all fishing in the 24 km. long river from the border to the fjord. The state finally acknowledged this right in the new Salmon fishing law of 1964.

A system of rights focused on fishing helps maintain the community boundaries and even comprises officially state owned areas. In this respect the community boundaries correspond to differences perceived in the control of resources.

Individual speculation, court cases, and tension between inhabitants manipulating Skolt, Finnish and Norwegian identity have caused upheavals in the Salmon Fishers' Association and at times challenged its existence. The Lappish Movement has also tried to enter here, but the association has always been able to channel such conflicts and has survived. It should be kept in mind that the Salmon Fishers' Association manages resources which are collectively owned by the members as long as they are in the valley. The activities of the Salmon Fishers' Association have jokingly been called 'minibolshevism'. But none in Laxefoss would consider this an appropriate expression for reindeer breeding, as reindeer are owned individually.

The Reindeer Breeders' Association was founded in 1911 but acquired new statutes in 1928.

Following a quarrel ten years ago there have been two boards of directors for the Reindeer Breeders' Association, each with a chairman in Laxefoss. The opposition between the two boards follows a right-left division. Right wing parties support first and foremost a few Samer who own and manage the reindeer flock once owned by all the members of the organization, but which today has a limited ownership due to various manipulations, entrepreneurial activities and the change from intensive to extensive reindeer herding and breeding. Such a change usually takes place at the expense of smaller owners[12]. These Samer themselves are supporters of and are supported by the Lappish revitalization movement. Together with related Samer who successfully exploited another comparable reindeer breeders' association in the township, in 1969 they founded a new branch association of the National Norwegian Reindeer-Samers' Association *(Norges Reindrifts Samers Landsforening)*. The new association was intended as an alternative to two old organizations, each of which split in two. Geographically the reindeer organization covers Laxefoss and the surrounding area. The largest left wing party, the Labour Party, supports the Laxefoss Finns and Norwegians who have lost their reindeer and a considerable number of Samer nearby who have also lost their animals.

The first Agricultural Association was founded in 1914. The present association, which grew out of a tractor association, is officially intended to help manage husbandry. The Association merely exists on paper, because 'when necessary we can make a common fist against the authorities'. After the war a tractor association (intended to manage the first tractor, received gratis from England) went bankrupt because of bad management: every member wanted to use the tractor as cheaply as possible, with the result that when the tractor broke down funds to repair it were lacking! People knew that this would happen but no one dared to take the unpopular initiative to set a higher price for renting the tractor. Another reason for trouble was that everyone needed the tractor during the same hectic summer month. This is typical of quite a few similar enterprises in northern Norway. (Compare Paine (1963) and Rudie (1963) on tractor innovations). The tractor was then sold to one of the inhabitants who used it profitably on his own fields and those of others until it finally broke down. The farmers in Laxefoss learned from this and all of them bought tractors. Today there are fourteen four-wheeled tractors, of which seven were bought new. There are also four or five two-wheeled tractors. This Association is a local branch of a national organization. A split in the national organization has caused some splitting in the local association also with several farmers leaving the Agricultural Association for political reasons. Before farmers had to be members of an association to get the very important state subsidies, but the law no longer requires this. This has not helped to activate the agricultural Association.

POLITICO-CULTURAL ORGANIZATIONS

Organizations which are local branches of national organizations may also be called politico-cultural organizations. The contact between the mother organization and its branches is frequently in the form of financial support going in both directions. Some branches must sell certain goods distributed by the 'mother' group.

In Laxefoss there are five organizations of social importance: the Local Labour Party Association[13] (founded in 1912); the Sports Club (founded in the 1920s); the Health Association (founded in the 1930s); the Church Association (founded just after the war); and the Lifeboat Club (founded in the 1960s). These organizations are responsible for social meetings, such as social evenings with bingo and dancing. Sometimes they are the only organizer, while at other times they cooperate with one or more of the other organizations. The local Labour Party Association, the Sports Club and the Lifeboat Club jointly arranged four bingo nights during the winter of 1971-1972, for which they earned approximately 2500 Nkr. which they invested in a record player with loudspeakers and a microphone. The clubs accumulate capital which is spent on social events. Most organized social events occur outside the hectic summer season (though common salmon fishing is in itself a social event). Social activities help people make it through the dark season when the sun doesn't come over the horizon.

Social evenings, dances and bingo cannot be announced in the local newspapers as is the habit in the area. The reason is that the 'athletics' hall of the school where the arrangements are held is not acknowledged as a 'public' meeting place. Therefore few come from outside the community (only some friends and relatives who live elsewhere in the periphery or in the center of the township). The only exception to this rule is the 'Laxefoss Skiing Competition' which is organized every year at Easter time outside the athletics hall of the school, and can therefore be announced. Many inhabitants of the center and periphery take part and consider it a real holiday. Finns from Finland also have taken part. At a jubilee of the Sports Club a few years ago, a Russian group participated. Once present at the competition, people are then informed that there will be a feast in the evening. During 1971–1972, however, quite a few Finns from Finland, Finnish Skolts and some Finnish Samer were able to drop in at the regular feasts because of the newly completed road. But they were often drunk and had hardly any money to spend. A culture conflict arose. At first Laxefoss people activated their Finnish identity and even translated all information into Finnish when they spoke through the microphone to please the visitors from abroad. On later occasions they behaved more and more 'Norwegian'. Finally, during the winter of 1972–1973 it was decided that the hall was not a public place, and the Finnish Skolts were forbidden to enter.

Other important meeting points in the valley are the three cafeterias, each of them with a beer license. This is a direct result of Finnish tourism in summer, in combination with the township's position as to licenses (the most liberal in the province). As the cafeterias are open year round, most of the time they serve the local population, while the two or three summer months make them an economic business. The cafeterias help keep the youngsters home by serving as their meeting grounds.

THE MEANING OF ORGANIZATIONS FOR INCORPORATION AND INTEGRATION

While resource management organizations incorporate to be able to protect local resources against outside forces, they work against these outside forces through the very system of law and order of the state. Politico-cultural organizations integrate the local population in the larger society by doing work which is aimed at larger political, social and cultural goals and which may be held in common on a nationwide basis. These organizations were founded on the local voting district, which follows the old school district, arbitrarily established by Norwegian administrators. They do not always coincide with perceived community borders, which can be a handicap as to the ability to found formal organizations on a community basis. Apart from Laxefoss, the voting district includes mainly settlements where Samer are a majority. As Laxefoss was the major settlement in this district, the Samer never played any part in the social activities of these politico-cultural organizations. This introduced opportunity costs which may have helped to stimulate migration from these settlements to the center of the township.

Resource management organizations are run by men, while women run the church, health and lifeboat organizations. Once a week there is a meeting of either the health or the lifeboat club. Clubs do not tend to respresent cliques, though in certain clubs some people and some neighbourhoods are more active than in others. At the health club one sings religious songs, while the meetings of the lifeboat club the songs are secular – but otherwise the meetings have much in common. There is much eating and drinking of non-alcoholic beverages. One of the main services to their members is that they provide a forum for gossip and a means for the women to discuss conflicts which are otherwise dealt with by their husbands. These organizations help unite the villagers and are a counterweight to tendencies of faction-forming in the community.

Men and women alike are active in the Sports Club and the local Labour Party Association. Both resource management and politico-cultural organizations strengthen the local feeling of belonggingness by the increasing success they have when they press township, province or state administrations to acquire something. But this does not deny setbacks[14] nor does it mean that there cannot be a minority of the members of these organizations who may disagree on a pollicy. The 1960s, in fact, show a series of conflicts within the clubs which people slowly overcame. The process of integration is cumulative and requires continual decisions. A number of persons also are members of nonlocal resource management and politico-cultural organizations such as trade unions, a cooperative in the township, or even a bingo club in the township. But local memberships are usually given priority.

SOME CONCLUSIONS

The small community is part of a process as are the lives of the individuals whom it embraces. The apparent stability produced by institutions is time and again challenged by individuals and cliques. This is no reason to neglect the study of organizations and institutions. Neither is it realistic to conceive of social life as consisting only of conflicts. I have tried to show the main forces which made people move to the valley which became 'Laxefoss'. I also tried to show how – in time – a sense of belongingness and cooperation developed in a complex multi-ethnic setting. Accounts of what happened are passed on from generation to generation as a charter. For me there was enough historical material available to check the data given. Ethnicity is one of the factors which determines which version one gets to hear. As a non-Norwegian I got to hear all sides.

It appears from my material that the sense of belongingness and social contacts in Laxefoss developed mainly from activities in, around and between formal organizations. The various ethnic identities were made commensurable to each other by organizations. These, just as the administrative system of the larger society, did not have ethnicity as the basis for recruitment, but focused solely on the management of local resources or attainment of social values. Naturally the various formal organizations do not always mobilize the same individuals, or the same number of members. And yet the net effect has been that the members of the small community have been able to develop common activities which have been to the benefit of them all. This has taken place in spite of differences in ethnicity and culture, and in spite of competition for scarce resources during which ethnic differences have been made relevant. By working through these formal organizations the inhabitants of Laxefoss have been able to press their claims as well as oppose various measures and laws of the state. As mentioned above, this picture deviates somewhat from what is often found in 'Norwegian' communities, where the local clubs are often rivals and are even founded because of existing rivalries. Laxefoss has managed well in withstanding and or accepting increasing external pressures, the corollaries of increasing integration in the Norwegian nation.

In a neighboring community where most inhabitants are Samer, further from the township center but with about as many inhabitants as Laxefoss, emigration has been stronger than in Laxefoss. The few formal organizations this community has are in fact organizations on paper only. The Laestadianist community there has disintegrated. In Veres Navolok,[15] a community with just over 500 inhabitants even farther from the center (but in the same township) and with a large majority of Finns as inhabitants, the population turnover has been almost zero for years. The number of inhabitants has tended to increase and there are reasons (new investments, e.g., in 1974 in a trawler) to believe that this tendency will hold. The community is not spread over a long valley, but highly centralized around a harbor. There are as many as three Laestadianist factions (since 1973 four), while the greater part of the non-Laestadianists is engaged in a few very active clubs. Laestadianism (to which about 50% of adults still adhere) is literally falling apart and its functions are being taken over by secular organizations. Increased communication with the outside world is responsible for this. The ecological possibilities for these three communities do not seem to be decisively different. But the ways these communities have been able to use local resources, and press the authorities to assist, differ. Possibilities for migrant labour in the center exist (and are made use of) for the three of them.

It has often been observed that the farther a community is situated from the center, the less integration one may expect. But distance from the center does not seem to be a decisive determinant for these small communities' ability to survive the integration process and political decisions favouring centralization (see below). Neither can degree of social stigma be seen as the determinant in explaining the survival potential. Both distance from center and social stigma, however, do add to the stability (low population turnover) of small communities. Where these stabilizing factors are found *and* formal organizations exist, we can expect a stable community with hope for its future existence.

Formal organizations have great importance in Norwegian social life, partly because of the peculiar politico-geographical shape of the country, and partly – I dare say – because of the climate. Boissevain (1968:21) observed that the climate affects the structure and size of personal networks. The presence of formal organizations in the environment makes them all the more needed on the local level, as they are the only adequate tool in local self defense. I believe that this applies to Norwegian small communities in general, irrespective of ethnic adherence. But in multi-ethnic communities these problems have extra dimensions, due to the presence of culturally non-Norwegian ideologies like Laestadianism, problems of culture contact, and confusing facts such as one person having several ethnic identities. Nation-based formal organizations are nationalistic implications of nationism (see Introduction). This nationalist aspect is more visible in northern Norway. Whether it justifies an expression like 'Norwegian neo-colonialism' as used by members of the Lappish (revitalization) Movement[16] is not as certain as they would have it.

As mentioned, ethnic non-Norwegian small communities often have a solidarity of their own which makes the introduction of Norwegian formal organizations very difficult. Where Laestadianism (an 'anti-colonialist' prophetic movement, see notes 6 and 7) has been strong it has only added to the problems by stressing likeness and modesty, while Norwegian formal organizations derive part of their strength from the presence of a board with a clearly defined hierarchy. Activities organized by clubs often amount to competition or dancing (which is also opposed). Laestadianism denounces competition (e.g., athletics) and Laestadianists therefore disapprove of sports, as well as books and TV (sometimes even radio) which show it. In Veres Navolok there is still no cafeteria and no beer license. The local youth is kept busy by a very successful football club. When this club some years ago was to get its first football field (which would be at the expense of potato fields of a number of Laestadianists) a referendum was held. The Laestadianists lost, and a major change in the community resulted. It cannot be argued that the introduction of formal organizations in Laxefoss was eased by the mere absence of strong social cohesiveness and kinship relations among the immigrants, and the presence of enterprising Norwegian schoolteachers. To Veres Navolok this also applies, but there no formal organizations formed before the war. Laxefoss obtained a road connection to the township in 1939 and Veres Navolok in 1963. Prior to that, both places were connected to each other and the township center by a local steamer. Veres Navolok had no boarding school, but it had a Norwegian fish buyer (which Laxefoss had not). And what is more, it can be argued also that elsewhere Norwegian schoolteachers or merchants have been active without having been able to organize people with lasting success in formal organizations. Robert Paine (1965) gives examples of this. This tempts us to conclude that the mere existence of more than one non-Norwegian ethnic group gave the presence of Norwegians a special meaning.

Someone had to solve the conflicts – in the last resort it was always the administration. The communities for which Paine (1963) describes entrepreneurial activity without its profits are solid Coast-Lapp communities where Laestadianism is a factor of importance.

My material leads me to conclude that on a local level, formal organizations based on ethnic identity can (at least in Norway, where homogeneous Lappish or Finnish communities rarely exist) only add to existing problems by mobilizing groups of people within a small community against each other. They can in this way even cause division within one ethnic group. I mentioned a community not far from Laxefoss where most of the inhabitants are Samer. The Samer are divided for and against the Lappish Movement, and this has caused a gap between Movement supporters and the others who have neither the need nor the desire to stress their ethnic identity.

In Laxefoss the revitalization movement activated some Skolts who are claiming old rights (from before the 1826 agreement) to fishing places in the river, the reindeer (now owned by the revitalization movement Samer in the community just mentioned), and to plots of land today rented from the state by the Salmon Fishers' Association. The Orthodox chapel has been restored to its old use. Once a year the bishop of Helsinki and Skolts and Orthodox Finns come from Finland to say high mass (there are no Orthodox believers in Laxefoss nowadays). This activity was organized in the 1960s by an Orthodox Finnish priest (a tourist) who contacted Norwegians (the township's committee for culture and history) in the township center. For them Samer and Skolts are exotic groups[17]. Most of the people in Laxefoss consider the Orthodox service a ridiculous event. They refer to it as a fancy-fair and 'picture-licking' (i.e. kissing the icons). Skolt identity is enhanced for the few who successfully can translate themselves into a tourist attraction. They show tourists the chapel and exploit tourist cabins and camping grounds. One of them manages to appear on television or radio programmes at regular intervals. But other inhabitants with Skolt blood are even more than before stimulated to hide their identity.

In other words, my findings confirm a theoretical observation made by Brox, who warned that apart from a needed mentality change for many Norwegians and others, there is a more important point to be made:

But, in my opinion it is more important to start and develop and press through measures which are to the advantage of all groups living in the periphery – irrespective of ethnic origin or identity. Efforts to reach such solutions will make Lapps coalition partners with the other people in the periphery, rather than competitors. This means that one gains some degree of success at the expense of society's power elite and not at the expense of other underprivileged groups in the periphery (Brox 1972: 32)[18].

When one of the criteria for membership of an organization is ethnic identity, systematic cleavages are generated. This can erode other multi-ethnic local organizations which are not organized around ethnic identity. It can split such organizations, as indeed happened with the Reindeer Breeders' Association. Such cleavages can only be avoided by having membership criteria which do *not* involve a social status which is *made into* an imperative one.

A class struggle or a women's emancipatory movement can cause structural change in society: equality before the law is a state principle but it has not yet been practiced everywhere. The Lappish revitalization movement is based on such perceived non-equality before the law, but it wants to *increase* this non-equality. This plural principle collides with the very foundation of the Norwegian legal system: the Constitution of Norway. Unlike economic classes or Women's Lib, it does not ask for *like* rights, but for *extra* rights. It could also have asked for *other* rights. This way the Lappish Movement ends up blurring the class differences among the Lapps themselves. At the moment one of the main problems of the Movement is that (apart from a few well meaning social scientists) it is being controlled by rich reindeer owners organized in the National Norwegian Reindeer-Samer's Association. The Lappish Movement embodies more formal organizations, but the most influential one is a sector-association focused on reindeer breeding. This in itself is symptomatic of the situation: it should be remembered that most are *not* reindeer breeders!

Formal organizations not based on ethnicity will make Lapps coalition partners with the other people rather than competitors. The same applies to groups among the Lapps – Samer and Skolts – as well as to Finns and Norwegians and to any other combination of these ethnic groups. It is necessary that such organizations try to force through measures which are to the advantage of all groups. In the periphery formal organizations should coordinate socio-political action – they should not divide people.

Laxefoss is an example of the result of corporate action. It provides illuminating case material. It also provides us with case material about the divisive effects the use of ethnic categories can have in the struggle for scarce resources in such a situation.

NOTES

[1] Fieldwork was carried out in northern Norway from June 1971 until May 1972. One semester at the University of Bergen, Sosial-Antropologisk Institutt and part of the fieldwork were financed by the Norwegian Ministry of Foreign Affairs. I am particularly obliged to Professor F. Barth. A postgraduate contribution by the University of Amsterdam covered another part of the fieldwork expenses, and Kari Storaas Gorter the rest. I am very grateful to Jeremy Boissevain for stimulating help and criticism. Trond Thuen (Tromsö University) was so kind as to read through a draft of this paper and help with his criticism.

[2] Laxefoss (a pseudonym) is situated in a fluvio-glacial valley and consists of 67 house-based households. Settlements along the river cover a stretch of 14 km.

[3] See also below in text: in 1891 – 94 Norwegian citizens; in 1971 – 203.

[4] For the concepts of 'ethnic identity' and 'ethnic group' see Barth 1969:13–16. But it should be kept in mind that there is no basis to call ethnic identity 'the most basic identity' as Barth does. Whether such a status is more imperative than other statuses (e.g., in connection with social class) depends on peoples' definition of a situation. Ethnic identities can appear as well as disappear; history has its own dynamic which people often try to arrest by codifying statuses. Reidar Grønhaug (Bergen University) has distilled such thoughts from the Turkish class and ethnic group situation which he studied on the spot.

In my paper, a Norwegian, Finn, Same, or Skolt is (a) someone who is a Norwegian citizen; and (b) someone who has Norwegian, Finnish, Lappish, or Skolt-Lappish as his mother-tongue and or considers himself a Norwegian, Finn, Same or Skolt, respectively. This definition follows one given by the Norwegian Ministry of Church Affairs and Education (*Kyrke- og Undervisnings-departementet* ed. 1962–1963). The above definitions give ample scope for ethnic identity management. Lack of somatic differences often makes such management all the more easy. Nation-states tend to use definitions of type (a) only. Members of a formal organization using ethnicity as a criterion for recruitment use definitions of type (b). Individuals choose among the various definitions.

[5] Compare with publications of Paine (1965) and Eidheim (1958, 1971a and 1971b).

[6] Paine (1965:180) expressed it very cogently. The preachers created a myth of universality of which the local community was the center and which was maintained independently of the church and the state. Worldly low status was transformed into spiritual high status.

[7] Paine (1965:7).

[8] See Barth (1960:4–5).

[9] My fieldwork material supports the following observation by Elias as highly relevant:

Ineffective or not, parties are symptomatic of a stage in the development of societies at which the integration of the state-population has become closer and at which it is no longer possible to take decisions affecting the lives of the population of a country entirely without regular channels of communication between decision makers and those affected by their decisions. The balance of power ... is no longer as uneven as it was in earlier stages of social development (1972:12–13).

Declining local political party activity (also in Laxefoss, see note 13) could point to an opposite trend. This danger is present in modern Norway as well as elsewhere.

[10] In 1971 there were 67 houses (households) with 56 parts in the Salmon Fishers' Association. Some have been stimulated to build houses in order to get a share in the Association. It has become easy to get loans for building a house. It is a way of self-employment and shows lack of work rather than affluence.

[11] The rules of the Salmon Fishers' Association are anchored in (obsolete) state law.

[12] This is because the animals of each owner have a separate earmark. A shareholders' association with one mark would eliminate these problems. Ørnulf Vorren pointed to this as early as 1950. The Soviet Union practices with great success one-mark systems. People (e.g., rich Samer) who benefit from the current system manage to block such amendments. This has resulted in what Vorren once called a 'policy of the great plains' (*viddenes policy*). In northern Finland, Tim Ingold (1973) analyzed the theoretical problem of small and big owners and we exchanged ideas on this.

[13] Some will argue that since the local Labour Party Association dominates the political scene in Laxefoss and since the Township Council usually has a Labour Party majority, this Association will have importance for resource management – be it in an indirect way. Though there are exceptions, this is highly doubtful. Most administrators at the top are no longer self-made township politicians, but professional experts (see also Trond Thven and Odd Handegård). As note 9 indicates, this may point to a coming crisis of grassroots democracy: efficiency against democracy.

[14] Official state plans envisage measures to keep the population ratio of northern Norway compared to Norway as a whole at the existing level of 11.7%. A regional plan accepted by the township envisages allowing the center to grow in absolute numbers, but not communities like Laxefoss: the number of inhabitants of Laxefoss is to be kept constant. This has implications for the township's economic and social policies (see note 17).

[15] A pseudonym.

[16] This concept is borrowed from Wallace (1956:264–281).

[17] As has been said before, countrywide economic policies of society's power elite are by no means without implications for communities in the periphery. The current economic system favors unbalanced growth, as do the regional plans of the government which keep harping on the

need to concentrate the population in so-called growth-centers of at least 1000 inhabitants (for Finnmark at least 500 inhabitants). When one takes the existing pattern of communities as a point of departure for planning, one needs a model designed to balance growth. Such a model needs rigid planning, which the power elite today is not prepared to carry out: it conflicts too much with old-fashioned liberalist ideology and vested interests. In Scandinavia, Gunnar Myrdal (1957) and Knut Heem (1974) have dealt with this problem. But as can be seen from the relatively small size of these growth-centers, the power elite has been forced to make important concessions as to size and degree of concentration of the population. Note 14 shows that they do not always dare to condemn smaller communities (like Laxefoss) either.

REFERENCES

Barth, F.
The Land Use Pattern of Migratory Tribes of South Persia. *Norsk Geografisk Tidskrift* 17, 1960.
'Introduction,' in *Ethnic Groups and Boundaries. The Social Organization of Culture Difference*. Bergen: Universitetsforlaget, 1969.

Boissevain, J. F.
Netwerken en Quasi-groepen. (Inaugural lecture). Assen: van Gorcum & Comp. N.V., 1968.

Brox, Ottar
'Sameproblemet som glesbygdsproblem,' in *Strukturfascismen och andra essäer*. Uppsala: Verdandi Debatt nr. 65. Bokförlaget Prisma/Föreningen Verdandi, 1972.

Eidheim, Harald
'Erverv og Kulturkontakt i Polmak,' in *Samiske Samlinger*, bind iv. Edited by Asbjørn Nesheim. Oslo: Norsk Folkemuseum, 1958.
Aspects of the Lappish Minority Situation. Oslo: Universitetsforlaget, 1971a.
Samane – ein avvikarkategori i storsamfunnet, eller eit folk med rett til ei framtid? *Menneske og Miljö i Nord-Norge* (Sosialdepartementet). Oslo: Universitetsforlaget, 1971b.

Elias, Norbert
Processes of State Formation and Nation Building. *Transactions of the 7th World Congress of Sociology, Varna, Bulgaria, September 1970*. Geneva: International Sociological Association, 1972.

Friedl, Ernestine
Lagging Emulation in Post-Peasant Society. *American Anthropologist* 66:569–585, 1964.

Handegård, Odd
Koordinering-Klassisk problem og aktuell hodepine i regionalpolitikken. Stensilserie A. Institutt for Samfunnsvitenskap, Universitetet i Tromsø, 1973.

Heen, Knut
Forelesningsnotat Samfunnsplanleggingsgruppen, 26.3.74. Institutt for Samfunnsvitenskap, Universitetet i Tromsø, 1974

Ingold, Tim
Statistical Husbandry: Chance, Probability and Choice in a Reindeer Management Economy. *ASA Decennial Conference 1973:* 'New Directions in Social Anthropology,' 1973.

Kirke og Undervisningsdepartementet
Innstilling fra Komiteen til å utrede Samespørsmål. Oslo: St. Meld, nr. 21, 1962–1963, 1962.

Kjellberg, Francesco
Politisk Lederskap i en Utkantkommune. *Tidsskrift for Samfunnsforskning* 1:74–90, 1965.

Myrdal, Gunnar
Economic Theory and Underdeveloped Regions. London: Gerald Duckworth & Co, 1957.

Paine, Robert
'Entrepreneurial Activity without its Profits,' in *The Role of the Entrepreneur in Social Change in Northern Norway.* Edited by F. Barth. Oslo: Universitetsforlaget, 1963.
Coast Lapp Society II. Oslo: Universitetsforlaget, 1965.

Rudie, Ingrid
'Two Entrepreneurial Careers in a Small Local Community,' in *The Role of the Entrepreneur in Social Change in Northern Norway.* Edited by F. Barth, Oslo: Universitetsforlaget, 1963.

Thuen, Trond
Samfunnsplanleggernes Politiske rolle. *Norsk Byggekunst,* n.d.

Wallace, Anthony F. C.
Revitalization Movements. *American Anthropologist* 58:264–281, 1956.

13

Samish Responses to Processes
of National Integration

Helle G. Snell and Tom Snell
University of Amsterdam

ABSTRACT

The Sames and their activities to protect ethnic identity are treated not as an isolated case, but as an example of the changing power relations between national centre and small communities. Assimilation and ethnic activism are seen in relation to large-scale processes in the encompassing society. Assimilation (on community and individual level) is seen as a condition of powerlessness. The Samish Movement, growing in signifi-cance, is the ideological instrument with which Samish communities now seek to become less functionally dependent on the national centre. This paper examines how Samish communities were caught up differently in national integrative processes; the conditions under which the ethnic movement could emerge; and how Samish communities now act on the new ideas of ethnic integration.

THE SAMISH MINORITY[1]

The Sames are a most divided people. By the expansion of more powerful and better organized peoples they were made subordinates of four different national governments. About 30,000 live in Norway, 10,000 in Sweden, 2,500 in Finland, and 2,000 in the Soviet Union[2]. They are linguis-tically divided into at least four groups speaking four mutually unintelligible dialects of the Samish language. The linguistic boundaries, which run from east to west, do not coincide with the north-south national boundaries. Within the Samish population there exist all gradations of mastery of the national language. In Norway, for instance, there are Sames who speak only Samish and those who count themselves as Sames although they speak only Norwegian. Concomitant with this, one finds great differences in the intensity and the content of Samish identification.

Furthermore, the Sames are occupationally divided. The most significant distinction is between reindeer-breeding Sames and those who make their living in other ways, including farmers, fishermen, seasonal construction workers, and full time wage earners. In Norway only 10 per cent are reindeer breeders, in Sweden 25–30 per cent. It goes without saying that the different occupatio-nal groups among the Sames may have important conflicting interests.

The bulk of Sames live in the northernmost provinces of Sweden, Norway, and Finland. In northern Norway we even find some municipalities in which Sames are in absolute majority. The *Southern Sames*, of whom there are very few (roughly 1,000 in Norway and 1,500 in Sweden), are almost exclusively reindeer breeders. They are dispersed in small groups (bands) over an enor-mous area along the Swedish-Norwegian border, from Lake Femund in the south to the Arctic Circle in the north (see map). Many Southern Sames see themselves as a minority within the Samish minority.

The Samish minority situation is thus characterized by many divisions. To find a common political

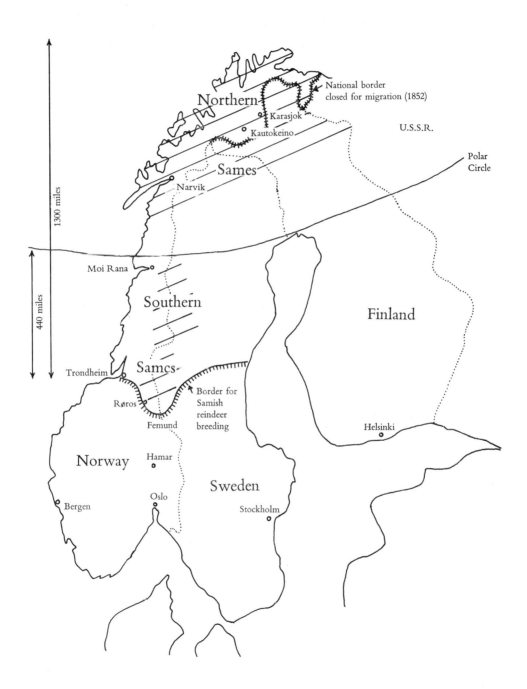

denominator, comman demands around which all Sames can rally, is extremely difficult, particularly in light of the traditional Samish social structure characterized by extreme political decentralization (Vorren and Manker 1962). Yet a Samish Movement has emerged in the years after the Second World War, presenting an ideology which aims to reach all Sames[3].

This article deals with the changing relations of power between the state and the small communities of which it is comprised. It deals with the relations of dependence between the two levels. The small communities here consist of people with a different cultural heritage from that of the majority of the population. This makes their relation to the state society in some ways unique; in other ways, however, they share the conditions of other small peripheral communities within the same national unit.

The explicit assumption is that these relations until very recently have been extremely unbalanced. Small peripheral communities, and certainly those with a deviant ethnic signature, have had little or no means to exert much influence on the content and direction of plans, decisions, and other activities taking place on the national level, but with profound bearing on conditions of life in these communities.

In Western European democracies, one of the most remarkable tendencies to appear in the last 25 years is that smaller *and* larger units than the traditional nation-state seek to seize control of a bigger share of the power functions which were previously monopolised by the state. Ethnic groups and groups defining themselves on the basis of common regional membership have come into action from below at the same time as international power structures like the European Common Market and NATO have emerged. This indicates, we hold, that a significant change of the traditional power balance (within and between nations) is gradually taking place.

The present article is a case study of the processes whereby small communities are gradually deprived of their local autonomy, functions, identity, and meaning up to a certain point when they seem to 'wake up' and seek to redefine the terms on which the two levels should be interdependent. By placing the Samish minority group in a historical perspective, it will be shown how Samish communities in various circumstances reacted to the overall impact of long-term processes of national integration and to decisions taken by the central government. Indeed, one of the main points will be to demonstrate how these external forces to a great extent even produced the variety of adaptations and divisions which the social map of the Samish minority situation shows us today. Two sections dealing with the differentiated position of reindeer breeders vis-à-vis non-reindeer breeders and the changes in the organization of Southern Samish reindeer breeding describe the influence of forces originating outside the Samish minority. By demonstrating how Samish communities were constantly forced to adapt to changed and changing circumstances, they illustrate the relative powerlessness of small communities which, we argue, has been the general picture until very recently.

What means do small communities mobilize in order to change things in their favour? In this case, the Samish Movement is the ideological instrument which has been constructed to obtain for the Samish minority as a whole a more favourable position in negotiations with the state authorities[4]. In the Movement, ethnic identity is converted into an organizational quality and ethnic solidarity is proclaimed to be both the integrative force to work with *and* the desired goal to work towards. The crucial measure of success will be how Samish communities act on the ideology of ethnic solidarity. To illustrate how and why two different responses to the new ideology are coming into existence, we shall deal in considerable detail with the Southern Sames – reindeer breeders organized in small herding units or bands. As will be shown, two currents, inchoate but discernible, are taking shape: the '*occupationalists*' and the '*culturalists*' represent two different ways of organizing ethnic identity corresponding to differences in their conceptions of the organization of reindeer breeding. The 'occupationalists' and the 'culturalists' find themselves in different opportunity situations and this, we argue, contributes strongly to the nature of their response to the appeals of the Movement[5]. The remaining part of the paper attempts to compare how other communities of Sames in Sweden and Norway, notably those outside reindeer breeding, are related to and affected by the new ideology. But first a brief account of the processes leading to national integration and to two fundamentally different Samish responses will be given.

NATIONAL INTEGRATION – ETHNIC INTEGRATION: A PARADOX?

In 1890 the Sames in Norway numbered approximately 20,000 according to the official census. That number was unchanged by 1930. By 1950 their numbers had dropped to barely 9,000[6]. This reduction can not be explained by a low rate of reproduction; on the contrary, the birth rate among the Sames is known to be extremely high as compared to that of the Norwegians. Reasons for the sudden and rapid decrease in numbers must be sought elsewhere. Processes taking place in the wider society during this same period provide us with clues for a further understanding of this reduction. These processes can most adequately be described as processes of increasing integration of the Norwegian nation-state. It is meaningful to view the reduction of 'registered Sames' against this background.

By national integration we refer to processes in society at large by which people become more interdependent and whereby the various regions of the country become more closely tied together in a national framework[7]. Let us briefly indicate some of these processes:

Norway gained complete national independence relatively late. Until 1905 it was united with Sweden, enjoying only relative autonomy in internal affairs. Independence was preceded by a period of consolidation of nationalist feelings. Long after 1905 Norwegian politics have been coloured by the desire to create a national self-image. Consequently, an image of cultural uniformity and national homogeneity was promoted and tolerance of divergent 'cultural arrangements' was very limited[8]. The 'politics of Norwegianization', a term that has been given to the Norwegian national policy with regard to the Sames, must be seen partly in the light of the young Norwegian state[9].

Industrialization of Southern Norway and transition from subsistence to cash economy in the country as a whole were greatly accelerated after independence. The traditional organization of economic activities was fundamentally changed.

In the process of social and economic integration of the nation, communities lose many of their traditional functions and become less differentiated. People grow more dependent on forces outside their immediate and traditional sphere of influence, i.e. forces outside the local community. Along with the 'defunctionalization' of local communities goes the increasing centralization of functions on the national level. The defunctionalization of the Samish communities meant that many of the functions which were formerly performed within those communities were taken over by agents of another culture, i.e. Norwegians.

Communications greatly improved as roads were built to break down the isolation of peripheral communities. The mass media further helped spread information to and from and about all parts of the country.

A national school system was designed, offering the same package of knowledge to every child. On the whole, the average level and spread of education was improved greatly. In the Samish communities, however, children who spoke only Samish were educated in a completely different language. Their own language was until the 1950s not only not taught, but not tolerated (cf. Dahl 1957).

These are some of the trends which have helped shape the Norwegian nation-state of today: a welfare state in which democratic values are highly respected. To the Samish population as a whole these processes of national integration meant that they were increasingly brought into contact with agents of another culture. They were integrated into the national economy. Many Sames, mostly those not engaged in reindeer breeding, increasingly adopted a Norwegian lifestyle[10]. The Samish language lost its traditional functions and became a serious handicap in the local arena dominated and controlled by Norwegians and their values. In some communities with mixed settlement everything associated with Samishness became stigmatized both by Norwegians and by Sames. 'The basis for their (i.e. the Sames') dilemma is that in order to achieve the material and social goods they appreciate, and to share the opportunities available in society, people have to get rid of, or cover up, those social characteristics which Norwegians take as signs of Lappishness' (Eidheim 1969:45).

It is not surprising, then, that many Sames did not feel any need at all to make their Samishness publicly known, when in the census of 1950 they were asked the standard question: what language is spoken at home? They had reacted to the changed circumstances by engaging in a process of assimilation, and this involved taking great pains to hide all manifestations of Samish identity. What *is* surprising, however, is the fact that not all Sames reacted in the same manner to the new situation brought about by the increased national integration; some decided to remain Sames and started to organize themselves on the basis of ethnic identity.

As mentioned above, in the years after the Second World War the Samish Movement got off the ground by offering completely new 'solutions' to problems of identity. While assimilation can be said to have been the traditional Samish reaction to situations of culture contact, the Movement now created a new alternative, an opposite strategy for identity management[11].

The new ideology stresses maintenance of cultural specificity and pride in and adherence to Samish identity. It seeks to dichotomize and unify at the same time: by emphasizing common Samish cultural symbols, their difference from Norwegian national symbols *and* the equivalence of Samish culture are simultaneously stressed. The Movement seeks to redefine and reactivate values: positive value and new meaning are given to cultural forms and expressions which are stigmatized by the dominant group. The Movement appeals to ethnic solidarity and cooperation to realize the desired 'refunctionalization' of Samish communities, many of them in a poorly differentiated and backward economic situation. Finally, the Movement seeks to redefine the ethnic boundary: by applying a wide definition to the concept of 'Same,' the Samish population in Norway was recently estimated at 40–50,000[12].

There is an apparent paradox in these developments. Until recently, processes were operative in society at large to produce national integration, and the predominant Samish reaction (assimilation) only seemed to prove the theories of the Melting Pot. Now, in important respects, the Movement counteracts national integration by establishing an ethnic frame of identification. This shift seems to imply a curious combination of powerlessness and a proud attempt to seize power. Furthermore, it seems to take place at a moment when the pressures to reduce the possibilities for cultural diversification are stronger than ever. We shall be able to say more about these questions in the conclusion.

REINDEER BREEDING AND THE POLICY OF 'A LAPP IS ALL RIGHT IN HIS PLACE'

Any discussion of Samish culture and identity must pay special attention to reindeer breeding, as it is considered the Samish occupation par excellence. It is certainly true that reindeer breeding is a traditional Samish way of making a living. Yet the key position which is frequently assigned to reindeer breeding as the 'core of Samish culture' needs some modification.

The state politics of both Sweden and Norway have strengthened the association between reindeer breeding and Samish culture and tradition. In both countries reindeer breeding is an exclusive Samish legal privilege[13]. The reindeer-breeding Sames are the only Sames who have been given specific rights, i.e. to own reindeer and to use certain natural resources.

It is outside the scope of this article to consider in detail the question of why reindeer breeding was ever made a Samish privilege. It is certainly possible that the respective governments were at least partly motivated by the intention to protect the vulnerable Samish economy from intruding outsiders. Our concern here is to show the (unintended) consequences of this policy.

The fact that only the category of reindeer-breeding Sames was noticed and given special rights by the central administration has led to a certain isolation of this group. In principle, it was the occupation which was protected and *not* the culture of an ethnic group. It is well known that protection is closely connected with dominance and control. Protection implies a relation of dependence – the protector is by definition more powerful, the one who can state the conditions under which protection is given. The rules and regulations for reindeer breeding, stated in the Law of Reindeer Breeding, specify the conditions which must be fulfilled if governmental support and financial aid are to be given. Reindeer-breeding Sames today find that in all aspects of their work situation, they are dependent upon the central administration. Lapp-inspectors *(Lappefogder)*, who are appointed centrally, make sure that reindeer breeding is practiced according to the law.

What reindeer breeders get in return, indirectly, has turned out to be a certain 'freedom' to act out their Samish identity. The fact that they were the only Sames singled out as 'somebody special' has made reindeer breeding the only sphere in which it is truly legitimate to be a Same. To be precise, Samish behavior is in all cases evaluated by Norwegians as being deviant. Inside the sphere of reindeer breeding, however, it is precisely this 'deviant behaviour' which is legitimate *and* which today can be, and is indeed, exploited by tourism. The notion that 'all Sames are reindeer breeders' is nourished and confirmed by the tourist industry. The romanticized and folkloristic idea of the Samish people – the stereotype of the strong, free, and healthy Same who migrates across the mountains with his herd – is a fiction. The grievance is that here culture has been confused with folklore: that particular image of the Samish people which corresponds with the popular stereotype is sustained by the dominant group and receives positive sanction and support from the government in a welfaristic sense. In this manner, the deplorable economic situation of a people is obscured and concealed, and the problems of Samish ethnicity degraded to reindeer-folklore.

It is commonly asserted that the policy of 'Lapps are all right in their place' = 'in their primitive turf huts,' 'with their reindeer,' and 'in their Lappish clothes,' is characteristic of the ethnic policy in Sweden. Indeed, for many years the official state policy there was even named *Lapp skal vara Lapp* (a Lapp should be a Lapp). This was accompanied by special regulations and provisions designed for the group of reindeer-breeding Sames[14]. It is true that the demarcation of the group of reindeer breeders has been much more rigorous in Sweden than in Norway, and that the Swedish reindeer Sames have received relatively more protection and financial support than their Norwegian counterparts. This fact is often taken to imply that Sweden has developed a specific ethnic policy while Norway has not. We would argue, however, that there is little fundamental difference between the two countries in this regard. In Norway, just as in Sweden, the right to own reindeer is defined according to ethnic origin. And in both countries *occupation* has thus been crucial for the ethnic policy, leading to increasing incorporation of the occupation of reindeer breeding into the national economy.

The occupational isolation and protected identity of reindeer breeding Sames have contributed to the alienation of many non reindeer-breeding Sames from their cultural heritage. The latter category of people was simply not recognized and their Samishness was ignored by the authorities. Everything was done to make it clear that there was no place for them unless they assimilated. The formation of the national Norwegian reindeer breeders' association (the NRL) in 1947 is a case in point. The intention of many Sames then – reindeer breeders and non-reindeer breeders alike – was to form a national, unifying organization based on ethnic principles and open to *all* Sames. At the first meeting of the organization, however, the government, through the interference of Lapp-inspectors, strongly supported the inclination of some reindeer-breeding Sames to create an occupational organization exclusively for reindeer breeders. The government thereby helped to make the internal division along occupational lines more pronounced (Otnes 1970:171).

SOUTHERN SAMES: CHANGES IN THE ORGANIZATION OF REINDEER BREEDING

Reindeer breeding is an occupation which sets clear upper limits on the number of animals that can possibly be fed in a certain area. This upper limit, in turn, determines the number of persons who can make a living within that area. This again is dependent on the minimum standard of living at a given moment. There has always been a flow of personnel between reindeer breeding and other occupations, but generally overpopulation in breeding has forced people to leave and find another way of making a living.

Changes in the organization of reindeer breeding can only be properly understood if they are placed in a broader context: certain historical events together with long-term processes in the encompassing society have called for these changes. This makes them illustrative of the enormous impact from the outside world on small communities with a distinct adaptation to the natural environment. As these changes appear to have repercussions for the way ethnic identity is experienced, by generating new and divergent opportunity situations, we shall proceed to describe them in some detail.

Until about 1900, the Southern Sames practiced intensive reindeer breeding – as contrasted to extensive breeding – which may be characterized by
– a relatively small number of animals (about 50) per houshold unit;
– intensive herding; the herd was continually followed by all family members, which made for very tame reindeer;
– the single family was in general the herding unit;
– extensive use of the reindeer for milk, cheese, meat, clothes, shoes, and tools;
– relatively little dependence on capital.

Changes in this form of reindeer breeding were brought about by many interrelated processes, which took place much earlier but the effects of which were felt much later because of the long distances.

In 1852 the Norwegian-Finnish border was closed (see map). This was a decision taken by the central governments of Russia (of which Finland was part) and Sweden (of which Norway was then part). This meant that Sames were no longer allowed to migrate with their herds between the two countries, and heavy sanctions were placed on trespassing. Both Finnish and Norwegian Sames were victims, as both groups traditionally migrated to and fro. Norwegian Sames looking for new pastures migrated in great numbers to northern Sweden, thereby causing overpopulation in Swedish Lappland. A struggle for survival began. The Norwegian Sames were better organized and applied a new strategy which eventually developed into the so-called 'extensive method': the animals of several owners were let free to spread over large territories, whereby they mixed with Swedish herds making these more difficult to control. It is a characteristic of extensive breeding that it cannot coexist well with the intensive method. The general result of their clashing is that small intensive herds are absorbed by big herds.

The Swedish Lapp-administration decided to force a number of reindeer-breeding families to migrate further south, where population pressure was less urgent. In this manner, the extensive method spread slowly to the Southern Samish districts, both in Sweden and in Norway. Around the turn of the century, traditional intensive breeding was permanently disrupted in most reindeer districts. This was the beginning of the more or less chaotic organization of reindeer breeding which even today characterizes so many southern districts. The transition from intensive to extensive breeding coincided with the transition from subsistence to cash economy with increasing emphasis on meat production. This again meant that each household needed a much larger herd to exist; today 400 deer is considered an appropriate number for an average household. The growing number of reindeer increased conflicts with peasants, who in Southern Samish districts are usually Norwegians. Already in 1883 this led to the first law on reindeer breeding which was principally designed to protect peasants and to regulate compensations for damage caused by intruding reindeer (Falkenberg 1949). The same law seriously limited the traditional freedom of movement. The Samish grazing grounds were divided into reindeer districts and the Sames were more or less arbitrarily assigned to certain districts and required to stay within them with their herds.

The extensive method has exposed reindeer breeders to profound organizational problems of which we shall mention only a few. In the first place, the permanently mixed animals (one band – several individual owners – one herd) call for changes in the relationship between herding (= the control and nurture of animals in the terrain) and husbandry (= the growth of herd capital and the formation of profit) (Paine 1964). Good herding is necessary for good husbandry; if herding is bad, animals will be lost to other districts. Effective herding of large herds, i.e. good control of animals, seems to be possible only with large capital investments (for fences, snowscooters, summer and winter dwellings, and cars). The necessary capital must come from productive husbandry, i.e. there must be enough choice alternatives to make selective breeding and optimal meat production possible. This in turn is totally dependent on locating and gathering as many deer as possible for marking in the summer and slaughtering in the winter. Loss of herd control means finding only a small percentage and consequently, the reduction of choices (forced slaughtering of whatever you have managed to fence in) and of productive capital (only a small percentage of the calves can be marked).

In the second place, the new extensive method of production necessitates *cooperation* of several households. In general, a labour force of 10–12 grown men is needed to work with the mixed herd. This calls for new kinds of decisions. Both work organization and economic planning now demand joint rather than individual decision-making, coordination and unanimity as to strategy rather than individualism. This is often very difficult to obtain. As one informant put it: 'formerly, in the good old days, every Same was king of his own mountain; but now we have democracy in the mountains *(demokrati på fjellet)* and that is the source of all our difficulties.'

In the third place, the growing number of reindeer necessary for the desired standard of living resulted in an ever-increasing pressure of people and animals on fixed resources. This overpopulation led to increased competition. When herding is not properly conducted, the problem of unmarked deer *(heløringer)* becomes more urgent. These are a constant source of conflict between bands. Bad herding reduces the possibilities of marking calves and thus creates more *heløringer* to fight over. An unmarked calf becomes a *heløring* when it is older than one year. According to the law, *heløringer* must be sold by the Lapp-inspectors and the profit used for collective purposes for the whole district. In practice, carrying this out is largely inefficient, making more or less rightful appropriation of these *heløringer* possible. It goes without saying that various strategies have been thought out and employed for this purpose, with the usual result that relations between bands are severed.

Finally, the extensive method has introduced new clashes between big and small owners. When herds are badly controlled and the finding percentage is small, big owners nevertheless usually find enough of their animals to make continuation of their productive capital possible. Small owners, on the other hand, will have to look for other alternatives, as husbandry for them has become like looking for a needle in a haystack. Some will try to find additional sources of income, but most will prefer to stay in reindeer breeding, for instance by becoming the paid helpers *(dreng)* of big owners.

As we see, extensive breeding – itself a response to external influences (border closure, migration policy, increasing involvement in cash economy) – has brought about the almost complete disruption of the traditional social organization. In general, extensive breeding has greatly increased the level of risk for reindeer breeders, at least as long as rigorous herd control is lacking. Uncertainty has increased along with pressures from the outside world. The consequences of these developments have been further exacerbated by demographic pressures from within. Moreover, the new adaptation to shrinking resources has engaged breeders in new relations of dependence. Relationships with members of the dominant group (buyers, Lapp-inspectors, agents of the national and local administration, local shopkeepers, etc.) have in many cases become more vital for their economy than intraethnic relationships. In both kinds of relationships, however, identity management will be an aspect of role-taking.

In the following pages we will discuss two orientations – two directions in which solutions are sought – reflecting two opportunity situations. We have found that bands of Southern Sames and individual members of different bands fluctuate between these two. We have called the exponents of these two orientations 'occupationalists' and 'culturalists' (cf. note 5).

SOUTHERN SAMES: ORGANIZATION OF ETHNIC IDENTITY – 'OCCUPATIONALISTS' AND 'CULTURALISTS'

The 'occupationalists' have found very drastic solutions to the above mentioned problems of herding and husbandry. In the 1960s, all old and wild animals were slaughtered. Thanks to extremely good pastures, very capable leadership, good relations with influentials, and, last but not least, early and sensible use of the snow scooter, a modern, rational, well organized, and very profitable reindeer breeding has been established.

Knowledge of the traditional Samish reindeer breeding was transmitted from father to son and learned by experience. In contrast, the meat-producing reindeer industry of the 'occupationalists' is increasingly replacing traditional expertise with modern, rational know-how based on scientific experimentation. This has entailed an important shift of values. In their eyes, modern breeding must drop many traditional customs and cultural rules. To stabilize herd continuity and to minimize clashes between big and small owners, joint ownership of the herd is propagated. The aim is to organize human and animal resources into a stockholding company with fixed membership and equal shares of herd and profit. This goes against one of the most basic characteristics of Samish reindeer breeding, namely the individual and very personal possession of an earmark – the necessary condition for individual and traditional husbandry.

To the 'occupationalists', ethnicity means above all the right to own reindeer and to exploit certain resources. Problems of ethnicity are mainly experienced in their conflicts with the peasants. The growing prosperity of these 'occupationalists' has caused envy among some of the poorer Norwegian peasants in the area. These peasants, to a much greater extent than the Sames, make ethnicity functional in the debates about the disposal of local resources. Peasants make use of so-called historical uncertainties as to who arrived first in the area, and question the right of the Sames to be there. Ethnic differences thus become rationalizations for discriminating behaviour in this particular setting where Sames are relatively more wealthy.

The Ministry of Agriculture, which controls reindeer breeding, is put under increasing pressure from both sides. The Sames argue for enlargement of their district; the peasants ask for removal of the Sames and try to demonstrate that their breeding inhibits alternative economic development of the region, notably tourism. It is remarkable that these 'occupationalists', in trying to counteract these most urgent pressures, *undercommunicate* ethnicity. Instead, they emphasize and try to demonstrate that their breeding is a more profitable exploitation of the local resources than tourism, for instance, would be. In other words, they fight the peasants and they argue with the Ministry of Agriculture not by referring to ethnic rights, but by demonstration of economic viability.

This undercommunication of ethnicity, along with the overcommunication of rational economic calculations of profit and productivity, provide evidence of the extent to which the reindeer management of the 'occupationalists' has become integrated into the national market economy. It also reflects the shift in the major relationships of dependence, now no longer between Sames in different districts, but between Sames in a single district and representatives of the local and national centres. To this may be added that many 'occupationalists' have intermarried considerably with locals. This also contributes to a certain isolation from other Sames. The old pattern of visiting and exchanging services within a Samish milieu is now disappearing. Isolation always makes for a certain mysteriousness which again easily leads to doubt and suspicion. Finally we must note that the 'occupationalists' have been leading supporters of the NRL (the reindeer breeders' association), an organization which actively supports modern reindeer management.

Most 'culturalists', on the other hand, cannot show such profitable and well organized reindeer breeding. They have only partly been able to solve the above mentioned problems which accompanied the transition to extensive breeding. The 'culturalists' ethnicity is expressed in numerous details concerning how to live with reindeer. They emphasize the value of the Samish language for the work with the animals in the mountains. They value Samish art and handicrafts, and they have active knowledge of the place and meaning of these cultural items inside the totality of Samish culture.

Between the 'culturalists' there is still much traditional visiting and exchange of information. However, relations with the 'occupationalists' are rather poor. It has long been a thorn in the side of the 'culturalists' that the 'occupationalists' can demonstrate such excellent breeding. Good reindeer breeding has always been a matter of prestige among Sames, and it grieves them that the 'occupationalists' have succeeded only by throwing overboard so many old and valued customs. They see the good relations which the 'occupationalists' have with the central and local administration as proof that government authorities do not really want to support *Samish* reindeer breeding but are solely interested in the economic aspects of that occupation.

One issue in the immediate past, the design of the new law on reindeer breeding, showed that what is really at stake is the question of who provides the central administration with the information which underlies decision-making. The formulation of a section of the law considered crucial for future reindeer breeding was also recognizable as the opinion of some leading 'occupationalists'. This caused the indignation of most Sames, but it especially supported the suspicion of the 'culturalists'. They saw it as collaboration with the central administration and this supported their doubt of the ethnic loyalty of the 'occupationalists'.

The 'culturalists' are threatened by increasing pressures on resources, increased levels of risk and uncertainty in herd management, competition between individuals and bands, and the prospect of losing a way of life in which until recently group boundaries and definition of self and others were fairly sure. These problems have led to greater *concern for ethnicity*, as it is the last minimum defense security they have in an uncertain world. To counteract the decisive influence of the 'occupationalists' and to demonstrate their rejection of the 'occupationalist' solutions, the 'culturalists' when interacting with 'occupationalists' increasingly take care to act in accordance with a value system which they still control better and on which they stand stronger: the ethnic value system. In this, now, they feel increasingly backed by the Samish Movement. The Movement comes to play a significant role in their thinking. In this most uncertain situation of the 'culturalists,' the ideology of the Movement offers some kind of solution. It reinforces and supports by positive feedback the already growing concern for ethnicity.

With the 'occupationalists' as a sort of catalyst, the 'culturalists' increasingly come to see their problems as ethnic minority problems and not so much as occupational problems. This raises such important questions as which new cultural forms are compatible with the native ethnic identity? Among some 'culturalists' we see the emerging tendency to revitalize a number of elements from the intensive breeding method. This clearly performs a function for the construction of a historical tradition in breeding and for the selection of signals of identity, which in turn can enrich and support the ideological basis of the Movement. The highly specialized and rational reindeer breeding of the 'occupationalists', on the other hand, is thereby seen by some 'culturalists' as having become superordinated to and separated from its ethnic meaning. The 'occupationalists' shift in value orientation does not seem to be compatible with native ethnic identity, as it has gone together with a decreasing commitment to ethnic idioms. But – with the increasing influence of the Move-ment – the 'occupationalists' make efforts to establish their version of the myth of traditional Samish reindeer breeding, too. When trying to convince a national forum of Sames about the advantages of their modern breeding, they overcommunicate those elements wich *are* compatible with a Samish tradition (for instance, collective use of natural resources), while undercommuni-cating those elements which are not (for instance, collective ownership of animals).

The NSR (the national organization of all Sames; cf. note 3), with its strong emphasis on the legal ownership rights of Sames to their traditional territories, provides the 'culturalists' with a more meaningful perspective as to the future of reindeer breeders and non-reindeer breeders alike. The Movement (the NSR) initiates new fields within which they can organize and communicate ethnic identity, and thereby widens their perception of group boundaries. Until this moment, the 'culturalists'' view of Samish culture and identity has been strongly bound up with reindeer breeding as a way of life. Reindeer breeding was experienced as a prerequisite for identity mainte-nance. As one 'culturalist' put it: 'I seriously doubt whether I would feel Samish if I did not live with reindeer.' In other words, the boundary of reindeer breeding was experienced as running concurrently with the ethnic group boundary. This was mainly due to the physical absence of any concentration of Sames in other occupations. Now the Movement helps to broaden their view of identity maintenance by offering a new frame of reference, a different boundary, which also comprises Sames in other ecological adaptations. This is particularly relevant for their perception of the future of their children, who, they realize, increasingly will have to find a living outside reindeer breeding due to the growing overpopulation in that occupation.

To the Sames who do stay in reindeer breeding, the above mentioned emphasis of the NSR on the preservation and even extension of the Sames' legal ownership rights provides a further stronghold against expanding hostile interests. Although it is not very possible that even ownership can stop industry and tourism, it is evident that stronger arguments and more convincing calcula-tions are necessary to force owners off their land than has been the case until now, when Sames were rarely even heard in response to plans for expropriation of their pastures.

WHAT HAS HAPPENED TO SAMES WHO ARE NOT 'IN THEIR PLACE?'

It is evident that one does not cease to be a Same by moving out of reindeer breeding. Yet, main-taining ethnic identity becomes really problematic only then. Neither in Sweden nor in Norway have non-reindeer breeding Sames been given any special protection or rights. On the contrary, for centuries they have been systematically deprived of almost all traditional rights. There exists no 'Samish Bureau' in the national government. In principle, Samish problems are dealt with like all other problems, that is, according to functionally specific criteria and in terms of the expertise required to deal with them.

The category of non-reindeer breeding Sames, which includes the majority, lives in circumstances which favour assimilation. As their cultural specificity is not protected in any respect, they are approached as ordinary inhabitants of peripheral communities inside the nation-state. In the local setting they have to compete with the non-Samish population for their share of the scarce resources. The rules of the competition as well as the prices are fixed by members of the dominant group.

The significant difference between Norway and Sweden lies not so much in the policy regarding reindeer-breeding Sames (cf. p. 170) as in the government policy concerning peripheral areas (*utkantspolitikk*). This has repercussions for the local alternatives available to Sames who are not in reindeer breeding. At this point it becomes important to see what has happened to the non-reindeer breeding Sames in the two countries.

THE SWEDISH CASE – RIGOROUS WELFARE PLANNING

In Sweden, national welfare planning has focussed very heavily on industrial development of the southern part of the country. In order to attain this goal, a rigorous long-term plan was designed by the central government. Industries were set up in the south and migration of labor from peripheral areas was stimulated and subsidized. The underlying view of future economic development presupposed, in the first place, that industrializing was the only modern way to progress. Secondly, it was assumed that small peripheral communities were not viable, measured in terms of cash income and productivity[15].

To make it attractive for people to leave their homesteads, large sums of money were spent for reschooling, favourable credit possibilities, cheap housing, and other social and economic services. These were offered to households willing to give up their subsistence existence. All this was carried out in Sweden on a scale which has been – to our knowledge – unmatched in other Western European countries.

The other side of this welfare adventure is, of course, the extreme stagnation of peripheral communities. No investments were made to stimulate local initiative or to develop local resources. This, in turn, made the old household-centered economic enterprise, in which independence and self sufficiency were highly valued, increasingly difficult. This policy, thus, forced people, however reluctantly, to agree to the state-fostered plans. Therefore, it is not surprising that most Swedish non-reindeer breeding Sames have not been able to retain their ethnic identity. In this way the expectation that they will automatically assimilate has become self-fulfilling. Leaving reindeer breeding does not mean ceasing to be Samish. But the necessity of simultaneously leaving the Samish habitat places non-reindeer breeding Sames in networks of dependence composed predominantly of non-Sames. The persistence of any cultural identity is dependent on the presence of a reference group of some size with which people can identify and within which communication is possible. In the process of economic integration on the national level, peripheral communities have been gradually deprived of functions, of capital, of people, and thus of viability. The 'ex-area assimilation' of many non-reindeer breeding Sames has been a consequence of this.

The Swedish regional policy is reflected in the Samish organizations. It is frequently asserted that the Sames in Sweden are much more united than the Norwegian Sames. People then refer to the fact that there are two Samish organizations in Norway – one for the reindeer-breeding Sames and one open to all Sames – while there is only one national organization in Sweden comprising all Swedish Sames. On the surface this is true. However, the interests of non-reindeer breeding Sames in the marginal, slowly dying, peripheral hamlets of north and central Sweden have never had a chance to be taken care of, because they run counter to the aims of national planning. The SSR (the national organization of Swedish Sames) may be strong as a pressure group for the interests of reindeer breeding, but it has succeeded mainly because its demands were not too much in conflict with the intentions of the welfare planners. Subsidizing reindeer breeding does not conflict with the interests of tourism, for instance, and tourism is of increasing significance in Sweden. But subsidizing Sames who are not reindeer breeders would be the same as subsidizing peripheral subsistence communities, and these are doomed to destruction in the welfare technocracy because they cost too much and produce too little.

It is significant that the only Samish organization which has managed not to be incorporated by the SSR is very radical and has not been recognized as a negotiation partner by either the Swedish government or the SSR. This organization (*Storuman-gruppan*) explicitly fights for the rights of non-reindeer breeding Sames to use the traditional Samish territories.

THE NORWEGIAN CASE – EMERGING ETHNIC POLITICS

Compared to Sweden, regional planning in Norway has been more or less chaotic. After the Second World War, which left most of Northern Norway considerably destroyed, a national plan was made for the reconstruction of the area, with the intention of centralizing the peripheral and isolated population in a few local industrial centres. However, these plans have not been carried out as rigorously as in Sweden. One reason why migration did not occur as intended was that marginal farming and other subsistence occupations did receive some state subsidies. Though this assistance was not much, it nevertheless meant that people were not forced by poverty to leave their homesteads and become industrial workers elsewhere. In northern Norway we still find a remarkably high percentage (almost 50%) of the population engaged in primary occupations. The Samish population in Finnmark (the northernmost province) lives clustered in relatively large numbers. In some municipalities they form a numerical majority. Their poverty is considerable and Samish identity here is associated by the Norwegian population with miserable economic circumstances. While all of Finnmark experienced considerable economic growth after 1945, the majority of Sames have not been able to participate in the development. Their economic position has grown worse: in absolute terms as a result of extremely high birth rate, and in relative terms in comparison to the remaining Norwegian population in the province.

Eidheim (1958) has studied the low rates of migration from rural Samish areas in Finnmark. He found that one reason Sames stayed in poor circumstances instead of migrating to industrial centres was that high social costs were connected with the change from a predominantly Samish milieu to a predominantly Norwegian milieu. Identity problems in Finnmark are crucial: the fact that Sames in Finnmark live and interact in great numbers has made it possible for them to retain language, family relations, habits, and traditions. All this makes it attractive to stay, even though the economic resources are not present to feed the growing numbers. Their low economic status in turn leads to stigmatization of their way of life. This again increases the social costs involved in migration – a vicious circle indeed.

It is not that Sames do not want to partake in economic progress, but rather that all long term plans for development of the region have been stipulated without regard to the ethnic composition of the population. Their refusal to migrate has been their only means of showing that they prefer ethnic security to economic progress.

While the Norwegian government policy regarding the Samish population until well after the Second World War was largely one of 'Norwegianization', we may nevertheless conclude that it has not been as 'succesful' as the Swedish policy. This latter policy has really contributed to the 'disappearance' of almost all Sames not engaged in reindeer breeding. The larger concentrations of Sames in the Northern provinces of Norway now provide the potential organizational basis for the ethnic policy of the NSR. The NSR tries, among other things, to demonstrate how the ethnic composition of the population here has led to the impoverished state of the Samish segment.

The argument is as follows: Ethnic identity places Sames in an opportunity situation which is fundamentally different from that of the remaining population. This functions as a serious drawback whenever Sames must compete with Norwegians. The reason for this is that the new economic opportunities offered by the state have been designed by Norwegians. They presuppose a cultura homogeneity which is not present. Therefore, to introduce *real* equality in the area the cultural heterogenity of the population must be recognized and considered in the development programs. Local opponents of these ethnic provisions, some of them of Samish origin, argue that is is growing increasingly difficult to single out the Sames due to much intermarriage over the centuries. They fear that such measures might introduce real discrimination in the area. They deny, in other words, that the 'welfare state' has widened the gap between 'rich' and poor along ethnic lines.

Others, for instance Brox, argue that the problems in Northern Norway have to do with the peripheral location and are the same for the whole population there. He does not pay any special attention to the ethnic component. His solutions are based on the view that the whole North Norwegian population has shown a definite unwillingness to leave the small local communities. If the state is willing to subsidize marginal areas (the case in Norway as opposed to Sweden), funds should be spent more according to the wishes of the local population and less according to techno-cratic plans decided on in Oslo. Local initiative and the development of economic enterprises based on local organizations should be stimulated (Brox 1966, 1969).

We can agree with his argument to a certain extent. But we are not convinced, and neither is the NSR, that this would be sufficient to guarantee that Sames are released from their discriminated position within the peripheral region. It is our opinion that a good regional policy – a la Brox's proposal – should be supplemented with formal and real recognition of cultural pluralism in northern Norway. This means, above all, that Sames should acquire the possibilities and the means to decide on their own premises what kind of education they want for their children, how and where to build their houses, and how to organize their economic lives. Most important, Samish opinions and demands concerning the crucial questions of disposal of the natural resources in their traditional territories should count much heavier on the local political arena than has been the case until now. As long as the resources in the Samish territories are administered primarily by and through Norwegian agencies, many of which are completely centralized, it is not very realistic to expect a significant change in the present disadvantageous position of the Samish population in northern Norway.

In the Southern Samish districts the absence of any concentration of non-reindeer breeding Sames is remarkable. Yet every generation of reindeer breeders yields a turnover of people. It appears that many have settled in towns like Hamar, Trondheim, Røros, or Oslo. In some respects this resembles the Swedish situation.

One generation ago, many of those who were made to leave reindeer breeding, because of popu-lation pressure or due to economic misfortune, settled in the direct vicinity, where they engaged in various primary occupations and maintained considerable contact with reindeer Sames. They were well known to our informants among the reindeer Sames. But *their* children and the children of reindeer Sames today, who cannot continue in reindeer breeding, are likely to leave (or have already left) the home communities. This is related to their level of education and to the language barrier, which is less of an obstacle here than in the northern provinces. All Southern Saems speak very good Norwegian, and consequently they have been able to pick up more at school than have Sames in Finnmark. Therefore they are better equipped to enter the Norwegian role-system and are more qualified for higher paying jobs.

The relatively unproblematic careers of non-reindeer breeding Sames from the southern districts suggest that stigmatization of an ethnic group has something to do with numbers. How can we otherwise explain this striking difference with Finnmark? The number of Southern Sames in the single local municipalities has always been almost negligible. Moreover, the shift to other occu-pations has taken place very gradually, over a long period of time. Consequently they have never constituted a massive threat in the competition for jobs. But perhaps even more significant than the question of scale is the fact that these non-reindeer breeding Sames did not display a 'way of life' which could readily be characterized as 'typical' of Samish ethnicity. They mastered the Norwegian language and they did not cluster in pockets of poverty. They did not, as in Finnmark, consume large share of the social welfare funds granted to the municipality as a whole. They behav-ed, in other words, as 'ordinary people' and dit not give any cause for moral complaints.

They did not display a 'deviant behavior' which could foster interpretations in terms of 'culture' or 'mentality,' and thus lead to stigmatization of the group in the local setting.

The physical absence from local Southern Samish communities of most non-reindeer breeding Sames has, as mentioned earlier, contributed considerably to the conception reindeer-breeding Sames here hold of the 'true nature' of Samish identity. However, we can observe a significant shift in this, too. A growing number of these non-reindeer breeding Sames now help to uncover the important evidence, which has always been stressed as a programmatic issue by the Samish Movement, that moving out of reindeer breeding does not necessarily entail loss of identity. Supported by the wider frame of reference, which is provided by the Movement, we see these Sames create new ways to articulate their ethnic identity. There has been a remarkable increase of innovative activities during the last five or six years. The establishment in 1972 of a local branch of the NSR in Trondheim, a town where many Southern Sames have settled upon leaving reindeer breeding, is significant. In addition, they have engaged in active work with the Southern Samish language, and they have organized Samish radio programs on the local station. A few have found work at the boarding schools for southern Samish children where they do valuable work. However few in number these Southern Sames are, they give evidence of a beginning of functional differentiation and of a broader ethnic basis of interaction.

CONCLUSIONS

In this article we have discussed variations in the use and relevance of ethnic identity between different communities of Sames. We have compared the minority politics of Sweden and Norway and found that these do not differ basically. In both countries the minority group was narrowed down to embrace only the occupational group of reindeer-breeding Sames. And in important ways the minority problems of this group were reduced to the problem of integrating the *occupation* into the national market economy. Tourism has exploited the folkloristic items which go along with reindeer breeding as a way of life. This has added to the special position of reindeer-breeding Sames. The non-reindeer breeding Sames were never recognized as a specific category. Their ethnic identity was ignored and consequently continuously threatened. We have tried to explain differences in identity maintenance between Norwegian and Swedish non-reindeer breeding Sames partly by referring to differences in the centralized politics these two nations pursue with regard to peripheral areas. Norwegian regional politics have made it possible (by social aids and subsidies) for clusters of Sames to stay in the periphery.

For a further explanation of the growing awareness of and concern for ethnic identity which we see manifested in the Samish Movement, we must return to what we have called the seeming paradox between national and ethnic integration. The paradox is between the long-term processes of integration of the nation-state which seemed to call for increasing assimilation of minority group members, and the rise of ethnic consciousness and an ideology which aims to integrate the Samish people in new relations of solidarity.

Now it appears that this paradox does not really entail a contradiction. Our conclusion is that the processes which led to increased integration of the Norwegian nation-state are interconnected with and have in important ways contributed to shape a situation in which the Samish Movement could emerge. It was not accidental or contradictory that the Movement came, nor that it came at that moment in history.

When more welfare came to Northern Norway, it became increasingly clear that the Samish population was badly equipped to compete on equal terms with the Norwegians for their share. They remained poor and powerless *because* they were Sames. But at the same time, the same welfare – brought about by the increased integration of the whole area into the encompassing society –

made *new tactical resources* available, resources which until then had been locked but which could now be exploited in new ways. Improved communications, improved education, and increased awareness of the necessity of organizing in order to pursue one's interests, together with conditions of economic progress, political stability and a generally increasing tolerance in the wider society enabled leading Sames to convert ethnicity into an organizational quality. Tangible gains are now perceived as accomplished by the Movement, and this again will increase the expected further chances of success[16]. The Movement has communicated insight in problems. The awareness that one's problems are not personal or accidental, but recurrent and structurally conditioned, is extremely operative as a mobilizing and consciousness-shaping factor.

In other words, the processes by which national integration was brought about had a double, not a contradictory, effect: the Samish Movement depended for its very origin on the new structural situation brought about by those same processes which until then had only seemed to reduce the conditions under which cultural difference can persist.

Understanding the dialectics between *cultural assimilation* and *cultural diversification* is no easy task. The interconnection between the two processes has not been given much attention, as they were usually treated as isolated, mutually exclusive minority responses. This is to a great extent due to the predominance of static and a historic paradigms in anthropological theory. The present article must be seen as an attempt, however tentative and incomplete, to demonstrate their interrelatedness against the background of large-scale processes in the encompassing society.

When assimilation and ethnic activism are taken to be strategies chosen to come to grips with minority status, which is by definition a status of limited opportunities, then the shift in adaptive strategy reflects the more general shift in the 'balance of power' between state and small communities. The notion seems justified that engaging in a process of assimilation reflects an opportunity situation in which assimilation is left as the only realistic alternative. Assimilation can thus be viewed as the extreme consequence (in the case of ethnic communities) of the general processes of defunctionalization of small communities, whereby not only increased functional dependence on the national administration, but also cultural uniformity is brought about.

The Samish Movement exemplifies the general emancipation and growing self-awareness of ethnic minority groups which the period following the Second World War has witnessed. All these movements seem to operate on the same two levels: by reactivating cultural identity, self-esteem is regained. This is converted into new bonds of solidarity which are used instrumentally to win more functional autonomy to the communities. These movements seem to emerge at a time when the national governments are relatively less preoccupied with national integration than previously, and are increasingly engaging in processes of internationalization. Nation-building is largely finished in Western Europe. In the world today it has become increasingly clear that a growing number of problems are no longer national, but of a worldwide nature. Solutions can no longer be found on the level of single nations, but must be sought on a supra-national level, in international cooperation.

But the processes of ethnic integration do not stop at the national border, either. As regards the Sames, Nordic Samish Council (*Nordisk Sameråd*) has existed since 1953. It is an inter-Scandinavian council in which Samish organizations from Finland, Sweden and Norway are represented. With cumulative success it has functioned as an instrument of pressure toward the respective central governments. More recently, in November 1973, the Arctic Peoples' Conference was held in Copenhagen, where Sames, Indians, Eskimos and Greenlanders gathered together. The main theme of the conference was the present energy crises and the worry of these peoples that the sharply rising prices of raw materials will lead to increased exploitation of their territories, where valuable energy resources are known to be located. Awareness of common problems and common uncertainties thus mobilized ethnic minority groups to form coalitions and to cooperate on an international level as well.

The extended relevance of ethnic activism is that it highlights problems which have not always been perceived as such, but which may be typical of the welfare state. The problems of integrating in national society while keeping a sense of separateness, of participating in progressive welfare without necessarily losing a sense of identity, are not confined to ethnic communities, but have a much wider relevance. It might well appear that ethnic groups, and small communities in general, are now in a position not only to question the values of the welfare state, but to provide some of the values we need to obtain more human well-being.

NOTES

[1] In the present paper we have preferred to use 'Same' and 'Samish' instead of 'Lapp' and 'Lappish'. The most important reason for this is that Same is closer than Lapp to the name which the Sames apply to themselves. Besides, the word Lapp is, in the Norwegian language, loaded with negative connotations.
Anton Blok, Jeremy Boissevain, Peter Loizos, Per Mathiesen, and Jojada Verrips have been so kind to read critically an earlier draft of this paper. They have contributed many valuable suggestions.

[2] Numbers are approximate due to imprecise countings; see also note 6.

[3] We use 'Samish Movement' largely in two ways: first, to indicate the organizational innovations which started with the establishment of a Samish association in Oslo in 1948 (Oslo Sámi Saer'vi). The organizational frame of the Movement is today the NSR, Norske Samers Riksforbund, which is the only nationwide organization in Norway with membership open to all Sames. The NSR was founded in 1968, and is constituted of a growing number of local branches in all parts of the country. Secondly, with Samish Movement we refer to various forms of behavior and cognitive representations which point to growing awareness of ethnicity.

[4] Eidheim has given an excellent analysis of the rise of the Movement as an innovative process. This article is in some ways a follow-up of Eidheim's study. Notably our discussion of how the Southern Sames are affected by the ideology of the Movement can be seen as a further application of the models for identity management presented by Eidheim (1972).

[5] The designations 'occupationalists' and 'culturalists' are not indigenous but our own provisional terminology. Both these terms refer to orientations among reindeer breeding Southern Sames and not to locally specific groups, although one can find 'occupationalists' relatively concentrated in specific districts of the South. For the 'occupationalists', reindeer breeding is the most important single factor within the whole of Samish culture. Their attitude towards reindeer breeding is increasingly based on rational, economic calculations. The 'culturalists' emphasize various cultural expressions of Samish identity. Reindeer breeding here certainly has a crucial position, too, but more as a way of life than in economic terms. Whereas the 'occupationalists' are relatively oriented towards Oslo, the national centre, where – in their eyes – the most important decisions regarding Sames are taken, the 'culturalists' are increasingly interested in what happens in the Samish core districts in Northern Norway, where the Movement is gaining influence.
The reader will note that our own material concerns the Southern Sames among whom we did fieldwork from May until September, 1971. In discussing Northern Samish communities, we rely on material collected by others. In particular, Eidheim's essays offer a most inspiring and useful frame for interpretation.

⁶ These numbers should, of course, be treated with some caution. Criteria used for the definition of a Same have not always been the same. In 1890 only descent was used, in 1930 both descent and language, and in 1950 exclusively language (*Innstilling avgitt av den norsk-svenske reinbeitekommisjon*). The relevant thing about these numbers is, of course, that they say something about the rapidity of the process of assimilation.

⁷ Elias (1971a; 1971b) has been much more comprehensive about how long-term changes in configurations of interdependencies are related to and take place simultaneously with differentiation and specialization of functions on a higher level of integration. We have found Elias' theory of inter-dependencies highly useful for our interpretation of processes of national integration in Norway.

⁸ The creation of a national self-image is reflected in concern with national history and national language. Glorification of the Viking era goes together with systematic nonknowledge of the origin of the Samish people. The construction of *ny-norsk*, which clearly had the function to decontaminate the Norwegian language from the marks of centuries of Danish colonial rule (until 1814), goes together with suppression of the Samish language.

⁹ The term 'politics of Norwegianization' has been introduced by Fidheim (1968:206). It indicates that 'there has been no official initiative explicitly designed to safeguard the cultural integrity of the Lappish population.'

¹⁰ See Eidheim (1966 and 1969) for an elaboration of the long-term processes of assimilation.

¹¹ We will discuss the cumulative effect of the Movement for the organization of inter- and intra-ethnic interaction later in this paper. Our concern here is above all to show that the Movement seeks to establish an *ethnic* complementarization of social institutions and values, a pendant of national integration.

¹² For example, according to *Nordkalott*, a Samish newspaper. The preoccupation with numbers and definitions as to what should be understood by a Same reflects the unwillingness of the central government to consider the *qualitative* aspects of Samish minority status. As one of the leading young Sames put it: 'It is usually not a problem for us to define this' (Magga 1973:2). Samish initiatives, for example applications for government subsidies of Samish schools, have recurrently been blocked by central authorities with reference to national standard norms as to the minimum number of pupils.

¹³ An exception to this is Finnmark, the northernmost province of Norway, where non-Sames are also allowed to own reindeer.

¹⁴ For instance, there were compulsory nomad-schools until the 1960s for children of reindeer breeders. Until the 1920s these schools were purposedly kept primitive in order not to 'habituate' Samish children to modern comfort (Ruong 1951).

¹⁵ In our discussion of regional planning in Sweden and Norway we lean heavily on Brox (1966 and 1972).

¹⁶ Of course, increased ethnic integration may create a new basis for conflicting local interests between members of different ethnic groups. Any process of integration solves some problems of relationships by creating a new basis for interaction and cooperation. In some respects this implies simultaneously new sources of friction and sometimes severance of traditional local bonds.

REFERENCES

Anonymous
Innstilling avgitt av den norsk-svenske reinbeitekommisjon. Utenriksdepartementet, 1967

Barth, F.
Ethnic Groups and Boundaries. The Social Organization of Culture Difference. Oslo-Bergen: Universitetsforlaget, 1969.

Brox, O.
Hva skjer i Nord-Norge? En studie i norsk utkantpolitikk. Oslo: Pax Forlag, 1966.
'Sameproblemet som utkantproblem,' in *Sjätte nordiska samekonferensen i Hetta*. Stockholm: Nordisk utredningsserie, 1969.
Politikk: bidrag til en populistisk argumentasjon. Oslo: Pax Forlag, 1972.

Dahl, H.
Språkpolitikk og skolestell i Finnmark 1814 til 1905. Oslo: Universitetsforlaget, 1957.

Eidheim, H.
Erhverv og kulturkontakt i Polmak. Oslo: Samiske Samlinger, vol. IV, 1958.
Lappish Guest Relations under Conditions of Cultural Change. *American Anthropologist* 68:426-437, 1966.
'The Lappish Movement: An Innovative Political Process,' in *Local Level Politics*. Edited by M. Schwarz. Chicago: Aldine, 1968.
'When Ethnic Identity is a Social Stigma,' in *Ethnic Groups and Boundaries*. Edited by F. Barth. Oslo: Universitetsforlaget, 1969.
'Assimilation, Ethnic Incorporation, and the Problem of Idiom Codification and Identity Management,' in: H. Eidheim, *Aspects of the Lappish Minority Situation*. Oslo: Universitetsforlaget, 1972.

Elias, N.
Sociologie en geschiedenis en andere essays. Amsterdam: van Gennep, 1971a.
Wat is sociologie? Utrecht: Het Spectrum, 1971b.
Processes of State Formation and Nation Building. *Transactions of the 7th World Congress of Sociology, Varna, Bulgaria, September 1970*. Geneva: International Sociological Association, 1972.

Falkenberg, J.
'Samene øst for Femunden,' in *Den norske turistforenings Årbok*, 1949.

Magga, O. H.
'The Reindeerbreeders Association of Norway.' Paper written for the Arctic Peoples' Conference, Copenhagen, 22-26 Nov, 1973.

Ornes, P.
Den samiske nasjon. Interesseorganisasjoner i samenes politiske historie. Oslo: Pax Forlag, 1970.

Paine, R.
Herding and Husbandry: Two Basic Concepts in the Analysis of Reindeer Management. *Folk* 6:83-88, 1964.

Ruong, I.
Nomadskolorna i Sverige, in *Sami Ællin, Sameliv. Samisk Selskabs Årbok*. Oslo: Universitetsforlaget, 1951.

Vorren, Ø., and E. Manker
Lapp Life and Customs. Oxford: Oxford University Press, 1962.